Rough
Against all
Oldham Rugby League

Craig Halstead

London League Publications Ltd

Roughyeds
Against all the Odds
Oldham Rugby League Club 1997 to 2017

Foreword

Twenty years ago, a group of four of us started out on an adventure. None of us could envisage the town of Oldham being without a professional rugby league team. That was our only motivation in setting up the consortium that would oversee the creation of a 'new' club. Fast forward to 2017 and yours truly is the only one left. I am still here for the same reason.

A lot has happened in that 20 years, and as it is Oldham RLFC, it goes without saying that it hasn't been easy. In different ways, it seems like we have crammed more into the last 20 years than some clubs have in 100!

It is fair to say that, with hindsight, had we known then what we know now it might never have happened. The very existence of the club is a constant battle. We all believed we could make a difference and I hope that most of the people reading this book will think we have. It is abundantly clear that there is no golden pathway back to the top of the sport for us and, like many other clubs, we will always be striving to make whatever progress we can, however small.

It is apparent from reading the various contributions to this book that the club has had a profound effect on people, many of whom, myself included, who supported the old club. These people will have been grateful when a new club was formed but for many other younger supporters the new club is the one they will have grown up with and followed from childhood. Reading all their memories and learning of the enjoyment Oldham RLFC has brought to them is a truly heartening thing. We all have our different memories, of course. A fan on the terraces or in the stands will have different recollections to somebody directly involved with the club, but regardless of that we have all been touched by the club's presence. We all love our club and to anybody who isn't interested in, or doesn't understand sport, they have no idea what they are missing.

Sport is unlike anything else. It can have you on the ceiling in terms of joy and excitement, then it can drop you to the floor in an instant. Those extremes of emotion happen because we love our club and are so passionate about it.

Over the last 20 years I have experienced plenty of elation, and despair, and I feel honoured to have been involved for so long. Nearly 500 players have worn the Oldham jersey in that time so we have provided opportunities to a wide range of playing talent. It is with considerable interest that I note the affection with which several former players have spoken about the club.

On a personal level, my outstanding memories include the first ever game on New Year's Day, 1998. The win in the Law Cup match that day was (appropriately) against all odds, because of the time constraints we faced in putting a squad together, let alone producing a winning team. To beat Rochdale Hornets, on their own ground, in our first match and in front of a crowd made up of mainly Roughyeds supporters, was fairy-tale stuff.

Three and a half years later came the amazing comeback win in the play-off semi-final, again at Spotland, and again against our local rivals. That was the kind of display in a game of such importance that I could only have dreamed of.

More recently, the promotion success of 2015 was such a relief after so many unsuccessful Grand Final attempts. The feeling of having achieved our goal at last made the day so much more memorable. Nobody begrudged us that success after coming so near so often.

There have been plenty of hard times too and this book would not be complete without discussing the tough times as well as the good. It is those experiences that have enriched the history of this club and brought people together, on and off the field, to fight the cause. Even after 20 years I am still a bad loser and it is that passion that has kept me going for so long.

I would like to thank the various people who have helped me to keep the club alive, especially through the difficult times, and without them we wouldn't be here now. Many would shy away from public recognition, some have specifically asked not to be given it, but they have my sincere thanks. They know who they are.

Like any club, we are eternally grateful to our hard working group of volunteers who enable the club to operate, especially on a match day. I take my hat off to those people who have stuck with us through thick and thin over the last 20 years. I know more than anybody that it hasn't been easy and we are lucky to have a loyal group of fans that have the same kind of determination that we have always tried to instil into our teams.

To conclude, we are where we are today thanks to the efforts of two teams – the one on the field which displays the Oldham badge so proudly and, just as importantly, the one off it. We have a special club which we all love and I hope that it will go from strength to strength in the next 20 years.

Chris Hamilton
Chairman

Support for the Roughyeds

I first met Chris Hamilton in 1991 when I received a call from my accountants' office on Lord Street, in Oldham. I was asked to come and meet my new accountant as my last one had moved on. On entering the new office it seemed there was a distinct change in the decor, the walls were full of sports memorabilia which was a good start. After our initial handshake, it was about 55 minutes talking about sport, mainly Oldham Rugby League Club and Oldham Athletic, and about five minutes on my accounts. That is how it tended to go with all our meetings.

After six years of knowing and working with Chris – he actually did do some work – another meeting was requested. On entering his office and after the customary banter about the weekend's results, we got on to the subject of the rugby league club and the trouble it was in. This was before the infamous shareholders meeting at the Pennine Way Hotel in Oldham in which the liquidator got the necessary support from the shareholders to wind up the club. I will never forget his first words on the subject. "I would love to sort that mess out," he said to me. I nodded and smiled, at which point he said, "Will you back me?" Jumping in without thinking I replied, "Of course!" I then went home and thought nothing more of it.

I didn't realise or appreciate at that stage how much guts this fellow had, as I would learn as time went by. Over the next several years we had our square ups believe you me, but I never once doubted that he had 'bottle' in abundance. We used to smile at a drawing on his office wall of an emu swallowing a frog. Just as the frog was inside the emu's beak in the last chance saloon, the frog's front legs are wrapped around the emu's neck. The caption on the drawing was 'Never ever give up!' Class!

Chris arranged a meeting with the Oldham Bears chairman and chief executive Jim Quinn and the rest of the board, which he duly attended with the intention of seeing if he could salvage the remains of the old club. Unfortunately the business was too much in the mire, nobody was going to salvage that.

Despite that we were still keen but we realised we would need some help. We decided to think of anybody who might be interested in joining and would be the same way minded as us. I was doing a lot of work with Melvyn Lord at Reddish Demolition Ltd, who also was an old friend of the family and an Oldham Rugby League Club fanatic. Melvyn had started his career working for my dad and started going to the rugby with him and a few mates, with me tagging along as the little kid. We spent many years travelling up and down on Sunday afternoons watching our beloved Oldham and now the time had arrived when the club needed our help. Melvyn was running his own successful business by this time and was in a position to put himself forward so he did. Chris was doing a lot of work with a guy called Stuart Hardaker and he agreed to join the gang so there was now four of us.

Things then moved along quickly after the old club was liquidated. We applied to the Rugby Football League (RFL) for membership under a brand new company. In return we got absolutely no funding, which in all fairness was correct, to compete against teams who were receiving a substantial amount of money. We managed to sign enough players to put a team onto the park, all self-funded, which from scratch is pretty good going. The burden was shared between the four of us, with Chris running the day to day business. He was the one who took the stick, delivered all the difficult jobs such as sackings, contract talks, dealing with the media and the spectators and for most of the time for nothing. I don't think he got paid a penny in the first few years as there was never any money left in the pot to pay him, he was always the last to see any money. We weren't multi-millionaires who could finance big time players coming in, in fact we sometimes had to beg, borrow or steal. There were always sponsors who didn't pay their dues on time, unfortunately that was commonplace. It is very difficult to recoup money off companies for sponsorship when they disappear! Although we had a couple of particularly difficult years, at no time was it easy regardless of how well we were doing, there was always something to bring us down to earth with a bump.

One of the main issues we had was the subject of finding a suitable venue to play. This was so endlessly time consuming and soul destroying. I am not being disrespectful to the committee of the 'old' club because I know what it is like to try and keep a professional sports club alive, but with Watersheddings as their 'home', they didn't know they were born. This was an annual problem for us, we could hardly ever set budgets until the last minute, we were always 'behind the black ball' or trying to operate with a gun to our heads it seemed. It was ridiculous. On several occasions Chris and I left the Ivory Towers of the Civic Centre with a skip in our stride thinking we were making progress with Oldham Council officers only to be deflated some time later in another progress meeting. Senior Council officials regularly failed to attend meetings and sent repeated apologies, we became sick to death of their apologies. I was the more cynical of the two of us, convinced the Council's strategy was to wear us out, send us around the block again in the hope that they we would get sick of returning. In my opinion, Oldham Rugby League Club meant very little to the Local Authority. I was convinced they were apathetic about the club and whether it prospered or just died. They have been guilty of some serious mishandling of us. The biggest mistake they made was when they bought Boundary Park outright from Oldham Athletic. That was an opportunity for our future to be secured, indeed all professional sport in Oldham to be secured. They took the bait and sold it back to the new owners of the football club for the same money they paid for it. That could still have been a Council owned community stadium, to this day, with all the surrounding land included. The new owners saw the potential. Was this a case of short-sightedness or favouritism on behalf of the Council? Make your own mind up.

Oldham Rugby League Club will always be my team. I could never go along with those who support a different team just because they are in Super League. Oh dear, how could you? I loved my early days going with my dad Alan and my mum Ellen, up and down the country, to every ground in the league. Watersheddings was undoubtedly a scruffy old place but it was our scruffy old place. Those days are gone now though. We are now in a position where we are at. People have to accept and understand that and get behind the club even more because it is still very difficult season in, season out to keep the club afloat.

Chris Hamilton is still there fighting the battles, and let me tell you, all the hearsay of different people showing an interest in coming in and wanting to take over, is all totally untrue. Apart from Bill Quinn, who became Chairman in 2007, in all my time of being on the board I think we had talks with two other people, and neither even made it to a second meeting. Like I said, Chris and I have not always seen eye to eye, but you have to tip your cap to him. He can sometimes be the most awkward, stubborn individual you will ever come across, but he also has a wicked sense of humour. Like the motto on that drawing on his office wall 20 years ago, 'Never ever give up!'

Sean Whitehead,
Oldham RLFC Director 1997 to 2009

TWENTY years – wow! It doesn't seem five minutes since, in another life as an *Oldham Evening Chronicle* reporter, I rang Chris (Hamilton) for the first time and asked if I was right to believe that he was the man fronting a consortium to launch a 'new' Oldham club following the death of the Bears.

The reply was brief, succinct but very revealing. "No comment," to an old hack who has been round the block a few times can be roughly translated thus: "Well, yes, there is something going on but I am not saying anything yet."

In the weeks and months that followed, and as Oldham RLFC (1997) Ltd started to take shape, the Gang of Four and its spokesman became household names in the town thanks to the many column inches on rugby in the dear old *Chron*. Union Street would never claim to rival Fleet Street, but the paper in those days was part of the town's fabric. It mourned the passing of the Bears and celebrated the arrival of the 'new' Roughyeds.

Two decades on and its press hall is silent, a victim of the internet and social media. Rest in peace, old friend. You will be sorely missed.

What happened to the Bears, and now to the *Chronicle*, should be a salutary lesson to everybody who is proud of this town and the institutions that carry its name. There are thousands of people here who love rugby league and say they are Oldham fans, but who do little to support the club that many of us have grown to love and treasure. Lessons from Watersheddings and Union Street are clear – 'Don't use it and you lose it.'

It has never been harder to keep a club afloat. Here at Oldham we are lucky to have a man at the helm with the heart of a lion, who has devoted the best years of his life to Oldham RLFC (1997) Ltd.

He has made mistakes and he will be the first to admit that there have been things he would have done differently with hindsight. But be sure of this: Roughyeds would never have reached this milestone without Chris Hamilton's expertise, determination, stubbornness maybe, but above all his amazing fortitude in taking knocks and repeatedly getting up off the canvas to go again.

Who was it who once famously said: "If you can bear to hear the truth you've spoken twisted by knaves to make a trap for fools or watch the things you've given your life to broken, and stoop and build them up again with worn-out tools." Rudyard K perhaps had in mind a man with whom I am privileged to have shared a slice of my life over the past 20 years - the first eight of them as the *Chronicle's* Oldham RL reporter; the rest as club media manager in a voluntary capacity.

In a classic case of poacher-turned-gamekeeper I have had my eyes opened by what it requires to keep a relatively small club like ours in business and by the extent of the stress and strain that rests on the shoulders of those with financial and decision-making responsibilities. We have had one or two crises over the years but despite relegation from the Kingstone Press Championship at the end of the 2017 season we have had plenty to shout about as well, including that wow-factor win at Hull Kingston Rovers in the 2016 Ladbrokes Challenge Cup and no fewer than seven Grand Finals and a Promotion Final.

My personal best memory: the sight of Sammy Gee, who didn't play that day, leading the victory chant on the field at Whitebank after the 2015 win against Keighley Cougars in the Promotion Final.

Second best? Same day, same game, same celebration when the RFL's appropriately-suited Brian Barwick was saturated with champagne as Lewis Palfrey uncorked it.

You couldn't script it, but that has been the story of much that has happened in the topsy-turvy life of the reborn Roughyeds between 1997 and 2017. Despite setbacks, difficulties, disappointments and cash crises that would have floored many lesser clubs, Roughyeds are still alive and kicking.

Happy birthday you beaut – and here's to the next 20 years!

Roger Halstead, Club media manager and former *Oldham Evening Chronicle* rugby league correspondent

Rugby league is interwoven into Oldham life and adds to our rich history.

Oldham Football Club was established in 1876 at a meeting at the Prince Albert Hotel in Union Street West. It became one of the founding members of the Northern Rugby Football Union in 1895 when a group of northern clubs came together to say their players could no longer play without compensation for lost wages. They decided to split from the Rugby Football Union when their proposal for payments was defeated.

The club became known as Oldham Bears from 1996 as the Super League was established. However, with the club facing financial difficulties, fans faced a turbulent time and, despite a proud 121 year history, the club went into liquidation in 1997. A consortium under Chris Hamilton then came together to form a 'new' club which would be known as Oldham RLFC (1997) Ltd with a nickname 'Roughyeds'. A new era had begun.

Oldham RLFC has had its ups and downs. There have been wins and losses, promotion and relegation and various stadium moves too! As in life, we will face good times and bad, we will face doubt, even failure, but it is in these moments that we learn the most about ourselves. And so it is with rugby league and with the Roughyeds. But there has certainly been plenty of grit, determination and passion at this club.

Sport can do so much to bring communities together. A club is a community – it unites us in a common endeavour as we coalesce around a group of players, whose hopes and dreams we share each weekend. And somehow, we come through it all, although it feels like a rollercoaster, week-after-week, season-after-season.

A club is held together by its players, management, backroom staff and, most importantly, its fans and volunteers. I salute you all. It is clear that the ethos of this club and this great game is built on this tradition of coming together. I have seen it for myself when I have attended games. And long may it continue.

Oldham has a proud heritage of producing great players who have gone on to inspire others and I have no doubt we will continue to do so. I hope we can grow the game across the Borough so more young people can feel the benefits of its ethos and tradition. I am trying to play my part with the 'Diversity in Rugby' project I launched last year with the Rugby Football League. Twenty years since its establishment, the 'new' Oldham Rugby League Club is a part of our community and I very much look forward to the next 20 years and beyond.

Debbie Abrahams MP
Oldham East and Saddleworth

I am delighted to provide this brief note to celebrate the 20th anniversary of the rebirth of professional rugby league in Oldham, at the end of 1997. Oldham is an extremely important rugby league town with a proud and long history in the professional ranks, until their untimely demise at the end of the second Super League season. History will no doubt record that the move from a winter to a summer season, together with the advent of full-time professionalism across the elite league, proved to be a tumultuous and traumatic period for many of the sport's greatest names. It is to the immense credit of Chris Hamilton and his colleagues over the years that they refused to stand back and allow the great club that Oldham is to disappear off the fixture list for good.

Re-establishing a professional club under such circumstances was never going to be a stroll in the park and it is probably fair to say that in the intervening period the club and its management have laboured under exceptionally stressful times to keep the professional rugby league flag flying in the town.

On the field, rugby league demands tenacity, perseverance and, above all, bravery and it is clear from the Oldham story of the last 20 years that these qualities are required in abundance off the field as well.

I am delighted and pleased to publicly recognise that Chris and his colleagues have amply demonstrated such an outstanding commitment to the sport over this time.

Nigel Wood
Chief Executive, Rugby Football League

The moons aligned, or possibly collided, in 1997. In the same year as I became Chief Executive of Sheffield Eagles, Oldham Bears played their last match at Watersheddings and were later liquidated. A consortium of businessmen, with Chris Hamilton as chairman, then took control of a 'new' club. Since then, the paths of Chris and I have crossed on many occasions in many different situations. The voyage which the club has sailed over that period, both on and off the field, has not only tested to the limit the resolve of the club and all associated with it, but has demonstrated the commitment and ingenuity of its captain at the helm.

During this period I have accompanied teams to play Oldham at Boundary Park, Hurst Cross, Whitebank Stadium and Bower Fold. I know Oldham have used other grounds too to stage 'home' games and

I understand how much effort it takes logistically, professionally and emotionally to make these moves work. To not only move a club and a team, but also your crowd, and hold it intact is Herculean and huge credit must go to Chris and those around him that make it happen.

This journey, though, is nothing in comparison to the one that the club has taken on the field of play. To manage them both in tandem is a feat barely comprehensible. To witness the birth of the 'new' club in the bottom tier and the subsequent trials and tribulations through the various league structures, coming so very close to Super League in 2001, and then relegation to National League Two in 2006, may have been professional sport, but nevertheless has been painful, even for those not directly involved with the club. Then there were the repeated unsuccessful attempts to win promotion in such dramatic Grand Final circumstances. I have personally been witness to several of these occasions which perhaps provide my most poignant memories over the last two decades.

The emotion involved in the failed sixth attempt to win the third tier Grand Final in 2014 at Headingley, to a Hunslet Hawks golden point drop-goal, was a moment that I will remember for a long time. I telephoned Chris afterwards and genuinely feared for his well-being on the back of what had occurred. For a man who had truly thrown his life and soul into his club, this was sport at its most cruel. The following season, the most deserving of promotions was finally achieved, climaxed by the 31-20 win over Keighley Cougars at Whitebank. That day I knew there was no need to call Chris afterwards and a congratulatory text would suffice.

Nobody that day would have argued with the club's right to take its place in the Championship or indeed how hard-earned that victory had been. Oldham Rugby League Club has played a huge part in the history of the game having produced players and moments that have lit up the world's stage. The area is steeped in rugby league tradition from giants of the community game in Saddleworth Rangers, St. Anne's and Waterhead right through to the players produced that have contributed to international success and on that day the club represented it all. Chris Hamilton understands that heritage, it runs through his blood.

Ralph Rimmer
Chief Operating Officer, Rugby Football League

When I was requested to write a short article as part of the book to commemorate 20 years of the 'new' Oldham RLFC I had no hesitation in agreeing to write it.

I have been a rugby league supporter for more years than I care to remember having supported Saddleworth Rangers, Leeds Rhinos,

Sheffield Eagles and Oldham Bears, going to watch games whenever I could.

After the demise of Oldham Bears in 1997, professional rugby league was reborn in Oldham soon after. A consortium of four businessmen, led by chairman Chris Hamilton, worked wonders to get the 'new' club up and running in very little time.

It was after the formation of the 'new' team that I started to go to Boundary Park to watch the Roughyeds play. I met Chris at a match and eventually we became good friends. It soon became apparent to me how hard Chris Hamilton works to keep his beloved Roughyeds afloat. Believe me, he works extremely hard and puts in more hours in a week on the club's behalf than people would ever believe. Not only that, but I know it is a labour of love for him.

One of the requirements of being chairman of a professional rugby league club is that you have to attend the Rugby Football League's quarterly meeting with all the other club chairmen. I can tell you that matters arising at these meetings are often intricate and technical and Chris has always put his energies into dealing with such matters. In 2008 he was voted as Deputy President of the Rugby Football League and then, a year later, to indicate how highly he was thought of, he was voted to be the new President of the Rugby Football League.

During the years after the formation of the 'new' club, Chris worked hard to bring success to the club, enjoying some great results but also suffering some devastating losses in Grand Finals. He always shook off his disappointment, however, and pushed forward doing his best and getting the backroom staff and players in the right frame of mind to go again the following year.

After one such Grand Final loss at Warrington which would have seen the club promoted, I did not approach him as I saw tears of disappointment in his eyes. I rang him two days later and, heroically, he told me that he would keep on trying to achieve the goal of promotion. This is the measure of the man, he will never throw in the towel.

Chris Hamilton is a great confidant and whenever I have asked him for assistance on rugby matters he is only too happy to help. He has been a major player in keeping rugby league alive in Oldham for the last 20 years and he regularly supports charities, none more so than Dr Kershaw's in Oldham. He is honest, trustworthy and loyal, traits that have ensured Oldham Rugby League Club has been in good hands over the last 20 years. As a good friend of his, I also feel able to call him a real gentleman.

Chris Noble MBE
Chairman, Sheffield Eagles RLFC

Introduction

1997 was an eventful year in the United Kingdom. Tony Blair's Labour Party won the General Election, in so doing ousting the Conservative Party from office for the first time since 1979, Princess Diana tragically died in a car crash in Paris throwing the country into unprecedented mourning, sovereignty of Hong Kong, the largest remaining British colony, was transferred to the People's Republic of China and Channel 5 was launched.

In sport, Sunderland Football Club's Stadium of Light, Stoke City's Britannia Stadium and Bolton Wanderers' Reebok Stadium were opened by the Duke of York, Sir Stanley Matthews and John Prescott respectively. Australia beat England to retain cricket's Ashes and former Oldham RLFC star, Tommy Martyn, won the Lance Todd Trophy as man of the match in St Helens 32-22 victory over Bradford Bulls in the Challenge Cup Final.

In music, Paul McCartney received a knighthood, Oasis released their third album *Be Here Now* and Elton John's *Candle in the Wind* remake was released in tribute to Princess Diana.

On a personal level, my son Reece Thomas Halstead was born, while, locally, the biggest story of the year, certainly in sporting circles, was the sad and painful demise of Oldham RLFC, or Oldham Bears as they were known at the end, the detail of which I discussed in my first book *From Watersheddings to Whitebank – An Oldham Rugby League Memoir*, published by London League Publications Ltd in 2015. As the rugby league fraternity of Oldham struggled through their autumn of discontent, failing in many cases to understand or come to terms with how a club 121 years old could go into liquidation so quickly, it seemed only a matter of time before a new reincarnation of the club would appear on the sporting horizon.

As autumn drifted into winter and Christmas approached, Oldham supporters were given the present they all wished for and dreamt of – a new club, Oldham RLFC (1997) Ltd, was established and given the green light by the Rugby Football League to take its place in the following year's competition. To anybody with professional rugby league in Oldham at heart, it was such a relief that hardly any time it seemed had elapsed since the old club had died to the new club rising like a phoenix from the ashes. With directors Chris Hamilton, Sean Whitehead, Melvyn Lord and Stewart Hardacre at the helm, the new club gave supporters hope for the future and something to look forward to in 1998 and beyond after all had seemed lost.

Now, in 2017, the 'new' club is celebrating the 20th anniversary of its formation. There have been many ups and downs over the two decades – it was ever thus being an Oldham fan – but despite several disappointments, Grand Final defeats and ground issues, the good times that the club has experienced, and there have been many, make supporting the club so very worthwhile. Now, 20 years on, I look back from a personal perspective and I realise that, undoubtedly, the presence of a competitive Oldham team, forever striving to be as good as it possibly can be, has enriched my life so very much that I find it hard to comprehend what life would have been like without one. I love my rugby league so I'm sure that if there had been no Oldham RLFC since 1997, I would still have watched the sport live, probably in Super League. But I am also certain that I would not have enjoyed it anything like as much, or got as excited about it, as I do now watching Oldham. To me, and I know this applies to many other fans too, watching Oldham is what rugby league is all about. I would like to take this opportunity to thank the members of the consortium in 1997 for re-establishing the sport at professional level in the town so quickly after the Bears demise and to everybody concerned in ensuring the club has continued to provide a team to entertain us in the years since then. Here's to the next 20 years and many more after that.

Craig Halstead

Craig Halstead, with Chris Hamilton, prior to the Bower Fold match against Halifax on Good Friday, 2016. (Photo David Murgatroyd).

Thank you

London League Publications Ltd would like to thank: Craig Halstead for his very thorough work; Chris Hamilton for the idea and his support; everyone who contributed to the book, through interviews or providing photos; Steve McCarthy for designing the cover and the staff of Ashford Colour Press Ltd for printing it.

Prologue

Thursday 23 June 2016 is a day that will long live in my memory. The nationwide referendum relating to the United Kingdom's membership of the European Union took place that day, and I was employed by Rochdale Council as a Presiding Officer in a polling station in the borough. Although I now live and work in North Wales, I have maintained my involvement in electoral duties that I carried out as a former employee of the Council. But this is definitely not why I won't forget that day.

Just after lunch-time, I received a telephone call from a representative of the BBC *Songs of Praise* programme telling me that I was a winner, along with 31 other lucky people, of a competition ran jointly by the BBC and the Rugby Football League in which a choir was to be formed to sing the traditional Wembley hymn *Abide with Me* prior to the Challenge Cup Final later that summer. I had applied more out of hope than expectation a few weeks earlier, the requirement of the organisers being that I had to demonstrate support for a rugby league club, professional or amateur.

Since I was five, I have supported the two professional clubs in Oldham, the original club, founded in 1876 that went into liquidation in 1997 and more recently, Oldham RLFC (1997) Ltd, the old club's successor, which has continued to provide the town of Oldham with a professional club since then.

As my mind wandered away momentarily from voting slips and ballot boxes that day, I thought how wonderful and emotional it would be to represent my club on the big stage at the home of British sport and how much I had the current Oldham club to thank, for without their presence since 1997 this unique experience would never have happened for me. I felt then, and still feel now, very humble at being given the opportunity I was given and it's all down to Oldham Rugby League Club.

The organiser's rules stipulated that one supporter of each of the clubs that had reached the last 16 of the Challenge Cup that year would be guaranteed a spot in the choir. How fortunate it turned out to be for me then, that my team had produced one of the Challenge Cup competitions greatest ever shocks by winning convincingly at Super League club Hull Kingston Rovers in the last 32, thereby earning a last 16 shot at eventual finalists Warrington Wolves. Equally significantly for Oldham supporters, of course, was that the fantastic win that had catapulted the team into the spotlight overnight, also meant a dream was to come true for one of us some weeks later. I was the very lucky recipient, but I can only reiterate that I owe one of the best days of my life to the club, the personnel involved at the club, the chairman, the coaching staff, the players, the staff and the fans for making this all possible.

On 27 August 2016, the dream came true. I walked out alongside my colleagues in the choir, all of us resplendent in our club colours, in front of a Wembley crowd of 76,235 ready to sing my heart out. The Hull FC and Warrington Wolves fans gave us a huge cheer as we put into practice what our conductor, Steve Thompson, had taught us and with *Songs of Praise* presenter, Aled Jones, assisting we sang two verses of *Abide with Me*. I felt so proud, wearing my red and white hooped Oldham jersey, and ensuring my club was represented on this great day on the rugby league calendar. A colleague, Rick Farrell, representing Halifax, grasped his club badge with fervour while others including former professional referee, John Kendrew, now a keen Castleford supporter, and former RFL Disciplinary committee member and Huddersfield committee man, Neil Shuttleworth, took it all in their stride. For my part, I just tried to savour every moment, to ensure I missed nothing and had no regrets when it was over.

Earlier we had met Leeds Rhinos star Jamie Jones-Buchanan, one of the competition judges, and the BBC Sport anchor man Mark Chapman on the Wembley pitch. We had been introduced to rugby league legend Martin Offiah in the press conference room and to the First Lady of Rugby League, Lizzie Jones, who was there to present the cup to the winning captain. Throughout the whole experience Aled Jones had been the perfect host, calming our nerves and imploring us to enjoy every second.

It was a perfect weekend, one I will never forget ... and I owe it all to Oldham Rugby League Club.

Craig, middle of the back row, singing *Abide with Me* with Aled Jones in the *Songs of Praise* choir at Wembley in 2016.

Contents

1. Birth of a club   1

2. The Mike Ford era   13

3. Hurst Cross   27

4. The Steve Molloy years   37

5. An overseas invasion   51

6. Looking to bounce back   65

7. More Grand Final heartache   79

8. Mixed emotions   89

9. Whitebank Stadium – a home at last   99

10. A tough division to escape from   113

11. Welcome to a Bulls legend   129

12. Promotion at last   147

13. Challenge Cup magic   165

14. Fighting for Championship survival   181

15. Up the Roughyeds!   199

Appendix 1: World Cup call-ups 2017   213

Appendix 2: Appearances and scorers   214

1. Birth of a club

"Come on Oldham!" A lone voice, clearly in desperation, pierced the air from the far side of the Thrum Hall ground as Oldham Bears once more slipped painfully to defeat. It was August 1997 and, with rumours circulating that the club was in dire financial trouble and the end would be nigh if the club was relegated from Super League, the Halifax fans celebrated another home win. For us Oldham fans, we knew the writing was on the wall and only victory against Paris St Germain, in France, would keep us up. It didn't happen of course. Former Oldham star Andy Goodway's team won 23–12 and the Bears were relegated.

Brian Walker, in his excellent book, *Roughyeds .. The Story,* published by the Oldham Rugby League Heritage Trust, takes up the story: "The directors put the debt-ridden club up for sale but, with no takers, placed it into voluntary liquidation. Shareholders were officially advised that the Bears' directors had decided to commence liquidation proceedings in a letter circulated by chartered accountants, Pannell Kerr Forster, on 8 October, 1997 and at a meeting held at the Pennine Way Hotel, Oldham on 27 October, they learned that the estimated total deficiency was £1,198,908 although included in that figure was £310,859 being the value of the fully paid up ordinary shares. The liquidator got his 75 per cent of the shareholders vote in favour of the extraordinary resolution and Oldham RLFC was no more."

For a short time, it appeared that professional rugby league in Oldham was gone for ever. Oldham, such a proud rugby league town, how could this be true? The supporters, myself included, fervently hoped that a new club could somehow be formed, but how? And by whom? Within weeks, our worst fears proved unfounded. A group of men, who soon became known as the 'consortium' vowed to create a new Oldham club to continue the tradition of professional rugby league in our town. What a relief!

Led by chairman Chris Hamilton, a local accountant and former Head Boy at The Bluecoat School in Oldham, the consortium held a press conference at Boundary Park, the home of Oldham Athletic FC, and then at a packed Queen Elizabeth Hall to make public its intentions, its goals and hopes for the future. Chris remembers it all well: "It was a tremendously busy but exciting time," he said. "I had supported both the old club and Oldham Athletic, but this was my first involvement in the running of a sports club. The meeting at the Queen Elizabeth Hall was a night I will never forget. We were all extremely nervous but I knew that with my fellow directors, Melvyn Lord (vice-chairman), Sean Whitehead and Stewart Hardacre working alongside me, we could make a go of this.

When Roger Halstead, of the *Oldham Chronicle*, first telephoned me to introduce himself and ask initial questions about the consortium, I replied 'no comment, no comment' to each one. I was naive, but I had never dealt with the press before."

Roger, my dad, remembers the first time he visited Chris at his accountancy practice: "There were Oldham Athletic photographs on the walls. I wondered if I was in the right place at first. I soon realised that Chris, and his colleagues meant business though."

At the press conference it was announced that the Roughyeds nickname, so proudly employed by the old club, would be reinstated, that the club would play its home matches at Boundary Park in 1998 and that a 'Back to Basics' policy was to be instigated, clearly designed to emphasise that the club was going to start modestly, look to consolidate and then build over a period of time. After what had happened to the Bears it was reassuring and heart-warming. A team playing professionally in Oldham was what we wanted, not necessarily a team in Super League or a club spending money it couldn't afford in the quest for success.

Chris recalls: "We felt it was important that we made a new start, with new people, new ideas and new goals. A few people who had been associated with the old club wanted to be involved, but we wanted fresh faces around the place. Things had gone wrong at the Bears and we wanted a fresh approach."

In 1998, the rugby league structure consisted of the JJB Super League Championship, the First Division Championship and the Second Division Championship. As a brand new club starting from scratch, Oldham RLFC 1997 (Ltd), the club's official title, were awarded entry into the Second Division, a league comprising of only eight clubs. However, the fly in the ointment was that they were accepted without receiving a penny in central funding. "Not only that, but bizarrely, the Rugby Football League (RFL) forgot to put us in the draw for the Challenge Cup," continues Chris. "Obviously we complained about the oversight and, through Maurice Oldroyd, who was the Chairman of the British Amateur Rugby League Association (BARLA) at the time, we ended up with a number of amateur clubs coming forward to play us in a preliminary round tie, with Heworth from York being the club selected. That allowed the winners to take their place in the 'full' round. It was a tough baptism."

One of the major problems the board faced from the outset was a shortage of time. Remarkably, the first match was played on New Year's Day, 1998, just over two months after the fateful Bears meeting at the Pennine Way Hotel. As well as all the hurdles they had to overcome, and arrangements to make, with the RFL, with Oldham Athletic, and

2

others, they also had to begin the arduous task of appointing a coach, an assistant coach and signing a full squad of players.

Paddy Kirwan, the man who will be forever remembered in Watersheddings folklore for his try that knocked Wigan out of the Challenge Cup in 1987, was appointed coach with another local man, Mick Coates, well-known on the local amateur circuit as a coach of some repute, as his assistant. Players were snapped up one by one in the weeks leading up to Christmas, beginning with two hookers. Local lad John Hough, who went on to enjoy a long and successful career with the club, was the first after seeing service at Warrington Wolves and Darren Robinson, a fiery and skilful player, was the second.

John recalls: "It was a typical Oldham evening, cold and the rain was teaming down. I signed for the new club in the changing rooms at Breeze Hill School. Having enjoyed comparatively luxurious surroundings at Warrington that was a bit of a shock. I didn't realise until later in life though what a great honour it was to be the first player to sign for the club."

Veteran Paul Round, Afi Leuila, Joe McNicholas and Neil Flanagan, all of whom had played for the old club, were signed, the latter as club captain. Winger McNicholas was the scorer of the last ever try at Watersheddings, the old club's spiritual home, in the ground's last match, the farewell game against Swinton Lions in January 1997. "It was a great piece of centre play by Darren Abram that created my try. And I still have the match ball," Joe remembers with a grin. "I would like to take this opportunity to dedicate that try to a very special individual. Steve Gartland tucked me under his wing and helped with so many aspects of my game both on and off the field. This guy had a huge impact on me, as a rugby player and as a person. So 'Garty', that one was for you, mate!" Having scored 34 tries in 103 games for the new club, Joe moved to live in Australia in 2003 and is now Head of Strength and Conditioning for the Penrith Panthers Under-20s team. He recalls the early days well: "I remember like yesterday the day I walked into the club offices only to be told the Bears were finished. I also remember Paddy contacting me to say some local business associates were looking at forming a new venture and he wanted me on board to form part of the new squad. I still get goose-bumps now thinking about it because without Oldham Rugby League Club, and the good people that surround it, I would not be where I am now in the NRL. My days as an Oldham player have left me with the most amazing and unforgettable memories a footballer could ever wish for. The players, staff and supporters made my time as a Roughyed something I will never forget and something I am eternally grateful for."

It was announced that the club's debut match would be a hastily-arranged clash with local rivals Rochdale Hornets in the traditional Law

Cup season opener. Clearly it was imperative that 17 players were available to Kirwan and Coates that day so the signing of players became top priority. For some weeks Oldham had been chasing the signature of Ian Sinfield, the young Salford back-row forward and elder brother of future Leeds Rhinos and England skipper Kevin Sinfield. "Oldham had been trying to negotiate my release," remembers Ian. "I was desperate to play against Rochdale and the deal was eventually completed on New Year's Eve. I went to Chris Hamilton's office with my dad and signed on the dotted line at around 8pm that evening. Obviously it was an extremely proud moment for me because Oldham was my hometown club and I had supported the old club as a boy. Chris worked really hard to get the deal done and I appreciated that."

Chris chuckles when he talks about the Sinfield signing: "We had spent most of the day trying to contact John Wilkinson, the Salford chairman, but to no avail. Finally I decided to drive to The Willows and see him in person. I am glad I did because the deal was done that evening. I enjoyed my New Year's Eve that bit more knowing that Sinny was in the bag."

As I sat in the pub on New Year's Eve 1997, wearing my Oldham RLFC jersey, and waiting for the clock to strike midnight, thus heralding the dawn of another new year, an old pal shouted across a packed bar, "I thought they'd gone bust, mate?" "They have, but we are back! What are you doing tomorrow?" was my immediate response.

The following day – New Year's Day 1998 – saw the brand new Oldham team run out onto the pitch at Spotland Stadium. I told my mate that for once it wasn't important whether we won the Law Cup or not, all that mattered was a team representing Oldham RLFC was playing rugby league again, a team ready to fight tooth and nail for the badge once more. When I turned up at the ground that day, not quite knowing what to expect, and if truth be known, not knowing several of the players the new board had signed, it was with trepidation that we might get a good hiding, but also with a heady mix of pride, relief and joy that Oldham were back. The team wore a traditional red and white hooped jersey. That felt good. Not only had this group of players never played together before, they had not trained together for long either. For Oldham to win would take a Herculean effort; nobody but the most parochial of fans would have backed them to win that day.

Well, nobody wearing red and white on the Spotland pitch that day had read the script. Turning in a fantastic performance, full of guts and pride and with a terrific will-to-win, plus no little skill, the Roughyeds rocked Hornets from the kick-off, the forwards dominating the hard slog up front and the backs looking dangerous every time the ball was moved wide. Backed by a vociferous following of fans, swelled due to the feelings of shock and sympathy as a result of what had happened

4

to the Bears, the Oldham side scored six tries through McNicholas with two, Adrian Mead, Mike Prescott, Martin Maders and Sinfield, with six goals from the immaculate goalkicking of second row forward Brian Quinlan. The final score was an emphatic 36–16.

Skipper Neil Flanagan on the shoulders of Ian Sinfield after the 1998 Law Cup triumph. (Photo courtesy Ian Sinfield).

It was a surprising and wonderful result – real *Roy of the Rovers* stuff – and all the troubles of the past few months evaporated into the Rochdale air that afternoon. I recall with great pleasure the moment scrum-half Flanagan received the Law Cup and his ecstatic team-mates launched him onto their shoulders for the post-match photographs and celebrations. It had seemed like a home match due to the pre-dominance of Oldham fans in the 3,097 crowd and as the players made their way off after their lap of honour, I was already looking forward to the next match. Oldham were back, and the new club – Oldham RLFC (1997) Ltd – was up and running. McNicholas remembers the game well. "Playing in that first game at Spotland holds so many amazing memories but none more than scoring two tries to help us claim the club's first silverware. I recall one of my tries vividly. I received the ball on the left wing and stepped inside before veering out again to sprint clear and slide over the line."

Sinfield recalls: "Winning that day is undoubtedly one of my greatest memories, something I will always remember. In fact, I'd say it was probably the best day of my rugby league career as we were massive underdogs and literally a team that had been put together from scratch in a short space of time." Ten days later, the new team made their first trip into Yorkshire to face Hunslet at the South Leeds Stadium, a match I remember best for the debut of a player who became a real favourite over the next few years, Jason Clegg. 'Cleggy' was a product of the Littleborough RUFC and Littleborough ARLFC clubs and went to the same school as me, Wardle High School in Rochdale.

5

The four members of the consortium that relaunched the club in 1997: Sean Whitehead, Chris Hamilton, Melvyn Lord and Stewart Hardacre.

As a youngster, Jason had signed for Bradford Northern and I recall watching an 'A' team match at Watersheddings against Northern when 'Cleggy' was on trial there.

A week later came the first match at Boundary Park, the Challenge Cup Third Round preliminary tie against Heworth and the club's first competitive match. The Roughyeds played well again and won 36–14 with centre Sean Cooper and winger Craig Diggle each scoring two tries. A great crowd of 2,943 attended. However the team's involvement in the Challenge Cup ended in the next round with defeat at Widnes.

Extracts from the Oldham versus Heworth match day programme, 18 January 1998:

Sir Rodney Walker, Chairman of the RFL

It is with considerable pleasure that I welcome the new Oldham RLFC as a member of the Rugby Football League. The town of Oldham has, over many years, been a hotbed of rugby league and has produced many fine players, both amateur and professional. I feel certain that the public of Oldham will want to support the Directors of the newly formed club and, as Chairman, I would like to offer my best wishes to all concerned for a successful future.

Phil Woolas MP, Oldham East and Saddleworth

It is truly a pleasure to be able to send this message of support for the new season – one that many thought Oldham would miss out on. The welcome for the team at Spotland said it all, warm applause, genuine delight and gratitude to all the directors, players and off-field volunteers who made the resurrection possible. The result wasn't half bad as well! Oldham has always been a crucible for rugby league. To have professional rugby league without an Oldham side is as unbearable as it is unthinkable. Congratulations are due to all those involved. Best Wishes for 1998 and for many, many more years to come.

Councillor John Battye, Leader of Oldham MBC

Just a few short months ago, one or two cynics had us dead and buried so it is all the more pleasurable for the thousands of true Oldham RLFC fans – and I count myself amongst them – that today has finally arrived. Pinch yourself if you must but you needn't – the red and white hooped jerseyed players belong to the new Oldham RLFC – the Roughyeds are back in business and competing once again.

A special word of praise and admiration for Chris Hamilton, the chairman of Oldham RLFC, and his fellow directors who picked up the ball and ran with it, so to speak, against significant odds.

Paddy Kirwan, Oldham RLFC coach

I came back from holiday in early November, 1997 disillusioned with rugby league and in particular the demise of Oldham Bears. On discussing with the new board of directors, it was quickly apparent that they were genuine supporters who had done a lot of homework and had a similar love for the game that I do. Being on the same wavelength, I was delighted to accept the opportunity to coach the new team. Having Mick Coates alongside me is a big boost as his knowledge and respect within the local game means he is ideal for the job.

Ray French, BBC and the *Rugby Leaguer*

The Oldham directors have every right to feel pride in their achievements. The quartet have rescued a once great club and battled bravely against seemingly insurmountable odds to take their rightful place in the Silk Cut Challenge Cup. Today there will be thirteen Roughyeds, clad in red and white hooped jerseys, prepared to put their bodies on the line. What more could the good folk of Oldham want?

David Burke, *Manchester Evening News* and *The Times*

Rugby league without Oldham would be like Blackpool minus the tower. News that the Bears had gone into liquidation was devastating because Oldham are an institution in the game. Expansion around the UK may

7

be the modern thinking but Oldham epitomise the tradition and history of the 13-a-side code. Take away part of the heart and the body can't function. Thankfully, Chris Hamilton and his consortium have rescued Oldham who have now entered 1998 with a new confidence as well as a new team. Well done Chris and Co. for having the courage to step in and save rugby league in Oldham.

Robert Gate, rugby league historian
I am so glad Oldham were not allowed to perish. To me, rugby league without Oldham is almost inconceivable. Although a true blue and white from Halifax, I have always had a soft spot for Oldham, because, just like Halifax, it is a rugby league town.

Martyn Sadler, Editor, *Rugby League Express*
Rugby league is part of the history, culture and folklore of Oldham. It is hard to imagine Oldham without its rugby league club and thanks to Chris Hamilton and his fellow directors we will not have to. Being raised from the dead happened almost 2,000 years ago, if reports are to be believed, so the Roughyeds are following in auspicious footsteps.

Rugby league is a demanding game and rugby league people are used to facing challenges. The Roughyeds faced a challenge on New Year's Day at Rochdale and came through it superbly. I was delighted that my newspaper, *Rugby League Express*, was able to record that event.

John Huxley, *Sunday Mirror* and *Rugby League Express*
There have been times in the last few months when I have been afraid. Afraid that professional rugby league was a goner in the town of Oldham. For those of us who have had anything to do with the sport in Oldham – I worked for the *Chronicle* for four happy years in the 1970s – the club has become part of our lives while I recognise that there are people for whom Oldham Rugby League Club means everything. To be asked to contribute to an Oldham programme delighted me because I thought I may never have this privilege again.

We are lucky because there are people in the town who are dedicated sufficiently to rugby league to put their time and money into the club. They alone have made it possible to save the club. But they cannot do it on their own from hereon. In the end the measure of success of any professional sports club is whether they can field a team of paid players each week and whether sufficient people come through the gate to watch them and to make the club viable. Take either of these requirements away and you have trouble as the Bears discovered. To the people who had faith in the sport by backing the formation of the new club, I say a heartfelt thank you.

So the Roughyeds were back and it felt so good watching the team play. The league season began with a fine win at Workington and a narrow 12–10 defeat against now-defunct Bramley at Headingley. The victory at Derwent Park was a massive boost because Town were a Super League team only two years earlier. The Bramley game stands out in my mind because a kick at goal by winger Richard Darkes which would have tied the scores late in the game, shaved a post as it went narrowly wide. A victory at Doncaster followed before a second loss to Bramley, this one at home. Another great crowd of 2,921 attended.

A player who went on to make a huge impact in this inaugural season had joined the club by this stage – Michael Edwards. Another former Watersheddings old boy, 'Micky' had been a prolific try-scorer, mainly from scrum-half, in the old club's 'A' team in 1993–94 which went through the entire season unbeaten and won three trophies that year. He remembers: "Watersheddings was a wonderful ground to play at, such an intimidating atmosphere for opposition teams. However, I was delighted to sign for the new club, hoping to establish myself as the first-choice scrum-half. Imagine my surprise, or maybe shock would be a better description, when Paddy Kirwan pulled me to one side at training one night and told me he had a plan to play me at prop."

Paddy knew what he was doing though because Micky had a terrific year: "I like to think Paddy knew I was a solid defender and could break a tackle when in possession. I played slightly wider than a prop normally would and linked well with Afi Leulia, who was in the centre. I wasn't bothered where I played really, I just loved playing for Oldham. I even managed to score a hat-trick of tries once, against Workington Town at Boundary Park, and that in a pair of borrowed boots – I had forgotten to bring mine."

As the season progressed, the Second Division Championship split into two regions, East and West, to compete for the Red Rose and White Rose Championships. Each team played the other teams in their region with the two regional winners meeting in the Trans Pennine Cup Final. Some new experienced players had been signed, influential loose-forward Mick Martindale, big Joe Naidole, brother of former Watersheddings favourite Tom Naidole, and half-back Chris Wilkinson, who provided a steadying influence to a young side. Oldham enjoyed a 56–8 home win over Workington, a 25–20 win over a strong Lancashire Lynx outfit, who included another old club old boy Darren Abram in its ranks and a great 32–8 win over Barrow. As a result, the team qualified to play Batley Bulldogs in the Trans Pennine Cup Final. On 19 July, 1998, the club appeared in its first final, a great effort in its first season.

Although the team lost 28–12 to a home side who know how to play the Mount Pleasant slope so well, it was a pleasure to be there that day, stood behind the posts at the top end of the ground, cheering the boys on. One sad memory, however, was a serious injury to Batley and former Leeds and Great Britain forward Roy Powell, who it was feared had swallowed his tongue on the pitch. Play was held up for several minutes as he was treated by medical staff. Tragically Roy died a few months later after suffering a heart attack during training with his new club Rochdale Hornets.

Oldham finished the season in fifth place in the league, a commendable effort indeed. The club had done well in year one of its existence and much of the credit has to go to local born players who signed that year. As well as John Hough, Neil Flanagan, Ian Sinfield, Sean Cooper, Brian Quinlan and Mick Martindale, whom I have already mentioned, others born and bred in Oldham included full-back Steve Wilde, winger Chris Eckersley, stand-off Craig Barker, prop Martin Maders, whose father Denis represented the old club, and loose-forward Emerson Jackman. Quinlan was a fine goalkicker, Cooper a real handful at centre and Eckersley was a flyer, who certainly knew where the try line was. Sinfield recalls: "It was a thrill playing with so many Oldham born players and also with Paul Round, who was one of my favourite players as a boy and a real Watersheddings legend."

As the autumnal Tri Nations Championship approached, Roughyeds forward Graeme Shaw was named in the Scotland squad for games against Ireland and France. It was a very proud moment for Graeme, and indeed everybody connected with the club, when he was called up to represent his country in both games – an international call-up for a Roughyeds star in the club's first season.

In 1999, the majority of games were played out of town for the first time, at Spotland Stadium in Rochdale, as agreement could not be reached with Oldham Athletic for use of Boundary Park that year. So began the club's nomadic existence which was never to entirely leave it. A change on the coaching front saw Mick Coates take over as head coach following the departure of Kirwan after one year. Australian Graeme Bradley, a powerful centre from Bradford Bulls, took over the running of the club's newly formed reserve team. A few players left after one year, including the irrepressible Edwards, who then enjoyed a short spell at St Helens, coached by rugby league legend Ellery Hanley. Saints saw Micky as the man to provide cover for their talismanic hooker Keiron Cunningham but sadly, Edwards badly damaged the ligaments in a knee in an 'A' team game soon after signing and never played in the first team at Knowsley Road.

Some potentially exciting signings were made, French duo Laurent Minut, a full-back, and Emmanuel Peralta, a second row forward, arrived as did Australian scrum-half Daniel Brown, brother of current

1998 team group, the first year of the new club, with coach Paddy Kirwan and assistant coach Mick Coates (Photo courtesy Ian Sinfield).

Left: Man-mountain Jason Clegg, one of the most popular players to play for the club, 148 appearances between 1998 and 2003

Below: Graeme Shaw, the club's first international, when picked to represent Scotland in 1998

(Both photos courtesy of Oldham Rugby League Heritage Trust).

Newcastle Knights head coach and former Huddersfield Giants and St Helens coach Nathan Brown, and another Australian, big centre or wing Josh Bostock. Welsh international, and former Halifax Blue Sox Super League player, Mark Perrett, also joined the club.

Minut, Peralta and Brown all did well, but Bostock was desperately unlucky. He scored a fine try and looked good in a thrilling 8–8 draw away to Hull Kingston Rovers in a midweek match in March but then Josh received a bad knee injury at Hunslet four days later, which kept him out for the rest of the year.

As well as the overseas signings, an old favourite of Oldham fans from Watersheddings days joined the club as captain. Leo Casey arrived after service with Featherstone Rovers, Swinton Lions and Rochdale Hornets as well as the old Oldham club and was a powerhouse up front all season alongside John Hough and Jason Clegg. Although Casey, Hough and Clegg were the driving force behind the team in 1999, 'Cleggy' sees it differently: "I would say we were only part of the side and we couldn't have performed as we did without the support of the rest of the lads," he said modestly. "The front row got a lot of personal credit even though the team was struggling, but the contribution of the rest of the team should not be underestimated either."

The season began with two Challenge Cup victories. A comfortable win against the amateurs Eccles in the fourth round was followed by a terrific 18–10 win against Dewsbury Rams in the fifth round, played on a Monday evening at Spotland. Dewsbury, including former Bradford Bulls stars Nathan Graham and Paul Medley, went on to finish top of the newly-introduced Northern Ford Premiership (NFP) that year, so this result augured well for the Roughyeds.

The *Independent* said: "The sheer enthusiasm of the Oldham side, playing in exile in neighbouring Rochdale, proved decisive. Jason Clegg and the captain, Leo Casey, a popular choice as man of the match, were outstanding and typified Oldham's commitment while Daniel Brown, the Australian half-back, matched a high work-rate with some much needed creativity." However, defeat came in the next round at Whitehaven.

Unfortunately, the season's promising start didn't last and the team won only five and drew two of 28 games in the NFP. One of the wins was the highlight of the season, a 26–18 victory over Rochdale Hornets at Boundary Park. The match was billed as part of the 150th anniversary celebrations of Oldham Borough's municipal status. It was staged on Sunday evening, 13 June 1999 with an excellent crowd of 3,023.

A nail-biting 23–17 victory over Doncaster Dragons at Spotland in July was a major relief for supporters because it condemned the South Yorkshire outfit to the wooden spoon and ensured Oldham avoided that unwanted title. But in truth 1999 was a year best forgotten. Roll on the new millennium and a real upturn in fortunes.

2. The Mike Ford era

In 1985 the brilliant Australian stand-off half, Brett Kenny of Wigan, scored one of the best tries ever seen in a Challenge Cup Final at Wembley. Moving on to a wide pass he cut through the Hull defence like a knife through butter in an arcing run to score from the halfway line. It brought the house down. In the Hull team that day was Kenny's great mate, Peter Sterling, another fantastic half-back. "If Sterling was silver, then Kenny was gold," read a banner at Wigan's DW Stadium years later. But I digress. The pass that sent Kenny clear came from Oldham lad, Mike Ford, a prodigious young talent and as Wigan's first-choice scrum-half, with the world at his feet.

Ford went on to enjoy a terrific career as a player, giving outstanding service to Wigan, Leigh, the old Oldham club, Castleford (in two spells), Warrington and South Queensland Crushers as well as Great Britain, whom he represented on the Lions 1988 tour of Australia. He ultimately became a top class coach in rugby union, spending successful years as defence coach for Ireland, England and the British Lions and as head coach at Saracens RUFC, Bath RUFC and the French outfit Toulon. In 2017, Ford was appointed by Dallas Griffins in the USA to head up their rugby operations ahead of the launch of Major League Rugby (rugby union) in the States in 2018. But it was for his two years as head coach at the new Oldham RLFC, in 2000 and 2001, that I remember him best and where he really cut his teeth as a coach.

Despite brief spells coaching at Dukinfield RUFC and Bramley RLFC, his appointment at Oldham ahead of the 2000 season was the one that really set him on the way to the top as a coach. There is no doubt that Oldham were good for Ford in this respect, but equally it is very true that Ford was good for Oldham too. It was a terrific appointment by the board. Not only was Ford a fine coach in the making, but he was still playing at the time and was, therefore, able to control his team on the pitch as well as off it. While Mike was dictating proceedings on the pitch, his former Watersheddings team-mate John Henderson, who was introduced as assistant, looked after the dug-out.

Thankfully, Oldham were back at Boundary Park for the start of the new millennium and that, combined with the capture of Ford as player-coach and the signing of several new players, meant there was a lot of optimism among fans ahead of the season. Moving in alongside the boss Ford were five players from Bramley, his previous club. The Gibbons twins, Anthony and David, became great favourites as did full-back Mark Sibson, prop-forward Andy Proctor, who had played for the Roughyeds previously in 1998, and Australian-born Papua New Guinea international Tom O'Reilly.

13

In 1996, the Gibbons boys turned out for Leeds (the nickname Rhinos was added a year later) against Oldham at Watersheddings in the first Super League season, a match that was televised live by Sky Sports. Although they were highly regarded at Headingley, they were allowed to join Bramley and then move on to Oldham. Stephen Boothroyd, a junior rugby league coach in Leeds and colleague of mine in the *Songs of Praise* choir at Wembley in 2016, knows them both well: "I had the privilege of working with many talented youngsters in the Leeds City Boys Under-13s team and Anthony and David were two of the best. They had all the necessary handling, kicking, evasive and organisational skills needed to do well in the game and played in the 1987 Challenge Cup Final schoolboy curtain-raiser at Wembley. They turned professional for their local club as 17-year-olds in 1993, David making his debut towards the end of the 1994-95 season and Anthony in October 1995, at Oldham. They both played in the first Super League season in 1996 and despite giving a good account of themselves were among 20 players who left the club that year, paying the price for a poor season for the team.

After a loan spell at Keighley, they both had two and a half years at Bramley, before signing for Oldham in 2000. Both of them now have sons who are making good progress in the junior and schoolboy game in Leeds."

Chris Hamilton grins as he recalls a trip to the Rugby League Disciplinary Committee with one of the twins. "I think it was Anthony, but I couldn't be sure, you just could not tell them apart. Anyway, both these lads were so tough, not only on the pitch but in training too, great lads. On this occasion, however, Anthony was a nervous wreck." He clearly didn't care too much for having to face the disciplinary committee. "Remind me to never get sent off again Chris," he said to his chairman as he left the room.

In the three seasons they were at the club, 2000, 2001 and 2002, Anthony scored 36 tries in 88 appearances, mainly from right centre and David scored 37 tries in 94 appearances, mainly from stand-off. Not only did they produce such remarkably similar statistics – one more try for David, although Anthony did kick a drop-goal too – they also played in very similar styles. Indeed, if it wasn't for the numbers on their jerseys, people were rarely able to tell them apart. They were both tremendously tough competitors, hard as nails, and never took a backward step. Neil Roden, who joined the club mid-season in 2000, enjoyed playing alongside them: "The Gibbons boys were great lads, ideal team-mates when the going got tough on the pitch," he recalls.

Sibson proved to be a very astute signing too. Extremely dangerous with ball in hand when attacking from deep, he possessed the uncanny ability of being able to gracefully slide through an opposition defence

14

and then had the pace, more often than not, to capitalise on the break and score. I would say that in full flight he was one of the most exciting attacking backs I have witnessed in an Oldham jersey in the last 20 years. "I had played for Huddersfield Giants briefly, as well as Bramley, before joining Oldham, then Batley and Hunslet after, but no other club felt as big as Oldham," he said. "Playing at Boundary Park, it felt like the whole town was behind us. I remember what a great set of fans we had. It felt like we could beat anyone there and it generated a great atmosphere. Mike Ford built a team full of hard-working players, genuine people, typified by the Gibbons twins. I spent the majority of my career with them, at Bramley, Oldham, Batley and Hunslet and we built up a great understanding."

'Ziggy', as Sibson was known to his team-mates, raced in for 60 tries in 91 games, a great effort. In 2000, his 23 tries left him joint fifth in the sport's top try scorers list and he twice scored four in a match, against Wigan St Judes in 2000 and Queensbury in 2001, both at Boundary Park in the Challenge Cup. He continued: "My favourite try came in a match against Doncaster Dragons at Boundary Park. I'd just dropped a high kick near the posts which they scored from so I was feeling pretty low. Almost from the restart 'Fordy' passed me the ball, he knew the best thing for me was to get hold of the ball again after my mistake minutes earlier. One of the opposition stepped out of the defensive line leaving a gap. I went for it, managed to break clear and outpaced the cover before rounding the full-back. I never wanted to let my team-mates down and felt that I had made up for the mistake in the best way possible."

Proctor had made a big impression on Ford at Bramley and was immediately made club captain on his return to the Roughyeds. Other notable signings included former St Helens and Salford flyer Joey Hayes, prop Wes Rogers, another Oldham lad, from Swinton Lions, loose-forward Kevin Mannion from Rochdale Hornets and most significantly of all, young Durham-born centre Pat Rich from Keighley Cougars. Interestingly, Sibson, Mannion and Rich had all represented their country as student internationals.

Hayes had toured New Zealand, Fiji and Papua New Guinea with Great Britain in 1996 and had been a regular on Saints' right wing prior to his switch to Salford. He proved a real hit on Oldham's right flank too, forming a formidable partnership with Anthony Gibbons and eventually scoring 28 tries in 51 games over three seasons. I remember Joey scoring a spectacular try for Saints against Oldham Bears at Boundary Park when he got on the end of a teasing Bobbie Goulding cross-kick and he was equally dangerous when chasing Ford or Roden kicks to the corner in an Oldham jersey.

When Oldham fans with very long memories, or perhaps those whose fathers or grandfathers passed on tales of yesteryear, talk of 1950s great Bernard Ganley being the best goalkicker in the history of the old club, then Pat Rich got as close as anyone in the decades since to matching the great man's abilities with the boot. In two seasons under Ford, Rich kicked 254 goals, from all angles and distances, to prove conclusively that he was, indeed, a goalkicker of the highest class. Pat was also a fine centre too, extremely strong defensively and scorer of 17 tries in the same two-year spell.

His father and brother used to travel from Durham to watch him play, rarely missing a match, and I know they were extremely proud of his achievements in the game. Quite by chance, my dad and I bumped into Pat's brother at the London Stadium (formerly the Olympic Stadium) after the England versus New Zealand match in 2015 and he told us that the Oldham club had made an indelible mark on Pat and that he cherished every minute he wore the Oldham jersey. As a fan, it was great watching him too.

The Gibbons twins, Sibson and Rich used to travel to Oldham from Leeds together for training and on match days. "We spent a lot of time in a car on the M62, and most of that time was spent laughing," remembers Ziggy. "I was part of a back three [full-back and two wingers] with Joey Hayes and Joe McNicholas and we also became good friends."

As mentioned, Neil Roden began his long association with the club – apart from a brief spell away when he played for Batley and Leigh – mid-season in 2000 when he joined alongside another product of the famous Wigan academy, Phil Farrell, younger brother of Wigan and Great Britain legend Andy Farrell. Phil's twin brother, Chris, arrived at the club a year later. "I learned a lot from Mike Ford," recalls Neil, "not only because he was a fine coach but also a half-back like me. I played in the halves alongside David Gibbons for much of Fordy's two years at the club, with Mike on the bench ready to come on and perhaps turn a game our way if it was tight."

Sibson speaks extremely highly of Roden. "Neil joined the club in my first season and went on to become a club legend. A big character and someone I still consider a friend. I lost count of the number of tries he created for me as well as scoring a few himself too." Phil Farrell also gave terrific service to the club, captaining the side for much of the time. "Faz' was the best captain I played under," says John Hough. "He told it how it was and he led by example."

In the first half of the 2000 season, Oldham's bitter rivals Rochdale Hornets had acquired the services of former Western Suburbs second-row forward Shayne McMenemy. Unfortunately for them, things didn't work out for McMenemy at Rochdale, and when he was released following an internal dispute, Oldham pounced for his signature, particularly as Tom O'Reilly had suffered a bad leg injury around the same time. Shayne was a fine experienced forward and proved to be a formidable force in the Oldham pack for the remainder of the year.

"I enjoyed playing for Mike Ford," he recalls. "He was so clinical, he knew exactly what he wanted from his players and everyone respected him so much. This, I guess, was reflected in our performances. I enjoyed the challenge of proving myself in the English game because the NFP was a tough competition. We had some great players, John Hough, big 'Cleggy', Phil Farrell, Neil Roden, the Gibbons twins to name but a few. In one of my first games for Oldham, I kicked a winning drop-goal against Rochdale at Spotland, which was satisfying being it was against my old club. We had a great camaraderie, being the only Aussie the boys used to rib me a bit but it was all good banter."

McMenemy played just one game in 2001, against Barrow at Craven Park, before the Super League clubs started sniffing around him. "My ambition was to play in Super League," Shayne continues, "so when I heard that Halifax, then a top-flight outfit, were interested in me, I pushed for the move." After his spell at The Shay, he moved on to Hull FC and played a starring role in their 2005 Challenge Cup Final victory over Leeds Rhinos at the Millennium Stadium in Cardiff and then appeared in the 2006 Super League Grand Final against St Helens.

On moving back to his homeland, he became captain/coach of the Western Reds, based in Perth. "We would fly to Sydney every other week to play," he recalls. "I then started a Physical Training business and worked as a strength and conditioning coach at Parramatta Eels for several years before becoming Head Coach at Narallen Jets who play in the Group 6 competition. Playing for Oldham, however, was definitely one of the most enjoyable years I had in rugby league."

As a break from the monotony of pre-season training, Ford took his troops to Plymouth to spend some time with the Royal Marines. Sibson remembers it well: "We spent a night on Dartmoor in January and half an hour in the ice-cold Western English Channel. It helped to create a steeliness and mental toughness that defined the team. The team spirit developed in that side was the best I've had the privilege to be a part of. We weren't the most talented group but we would never give up and would do anything we could to come out winners."

The team's performances were steady, if not spectacular, from the outset in 2000, with a cracking win, 31–20, at Widnes, being an early highlight. A heavy defeat away to Featherstone Rovers soon followed, however, but this disappointment proved to be the catalyst for a superb winning run of seven straight victories in the NFP, including the win at Rochdale where McMenemy dropped the winning goal and a splendid 32–12 win away to Hull KR. Prior to the play-offs the team won five of the last six league games, including an excellent 27–10 win over Leigh Centurions at Boundary Park, a match in which John Hough scored twice, and a great 32–0 drubbing of Featherstone to avenge their earlier defeat by Rovers. Hooker Hough had a superb season in 2000. He was an ever-present with 33 appearances and also finished second in the club try-scoring charts with 18, behind Mark Sibson, who scored 23.

The play-offs began with another win over Hull KR, this one at Spotland, as Boundary Park was unavailable that weekend. Another major signing had been made three weeks earlier when, in a bid to push for glory in the play-offs, Steve Molloy, the vastly experienced former Warrington, Leeds, Featherstone Rovers, Sheffield Eagles and Huddersfield prop joined on loan. Molloy was a powerful presence in the front row and later returned to the club, eventually becoming player-coach, in 2002. The major highlight of the 2000 play-off campaign, however, was a thrilling tie at Doncaster that Oldham won in extra time. McMenemy remembers it well: "Doncaster were a fine side that year and after 80 minutes the scores were locked. We played another 10 minutes each way and we came out on top. It was a great feeling. Unfortunately, that sucked the energy out of us for the next game at Leigh, where we went down narrowly."

So the play-off campaign was over but Ford and his troops would be back the following year to mount a serious push for the Holy Grail of Super League which everyone coveted.

In 2000, the team's last match at Leigh was on 23 July, so it seemed a long time before the 2001 season began, ironically in December 2000. In the meantime, the Roughyeds welcomed a South Sydney Juniors team from Australia to Boundary Park on 19 November. Michael Curin, a historian at the South Sydney club, takes up the story: "The match was one of three played by the team on a short tour of the North of England, which they called the Ambassadors Tour. The idea was to give experience to a young squad of players and to help raise awareness of, and funds for, our club's fightback cause." One of Australia's most famous clubs, Souths, were ousted from the competition in 1999 when the Australian Rugby League decided to reduce the number of teams and it was a pleasure to welcome the famous green and red jerseys that the young Australians wore with pride that day. The Souths squad had some fine young players in it and the match with a strong Oldham side finished 14–14.

Future Oldham forward Tere Glassie turned out for the visitors that day: "I was in the UK for the 2000 World Cup with the Cook Islands. As I am a South Sydney junior, I linked up with them after our World Cup campaign ended and had a run," recalls Tere.

18

The Gibbons brothers, Anthony and David, third left and third right on the
front row, seen here in a Leeds Boys team with coach Stephen Boothroyd.
Both came to Oldham with Mike Ford in 2000.
(Photo courtesy Stephen Boothroyd).

Former Wigan youngster Phil Farrell, 'the best captain I ever played under',
according to John Hough.
(Photo courtesy Oldham Rugby League Heritage Trust).

Chris Hamilton explains how the match came to take place: "I was involved in arranging the tour along with an Australian agent friend of mine, Mick Robinson. Mick spoke to an acquaintance of his at the Souths end and it went from there. They played three matches, against ourselves, Keighley Cougars and Warrington Wolves. Of course, when the opportunity arose, I was delighted to welcome them to Oldham. It was quite a coup that they chose to play us and was a proud day for our club."

South Sydney were finally re-admitted to the NRL in 2002 and their journey back to the top was complete in 2014, when they won the NRL Grand Final with a team comprising the English brothers Sam, George and Tom Burgess.

2001 remains a year of mixed emotions for all associated with the club. Remarkably, having been formed only four years earlier and having started on the very bottom rung of the league ladder, the team got to within one win of reaching the promised land of Super League. Just 80 minutes rugby league away from joining the big hitters of our game, Wigan Warriors, St Helens, Leeds Rhinos, Warrington Wolves et al. It was a wonderful achievement, yet one tinged with frustration that they were so near yet so far from achieving a major goal.

Along the way 2001 produced some magnificent memories for the fans, exciting matches, spectacular wins and a play-off series that could not have been scripted. Super League coaches these days often refer to the 'business end' of the season, the last few weeks, the play-offs, where the prizes for victory are so great and where the team needs to peak. Often defeat or below par displays in the first half of a season are forgotten if the team gets it right when it matters most. This was exactly how it was for Ford's Oldham in 2001.

The season began well enough with two away wins in Cumbria, against Barrow Raiders and Workington Town, before a Christmas Eve 2000 classic saw Rochdale Hornets beaten at Spotland in front of a bumper gate of 3,402. Another terrific win, against Widnes Vikings, on New Year's Day, 2001 – attendance 3,471 – saw new winger Danny Arnold, scorer of 59 tries in 107 Super League matches for St Helens, Huddersfield Giants and Castleford Tigers, cross twice to help Roughyeds to victory. However, despite a 56–2 win over Chorley Lynx (Lancashire Lynx were re-named Chorley Lynx after the 2000 season), a match in which David Gibbons scored four tries, and a 52–6 triumph over Gateshead Thunder, when Mark Sibson and Neil Roden both scored hat-tricks, a grim midweek loss to Whitehaven at Boundary Park in March saw the early promise begin to evaporate. I recall that Ford looked visibly shaken in the Clayton Arms after the game that night. Two bad defeats over Easter against Rochdale Hornets at home and Widnes Vikings away followed. But there was little doubt in my mind, and I'm sure in many other fans minds, that Ford would turn things around and sooner rather than later.

Although Shayne McMenemy was proving a big loss, the mid-season arrival on loan from St Helens of Kiwi second-row forward Bryan Henare and a remarkable surge of form from local lad Keith Brennan provided the impetus for a major upsurge in form as mid-summer arrived. Henare was a great influence on the side: "I was very happy at Oldham, my young family and I were made welcome straight away and I think I played some of the best football of my career there. I played rugby league for nearly 35 years and my only regret is leaving Oldham when I did, in 2002. We had a good side with good players, and it was a pleasure to be part of it."

Keith Brennan's story was a fairy tale. He had played amateur rugby league, for Waterhead, Higginshaw and Shaw as a scrum-half and joined Oldham in 1999, with the intention of staking a claim for the number seven jersey. He played seven games in 1999 and five in 2000, but it was a positional switch to hooker the following year that really kick-started his career in the professional ranks. John Hough had been a mainstay of the side in the middle of the front row since day one in 1998, but with Brennan in the form of his life Hough had to be content with a place on the bench for several matches. Oldham were certainly blessed with two outstanding number nines. Indeed, the front-row was a real strength that year. With Leo Casey, Jason Clegg and Andy Proctor still going strong, competition for places was intensified with the early season capture of Chorley Lynx workaholic Paul Norton and the presence of juggernaut Danny Guest, usually introduced from the bench. Opposition teams found the Oldham front-row a formidable proposition to play against.

The team went on a superb late season surge for the play-offs, winning 11 out of the last 12 games in the NFP to nestle in nicely behind Leigh, Widnes and Rochdale in the final table. The run began with a tight 9–8 victory away to Batley Bulldogs with youngster Gavin Dodd delighting Oldham's fans with a winning drop-goal. More about Gavin to follow. Keith Brennan notched a classy hat-trick in the reverse fixture at Gateshead as Roughyeds romped home, 50–20, and then scored two more in a 26–16 win at Keighley.

The first play-off outing against Leigh, at Hilton Park, was a stunning match. Leigh had been tremendous all year, finishing nine points clear at the top of the table. But as is so often proven, league placings count for little in play-off ties, and Oldham were in a rich (no pun intended) vein of form and very confident. Keith Brennan put over an early drop-goal to ease nerves, but then went off injured. John Hough replaced him and almost immediately forced his way over from dummy half. So Oldham had their noses in front, but a crucial decision by referee Colin

21

Morris on the stroke of half-time had a major bearing on the result. With the home side attacking strongly it appeared that a Leigh player was tripped as he went for the line. The Leigh fans howled for a penalty try – the ball carrier looked a certain scorer – or at least a penalty and a red card for the culprit. But to their disbelief, and to the Oldham contingent's relief, Mr Morris, after a lengthy consultation with one – or maybe both – touch-judges, turned down their pleas and gave Oldham a penalty instead for an earlier offence.

This meant that Leigh had to come from behind in the second half and put a different complexion on the match altogether. Oldham defended magnificently after half-time, repelling Leigh's attacks time and again. Although they did fall behind briefly midway through the half, they stormed back from the kick-off, Mark Sibson, as was his want, scything through the Leigh left-centre position to restore Oldham's advantage and stun the home crowd. Still Leigh pressed right to the hooter, but the brave Roughyeds held firm and clung on to win 15–14. What a fantastic result!

Leigh had a second chance, but lost to Widnes and were out. The play-off series was wide open with Widnes, Rochdale and Oldham all fancying their chances. My dad, Roger Halstead, who had missed very few Oldham matches – old club or new – since he began to cover the old club's fortunes for the *Oldham Chronicle* in 1964, was in Australia as media manager on a North West Counties amateur tour at the time: "Although I thoroughly enjoyed the tour and wouldn't have missed it for the world, I was so frustrated at missing the play-offs," he said. "My mind was very much with the Roughyeds while in Sydney and I couldn't wait to hear the results. The win at Leigh was obviously a great one for the team."

Next up for Oldham came a massive derby meeting with Hornets at Spotland. Coached by former Oldham, Rochdale and Wigan hooker, Martin Hall, Rochdale were a force to be reckoned with at home with Oldhamers prop Danny Sculthorpe and centre Matt Calland, huge influences. For an hour they looked like a team capable of reaching the Grand Final, playing some exciting attacking rugby and scoring some fine tries. I was worried, very worried, and I know other Oldham fans were too. At half-time, with Hornets well ahead, Chris Hamilton was speaking to Emma Rosewarne from the RFL: "Emma commented on how well Rochdale were playing and that they were looking good to win the whole series as the Grand Final was also at Spotland," Chris remembers with a smile. "I told her that this match was far from over, we were definitely not out of it. I really believed we would come back and win."

In the third quarter of the match, Rochdale continued to impress and built up a seemingly invincible lead of 32–14 with 20 minutes

22

remaining. Were Oldham dead and buried? It certainly appeared that way. But nobody in black and orange, the team's away kit, believed they were, that is for sure. "We still believed we could win, we were always still in it," recalls Bryan Henare. "Mike Ford was inspiring us, out there on the pitch, and Jason Clegg was leading from the front. It was never all over with 20 minutes left."

What followed was pure theatre from an Oldham fan's point of view. Beginning to play catch-up rugby, and with Hornets noticeably tiring, Hough and Casey forced their way in for tries and with Rich converting both, the deficit had been reduced to just six points and Roughyeds were within striking distance. There was still sufficient time left and the Oldham fans, packed into the Willbutts Lane stand, sensed blood and raised the volume to roar the boys on. Rochdale's problem at this point was that they just couldn't get the ball back, another score from them would almost certainly have taken it away from Oldham once and for all. But, playing with gay abandon and throwing caution to the wind, Oldham moved the ball left at speed to allow McNicholas to cross in the corner and with the Oldham fans directly behind him, Rich slotted over a beautiful touchline conversion – one of nine successful kicks from nine on the day – to bring the scores level. Cue major excitement and delirium.

"I watch the semi-final comeback win against Rochdale at least once every week on DVD," said McNicholas recently from his home in Australia.

The game was Oldham's for the taking now, but the nagging worry was that one mistake, one dropped ball, could return possession to Rochdale and give them a chance to win the match and render the stunning comeback meaningless. It didn't happen. Only a few minutes after levelling the scores, Roughyeds scored a fantastic try worthy of winning any game. Henare, the scorer, reflects on it: "I crossed the line, but I think the ball must have passed through the hands of everyone on the team, it was a sensational team try." It certainly was. My lasting memory of it is a looping pass from David Gibbons deep in Rochdale territory which found Ford with oceans of room to draw the last man and send Henare behind the posts.

Rich converted and then Ford put the icing on the cake with a last-gasp drop-goal to clinch the win. The player-coach then ran half the length of the pitch with his arms in the air to celebrate with the fans. It was a magic moment. He knew, as we all did, that there was no way back for Hornets now. The comeback was complete, the spoils of victory belonged to us. What a great feeling. Chris Hamilton's half-time hunch that we would come through in the end had proved correct: "I still remind Emma of our half-time conversation when I see her to this day."

Paul Norton, workaholic front-row forward, signed from Chorley Lynx in 2001. (Photo courtesy Oldham Rugby League Heritage Trust).

Ford was fulsome in his praise of Rich after the game: "Pat won us the football game. Every week he's mithering for footballs to practice with. They scored one more try than us, but Pat's kicking won it for us."

Soon after I arrived home, I rang my dad to tell him the great news but he already knew, of course. I have no doubt that a few drinks – probably non-alcoholic as my dad rarely drinks beer – were enjoyed in Sydney that night, as well as in Oldham.

Just six days separated the famous win at Spotland from what we all fervently hoped and believed would be an even more famous win at the same venue. So it was then that on Saturday 28 July 2001, the biggest day in the short history of the new club arrived. All roads it seemed led to Rochdale once more. I had been in North Wales for a short break after the semi-final win, but recall driving back to Oldham midweek to ensure I was able to purchase a ticket before the club's allocation ran out. Missing out on the Grand Final was not on my agenda. A full house was expected for the NFP Grand Final and, with thousands more watching live on terrestrial television, it promised to be a great occasion.

Oldham fans were there in force, of course, as were Widnes supporters, who had seen their team play in so many big matches over the years. A crowd of 8,974 produced a cracking atmosphere on a warm summer's day.

Oldham lined up as follows: Sibson, Hayes, A. Gibbons, Rich, McNicholas, D. Gibbons, Roden, Casey, Brennan, Norton, P. Farrell, Henare, Mannion. Subs: Ford, Guest, Hough, Clegg.

Widnes included former Oldham Bears Paul Atcheson at full-back, Martin Crompton at scrum-half and Joe Faimalo and Chris McKinney on the substitutes' bench as well as future Roughyeds Damian Munro, Chris Percival, Simon Knox and Tommy Hodgkinson.

Munro casts his mind back to the big day: "As our team coach pulled in to the stadium, masses of people were gathered outside including lots in red and white glaring at us. As an Oldham lad, I had mixed emotions that day. My earliest rugby league memories were watching my dad Geoff playing for Oldham in the early 1980s. I went home and away with my grandparents on Barlow's supporters coaches where I took part in the first try-scorer competition. I always hoped I would pick out my dad's number. I followed Oldham into my teens and always hoped I would play for them which was every boy's wish to play for his hometown team. At the final in 2001, all my family were present at the match, some supporting Oldham."

Chris Percival signed for the club in 2003 upon leaving Widnes but all at Oldham Rugby League Club were stunned and saddened to hear of Chris's untimely death from throat cancer aged 30 in 2010.

Back to the match and, in truth, it seemed it was perhaps a game too far for Oldham. The Vikings were the better team and fully deserved the win.

'Dream on hold' – extracts from the *Oldham Chronicle* match report, Monday 30 July 2001

The agony of losing was written over the faces of the players and everyone connected with the Oldham club. By now that should be replaced by the glow of achievement and the realisation of just how far the team has come in two seasons under Mike Ford. When it came down to it, Oldham could not repeat the heroics of the last three weeks.

In glorious sunshine, in front of the live television cameras, in the biggest game of this new club's short history, the players themselves will be the first to admit they did not do themselves justice. It was the Roughyeds though who scored the first try after just nine minutes. On the final tackle, deep inside the Vikings half, David Gibbons launched a high kick into the sunshine. As winger Chris Percival let the ball bounce, Keith Brennan was quickest to react and ran in 15 yards from the posts. But a nervous Pat Rich could not repeat his form from last week and missed the kick. After Steve Gee scored Widnes's first try, Oldham were never in front again, although they had the chances. Rich was held up inches short after a Roden high kick and with Ford taking to the field Oldham began to mount some pressure.

However Widnes extended their lead through Jason Demetriou just before half-time. The Roughyeds were still in it though until a controversial try from Phil Cantillon put daylight between the sides. It took several reruns on the big screen, but the video referee gave the benefit of the doubt to Cantillon and the Vikings led 14–4. It was, however, no surprise when Demetriou ran in for his second try before Munro scored another against his hometown club. In the final 10 minutes Oldham were rewarded at last. Ford and Mannion linked up, with the big Number 13 somehow squeezing the ball out to Ford who scored his 151st and final try of his distinguished career. Then in the final moments the score was given some respectability when David Gibbons broke clear, passed to Ford, who returned the earlier favour to send Mannion in under the posts. Rich converted, but it was to the accompaniment of the hooter. The Roughyeds were defeated but not disgraced.

Ford said: "They are all pretty gutted at the moment. The sad thing about it was that we never really gave ourselves a chance. At half time, at only 10–4 down when we were not playing well, I thought we had a real chance still. But we did not control the ball and made too many mistakes. I honestly do not think they could have given me any more than they did, but I can only say good luck to Widnes. We got a terrific reaction from the fans and I told the players to be proud of what they have achieved. But there is only one winner and that is Widnes."

Chris Hamilton said he was disappointed at the result and for the players but wanted to pick them up. "We didn't play to our potential and that is the biggest disappointment. We are a better team than we showed and there is nobody more disappointed than me. But these lads are never beaten until the hooter goes and today they didn't have the rub of the green, it was not to be. Now it is my job to lift everyone at the club and I want to put on record just how proud I am of everyone connected with this club. The team at the club also stretches to the supporters who have been magnificent."

The last word goes to Damian Munro: "Although I was obviously pleased Widnes won and we were eventually awarded a place in Super League, I do remember looking at the Oldham fans that day cheering their players and hoping I would one day get to turn out for my hometown team. In 2005, my dream was to come true."

On a personal level, Chris Hamilton was beginning to impress the powers-that-be at the RFL. As a reward for his efforts in leading the consortium in late 1997 he was appointed in late 1998 to be deputy chairman of FASDA (the Association of First and Second Division clubs) and subsequently was also appointed to the RFL Operations Board. He was then appointed chairman of the APC (Association of Premiership clubs) in December 2000 and along with this went an automatic seat on the RFL board. In 2001 he was honoured to be named as team manager of the England squad that took on Wales at Wrexham.

3. Hurst Cross

Since the formation of the new club in late 1997 and that first competitive fixture against Heworth in early 1998, Boundary Park and Spotland, the two local Football League grounds, had been 'home from home' for the Roughyeds. Oldham Athletic's stadium on Sheepfoot Lane had been home base in 1998, 2000 and 2001 with Rochdale FC's tidy ground doing the honours in 1999. All this was to change, however, in 2002. A change of ownership at Oldham Athletic meant that the satisfactory rental agreement the Roughyeds had signed up to previously counted for nothing. Worryingly it soon became apparent that the two clubs were miles apart and a move away from Boundary Park was inevitable. Spotland was also unavailable so for the first – and by no means the last – time Oldham RLFC were homeless.

Since Watersheddings closed, many supporters of the old club and indeed the new one – myself included – had bemoaned the absence of terracing on the grounds used since and how the terrific atmosphere generated 'up on the hill' could never be replicated in all seater stadia. True, the Sandy Lane end at Spotland was still terraced, but an old-fashioned ground with terracing on three sides and perhaps a small main stand for those who preferred to sit, was much missed.

Who would have thought then, that in 2002, Oldham would be calling 'home' a small ground just outside the town's boundaries, but satisfying the need of many fans, to be able to watch the rugby standing up, behind the posts perhaps, being able to change ends at half-time and to get close to the side of the pitch. A warm welcome it was then to Hurst Cross, the home of semi-professional non-league football club Ashton United as the club's new landlords.

I for one loved it, the nearest thing we had experienced to Watersheddings since the halcyon days at the top end of town. Don't get me wrong, however, the facilities were inferior to those at Boundary Park or Spotland, and consequently the worry was that it wouldn't suit everybody, particularly as it was out of town, and attendances may drop as a result. The club's worst fears were to materialise unfortunately with the NFP average attendance falling from 1,840 at Boundary Park in 2001 to 1,149 at Hurst Cross a year later. The corresponding fixtures against Leigh painted a particularly grim picture, a gate of 1,526 in 2002 compared to 4,747 in 2001, an attendance two thirds less than the one a year earlier against the same opposition. The negative effect on the club's finances was obvious.

The move from Boundary Park, however, was just the first of three major bombshells to hit the club within a few months in late 2001 and the first half of 2002. The old adage that things like this usually come in threes came so frustratingly true. Chris Hamilton takes up the story: "Following the great year we all enjoyed in 2001 culminating in the near-miss in the NFP Grand Final, we were determined to make a major push again a year later. Most of the squad had re-signed and we enhanced it by bringing in two vastly experienced forwards from Widnes Vikings: Simon Knox and Tommy Hodgkinson. Both had been key men in the Widnes team that beat us at Spotland and we knew they were fine influential players. I was as confident as I could possibly have been that we would go really well again. Then the realisation struck home that we would have to leave Boundary Park."

As well as Knox and Hodgkinson, young centre, Jon Goddard, joined on loan from Castleford Tigers, goalkicking stand-off John Braddish arrived, also on loan, from St Helens and Cumbrian winger Will Cowell arrived from Warrington Wolves. The squad looked strong and with Mike Ford still at the helm, the season promised much.

Hardly had the season started, however, when bombshell number two struck. Ford announced his resignation from the Oldham head coach role to take up an offer to act as defence coach with the Irish rugby union team. It was a real bolt out of the blue and one the club could definitely have done without. Former Oldham centre, Phil Larder, a regular first-team player in the 1970s, and a man who became a top class coach in both codes of rugby, had a part to play in Ford being courted by Ireland. In his splendid book, *The Iron Curtain – My Rugby Journey from League to Union*, Larder says: "Union coaches had learned from observing my defensive sessions with the 2001 British Lions after that year's tour to Australia had ended. Clive Griffiths, another man with a league background, like myself, was appointed as defence coach by Wales immediately after the Lions tour finished. Irishman Donal Lenihan, the tour manager, then contacted me with a shortlist of professional rugby league coaches and asked for my recommendations. I pointed him in the direction of Mike Ford, a former pupil of mine at Saddleworth School in Oldham, who had impressed me when qualifying through the Rugby League National Coaching Scheme – so much so that I had taken an interest in his subsequent coaching career. Donal took my advice and appointed Mike, who did an excellent job as defence coach with Ireland before going on to work with the 2005 Lions and England at the 2007 World Cup in the same capacity."

So the Ford era was over. It had been an exhilarating two-year ride but the board were not prepared to let the grass grow under their feet and quickly made plans to find an experienced and quality replacement. John Harbin was born in Yorkshire, but had moved to live in Australia with his parents as a child. Having spent his formative years in Queensland, and played his rugby league there, he was steeped in the Australian way of thinking about the game. On returning to England later in life, he became head coach at Wakefield Trinity Wildcats and then chief executive of Dewsbury Rams. Having made a big impression in Yorkshire, he appeared to be an ideal choice to take up the coaching reins at Hurst Cross and was appointed soon after Ford's departure.

Harbin remembers: "I wasn't enjoying the chief executive role at Dewsbury, I was much happier out on the training pitch with the players than sat behind a desk in an office. Andy Fisher, the coach, was a good friend of mine so I certainly wasn't going to interfere on the coaching side. I just happened to be talking to Chris Hamilton in the corridor after a Dewsbury versus Oldham match and the seeds were sown there and then for my move to Hurst Cross. It was a relief to be on the coaching side again."

One of Harbin's first matches in charge of his new team was a mouth-watering Challenge Cup tie against mighty St Helens. The Roughyeds had seen off the amateurs of West Hull at Hurst Cross in the third round, a match in which Mark Sibson scored a fine hat-trick. In a foretaste of things to come a decade and a half later, the fourth round tie against Saints was switched to the home of Stalybridge Celtic Football Club in Tameside, only a few miles up the road from Hurst Cross. Bower Fold was a fine compact ground with two stands, more than adequate terracing and a much larger capacity than Hurst Cross. It was an ideal venue for the visit of the Super League giants and attracted a fine crowd of 4,089.

Saints showed Oldham tremendous respect by fielding most of their stars including Kieron Cunningham, Paul Sculthorpe, Chris Joynt and Sean Long and won comfortably, 40–6, but Oldham played with a lot of pride and never gave up. "It was a bitterly cold rain-swept day," said Harbin. "I really couldn't fault my team. They displayed a lot of spirit and tenacity." Jason Clegg recalls: "Playing against Saints, with all their stars, is the one match that sticks in my mind more than any other. It was a great occasion."

"I recall two more fine performances during my time at Oldham," Harbin continued, "a great win over Featherstone Rovers and another against my old club, Dewsbury Rams, both at Hurst Cross." The RFL introduced a mid-season competition, the National League Cup that year and the win over the Rams was one of six matches Oldham played in it. It is best remembered for a great performance from stand-off Gareth Barber, who scored three tries and kicked seven goals for a terrific 26 points. "It was a great night for myself and for the team," recalls Gareth. Oldham qualified for the quarter-final, beating Hunslet Hawks and Batley Bulldogs as well as the Rams, before losing to eventual cup winners Huddersfield Giants. Giants were in Super League a year earlier and were coached by future Great Britain supremo Tony Smith. They went on to win the trophy.

Local lad Gareth Barber, in goalkicking action, landed 80 goals in 2002 despite sharing the kicking duties with John Braddish.
(Photo courtesy Oldham Rugby League Heritage Trust).

Left: Joe McNicholas, represented both the 'old' and 'new' Oldham clubs.

Bottom: Powerhouse prop-forward, Danny Guest, destructive when used as an impact substitute

(Both photos courtesy Oldham Rugby League Heritage Trust).

However, as Harbin explains, things were not quite how he had hoped they would be at the club at the time. "Although the lads gave me all they had, both in training and on match-days, some of the facilities we had to use on training nights were not of the standard I was used to and, to be honest, expected for the level of rugby league we were playing at. Although none of the players said anything to me, I could tell that, as a group, they were disgruntled with the facilities too. I must re-emphasise though they were totally professional in all they did while I was coach and some, like Paul Norton, Joe McNicholas and Gavin Dodd stood out. I can't speak highly enough of these guys."

Harbin struck up a friendship with Oldham Athletic assistant-manager, Iain Dowie, and within a short space of time, he had been offered a job by the town's professional football team to join their coaching staff as fitness conditioner and sports psychologist. "Iain Dowie had a strong interest in Australian sport and he borrowed Australian Rugby League coach Wayne Bennett's superb book *Don't die with the Music in you* from me. It was about sports management and he loved it. He must have thought I could add something to their coaching staff and recommended my appointment. I agonised over whether to leave Oldham RLFC because I got on well with everybody at the club and I realised it didn't look great, so soon after my appointment there. But this opportunity presented itself to me and I knew I had to take it. If it hadn't I would have been more than happy to stay with the Roughyeds."

So as the 2002–03 football season began, Harbin had already carried out a pre-season training programme with Oldham Athletic. "I thoroughly enjoyed my time there, I was with the right mix of people at the right time," continued Harbin. This, however, was just the start of his career in the round ball game, moving with Dowie to Crystal Palace, whom they took into the Premiership, Charlton Athletic, Coventry City and Queens Park Rangers. "It was something special for me, running out with my team at Anfield and Old Trafford." After a short spell at Swansea City, Harbin then yearned for a return to his homeland and he took over the coaching reins at Yeppoon club in the Queensland Rugby League Central Division. "They were struggling when I arrived, but improved steadily and ended up quite successful. The standard in the 'Q' Cup is almost as high as the English Super League so I was very pleased."

His days in English football were far from over, however, and he soon linked up with John Sheridan, who was part of the squad at Boundary Park when he was there, at Plymouth Argyle. Further stints followed at Port Vale and Northampton Town before another rugby league coaching spell in Australia.

In June 2017, Harbin returned on a short-term basis to Oldham Athletic to assist manager Sheridan with pre-season training. "I always enjoyed working with northern clubs and northern people best," he offered with a smile.

So where did Oldham go from here, following Harbin's exit, bombshell number three. Results in the NFP and the National League Cup had been up and down all year, 12 wins, one draw and 10 defeats in 23 outings up to the end of June, so there was clearly a lack of consistency, hardly surprising in view of the coaching upheavals. Highlights of the year at that point had been the impact Gareth Barber was beginning to have in the side plus the emergence as first team regulars of two young players, both of whom went on to enjoy fine careers at the club, Gavin Dodd and Lee Doran. Barber had signed for Warrington as a youngster before joining his hometown club in 2001, and made seven appearances that year. It was in 2002, however, that he really made his mark as an accomplished and often exciting attacking stand-off. He made 38 appearances that year out of a possible 39, scoring 17 tries, kicking 80 goals and one drop-goal. He went on to play 138 times for the club and was a real fans' favourite.

Barber remembers the early part of 2002 well: "John Harbin was a focused coach and especially keen to push the younger players at the club. He gave me an extended run in the first team for the first time at Oldham which was just what I needed to help me develop as a player at that level. He also liked to vary his training sessions to keep them interesting and enjoyable, we often went swimming at Breeze Hill School for example, which was a break from the norm and very refreshing. Although subsequently I loved playing at Boundary Park, I also enjoyed turning out at Hurst Cross. Although the facilities weren't the best, it was a small atmospheric ground with supporters on all four sides and as a player that was good to see. I came to enjoy goalkicking in 2002 as well, particularly the extra responsibility that the job carries with it. It always felt good when the touch-judges raised their flags."

The careers of Dodd and Doran followed very similar paths. Both players worked their way through the reserve team at Oldham before establishing themselves in the first team and, like Barber, going on to play more than 100 first-team games, in Dodd's case 129 and in Doran's 112. Eventually both moved on, but not before they had left an indelible mark with supporters for their fine displays in Oldham colours.

Dodd played much of his rugby on the wing, but was equally impressive at full-back, while Doran was a speedy second-row forward who also turned out occasionally at centre. Dodd played 16 times in 2001 and Doran seven, but it was a year later that they came to the fore, Dodd scoring seven tries in 30 appearances, and Doran matching Barber's 38 appearances with 13 tries.

Doran says: "My favourite sport as a kid was football – I was a budding centre-half – and I didn't even play rugby league until I was at High School. But once I started playing the game I loved it and, as an 11-year-old, was lucky enough to play on the old Central Park ground in a curtain-raiser to a Wigan versus St Helens derby. You can imagine the size of the crowd. A few years later, I was delighted to join Oldham and made my debut at Leigh in 2000. Mike Ford was coach and he was a visionary – teaching us things in training that coaches are doing today, all these years later. His training sessions were rich in quality and I felt I learnt something new every session. In 2001 I was lucky enough to be selected for the NFP Under-21s side, a team that included some cracking players like Danny Sculthorpe, Rob Purdham, Neil Turley, Stuart Dickens and Jamie Rooney. We were coached by the late, great Mike Gregory and beat our Super League counterparts 27–20 in a match at Widnes.

Gregory was a phenomenal man with an aura about him, he commanded respect and had players running through brick walls for him. An England Under–21s tour to South Africa followed this match, but even though we beat the Super League team, only four of our lads were picked. In 2002 I established myself in the Oldham side and I was delighted to be a part of the club and the team."

As a supporter it was great to see young players like Barber, Dodd and Doran breaking into the first team and making a real impact. On-loan man Goddard, still in his teens for much of the year, also did well and stood up bravely to the difficult task of replacing Pat Rich at left-centre. His best days in an Oldham shirt were still to come, however, after finalising a permanent move from Castleford and enjoying a positional switch to full-back the following year.

Steve Molloy, the much-travelled prop who had played on loan for Oldham at the end of the 2000 season, had rejoined the club and, as an influential and experienced figure in the dressing room, seemed to be an obvious choice to take over the coaching reins, temporarily at least. So it was then that in early July, Molloy was appointed as player-coach until the end of the season. Chris Hamilton said at the time: "Steve needs to discover whether he can successfully combine coaching with playing. If he can, our association will hopefully stretch beyond the end of the season."

As the 2002 season had started for Oldham with a trip to Hull KR on 16 December 2001, it was developing into a long and arduous campaign. The National League Cup in the middle of the season had added to the fixture list and the season turned into one of the longest for many years, not finishing for Oldham until late September. A consequence of this was that Molloy still had plenty of time to stamp his authority on the side and put down a marker for his future coaching career in the weeks left before the end of the season.

He was provided with a major target because the RFL had decided to split the NFP into two divisions for the following year, the top nine clubs at the end of 2002 qualifying to play in National League One. It was a realistic and attainable goal and one that Molloy, his assistant Andy Proctor and the players set their stall out to achieve.

After two comfortable wins against Chorley Lynx and Swinton Lions, Molloy's men were then involved in the NFP match of the season, a thrill-a-minute encounter with league leaders and eventual Grand Final winners Huddersfield Giants at Hurst Cross. The Giants, fresh out of Super League and still full-time, were a formidable outfit at this level and had already beaten Oldham three times in 2002, once in the NFP and twice in the National League Cup. Their side included future England coach Steve McNamara at loose-forward, former Great Britain international Graeme Hallas, Papua New Guinea star Stanley Gene, a young Earl Crabtree – at centre, interestingly – star stand-off Chris Thorman, future Roughyeds full-back Paul Reilly and Oldham born prop Mick Slicker. Thorman was to come back and haunt Oldham again, eight years later, in York City Knights colours, but more of that later.

It was a huge task for the Roughyeds but, playing with tremendous spirit and heart, they gave the Giants the fright of their lives before falling agonisingly short, losing 32–30. It was a fantastic effort by the team and a superb match. "We really turned up that day and came so close to beating a full-time team coached by Tony Smith," remembers Gareth Barber.

Molloy was clearly beginning to exert his influence and make his presence felt as player-coach. Following this match the club had six NFP games to play, and it was crucial that they picked up sufficient points to sneak into the top nine, thereby guaranteeing themselves a place in the higher of the two divisions in 2003.

As it was they beat Hunslet Hawks, Workington Town and Keighley Cougars, all at Hurst Cross, and drew with Batley Bulldogs and Dewsbury Rams, the only defeat being an 18–17 loss to Rochdale Hornets at Spotland. It proved to be enough. Oldham pipped Dewsbury on points-difference for ninth place and Molloy had accomplished his task. It was a job well done by the big man and his players. The *Oldham Chronicle* said: "Molloy brought the best out of his troops and was a quick learner. He clearly had the ear of his men, who appreciated that, as a player-coach, he wasn't asking them to do anything he wasn't prepared to do himself. He mucked in, but he had the track record and the quiet, controlled authority to command respect. From what we have seen so far, he has the qualities to do well."

The play-offs featured all nine teams and Oldham, from ninth place, exceeded expectations by winning 19–11 away to fourth-placed Hull Kingston Rovers with Neil Roden an outstanding contributor to the win with two tries and a crucial drop-goal near the end. Neil recalls: "Hull KR away was always extremely tough, anything less than our very best was never enough to win there. We certainly produced our best that day." The team followed that by travelling to Rochdale in the next game and provided an encore to their win there a year earlier, this time triumphing by 20–6. Barber excelled, scoring two tries and kicking four goals. "I loved playing in the big games in front of good crowds, and this was certainly another of those," he recalls. Unfortunately the play-off run came to an end away to Batley Bulldogs in the next match when Roughyeds slipped to a 26–16 defeat. "I certainly didn't see that result coming," continued Barber, "we were playing well and I fancied us to win at Mount Pleasant too." But it wasn't to be.

It had been a long and demanding season for the players and this is illustrated by the fact that out of a maximum of 39 matches, Lee Doran, Barber and Jason Clegg all made 38 appearances, Jon Goddard and John Hough made 37, Neil Roden 36, Mark Sibson 35, Joe McNicholas 34, Bryan Henare 33, David Gibbons 32 and Danny Guest and Gavin Dodd 30. The defeat at Batley brought to an end a tumultuous season for all at the club. But with a move back to Boundary Park in the offing for 2003 and Molloy retained as player-coach, the future again looked bright.

4. The Steve Molloy years

With the traumatic 2002 season now consigned to the history books, fans looked forward to a more settled year in 2003. It was confirmed that the team would be playing at Boundary Park again and that Steve Molloy would be asked to continue as coach having done more than enough to earn another crack at it. With the NFP having been split into two, the club found themselves in with the cream of the teams outside of Super League, so it would be a tough battle week-in, week-out. Nobody was under any illusions about how tough it would be and to this end, several new signings were brought to the club. Australian prop or second-row forward, Dane Morgan, was a huge athletic man who had played in the NRL for Wests Tigers, North Sydney Bears and Melbourne Storm and, like his compatriot Shayne McMenemy in 2000, went on to have a huge impact.

Others signed included former Oldham Bears goalkicking stand-off Simon Svabic and Welsh international forward Chris Morley from Leigh Centurions, centre Iain Marsh and prop Martin McLoughlin from Barrow Raiders and former St Helens and Sheffield Eagles centre Paul Anderson, a man with 40 Super League appearances to his name. In addition, Jon Goddard had impressed sufficiently a year earlier for his move from Castleford to be made permanent. With Neil Roden, Phil Farrell, John Hough and Danny Guest all very much part of the furniture at the club and Gareth Barber, Gavin Dodd and Lee Doran now fully established, the signs were promising that a play-off place at season's end was a realistic goal.

Before the National League One season began in mid-April 2003, however, the RFL had changed things around by playing the National League Cup, now sponsored by Arriva Trains and known as the Arriva Trains Cup, as a starter to the season. Oldham found themselves in a group with Salford City Reds, like Huddersfield Giants a year earlier just relegated from Super League and still full-time, Leigh Centurions, Rochdale Hornets and National League Two sides Barrow Raiders and Swinton Lions. Unfortunately things didn't go to plan, and despite beating Barrow and Swinton home and away, the team under-performed against their League One rivals, picking up just one point from 12; a home draw with Rochdale. The Boundary Park loss to Salford was particularly gruelling to watch, the City Reds, including future Oldham forwards Paul Highton and Simon Baldwin, ran in 11 tries in a 62–4 victory stroll for them. Fans were certainly anxious, and looking for a big improvement, as the League season began.

As there were only 10 teams in National League One – Dewsbury Rams had joined the top nine from 2002 by winning a play-off – and, therefore, only 18 league fixtures, a run of victories could easily catapult a team up the league. A terrific 12–10 home triumph over Leigh Centurions in May was an early highlight, followed by three excellent wins in July, against Featherstone Rovers and Doncaster Dragons at home and Dewsbury away. Lee Doran was outstanding in this run, scoring eight tries in the three games.

The club, as always, were determined to make a strong push for the play-offs and, as in previous years strengthened the squad towards the end of the season. This time in came flame-haired utility man, Lee Marsh, on loan from Salford, Craig McDowell, a talented ball-playing forward from Huddersfield, winger Nick Johnson, on loan from Bradford Bulls and threequarter Chris Percival, from Widnes. A convincing home win over Batley Bulldogs in the penultimate league match of the season, when Nick Johnson, brother of Roughyeds forward Gavin Johnson, showed his class by scoring twice, set up a do-or-die battle with old foes Featherstone Rovers at Post Office Road in the final match. The equation was simple; win and the play-offs would be beckoning, lose and Rovers would make it instead. In effect, it was knockout rugby a week early and the old play-off buzz was evident around the club in the week leading up to the match.

The team produced arguably their best performance of the year and, with Morgan in stunning form, scoring a vital late try up the slope, and Keith Brennan dropping a late goal, the Roughyeds scraped home 19–14. This match was right up there with the best performances and results of the early years of the club as wins at Featherstone are something of a rarity and never easy to come by. So despite looking out of contention a few weeks earlier, Oldham had made the play-offs once more. Sadly, however, the great result away to Hull KR a year earlier could not be repeated and the Robins went bob-bob-bobbing along into the next round. So the 2003 season ended somewhat prematurely, but with definite hope for the following year.

Molloy was doing a fine job, particularly bearing in mind he was soldiering much of the heavy work as pack leader on the pitch as well. Gareth Barber pays tribute to the boss: "Steve was a team-mate of ours as well as our coach and it's far from easy having both jobs to contend with. He had a fine career as a player, playing for some top clubs, and he still had a lot to offer as a player at Oldham. As a half-back I always liked to follow him because he was always looking to offload in the tackle. As a player-coach you have to be able to trust the staff working alongside you and assistant Andy Proctor did a great job too."

Lee Doran agrees: "I held Steve Molloy in the highest regard. I was still a young player in 2003, in only my second full season, and it was a tremendous experience playing in the same pack as him."

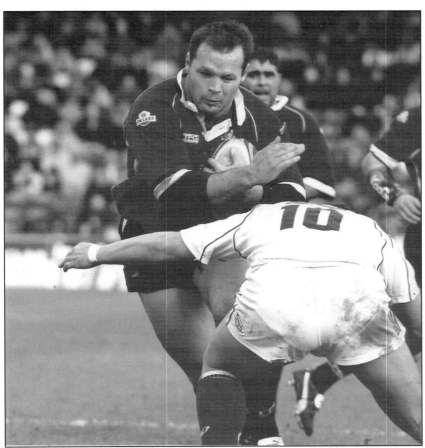

Player-coach Steve Molloy, a rock in Oldham's front-row between 2002 and 2004. (Both photos courtesy Oldham Rugby League Heritage Trust).

Andy Proctor, successful as a player, then as assistant-coach to Steve Molloy.

Lee Marsh, one of the late-season signings, made five appearances before the end of the year and said: "I thoroughly enjoyed the few weeks I had on loan at Oldham in 2003 and was keen to join permanently for 2004. We had a very good team, with some excellent players, and I knew we would be challenging again the following year."

Despite the late run to the play-offs, 2003 is perhaps best remembered for a particular incident in a match against Doncaster Dragons at the Belle Vue home of Doncaster Rovers Football Club in May of that year. Chris Campbell, son of top referee David Campbell, and himself a Super League referee of the future, had signed for Oldham a year earlier, scoring four tries in 12 appearances from the wing. He was a stylish runner with ball in hand and a valuable member of the squad. In 2003 he scored a further five tries in nine appearances. His big moment as a Roughyed came literally seconds into the match in South Yorkshire on 18 May 2003. With some fans still making their way into the ground, Oldham kicked off and frustratingly for Doncaster fans, right winger Paul Gleadhill knocked on close to his own try line. Campbell was quoted by the *Manchester Evening News* some years later as saying: "I remember it as though it were yesterday. I chased Gareth Barber's kick-off as hard as I could. My opposite winger fumbled the ball and I dived on it. Try! It was timed at seven seconds. It later appeared in a couple of rugby league publications, but it was never submitted to the *Guinness Book of Records* as a contender for the fastest try of all time in British rugby league. At the time I don't think we made as much of it as we perhaps should have done. After all, it's not just my record. It's one for the Oldham club as well. It's one we share, surely."

Chris Hamilton said: "It was even more remarkable because we kicked off and didn't have possession. Their player dropped the ball and Chris was alert enough to follow up and touch down." What a start! It only served to be a wake-up call to the Dragons, however, who soon got into the groove and eventually won 52–24.

So at the end of 2003, the new club had completed six seasons. At different times, four players, all of whom plied their trade where the on-field battle is at its toughest – the front-row of the pack – had sweated blood in the Roughyeds' cause. The term 'consummate professional' is often used in recognition of men who give their all on the field of play and who never take a backward step. Well, that term best describes all four – Leo Casey, Jason Clegg, Danny Guest and Paul Norton – Oldham heroes one and all. The man who packed down alongside them in the middle of Oldham's front row, John Hough, is perhaps as well placed as anyone to talk about them. Hough says: "Out of all the packs that I played in over my career the one with Casey, Clegg, Guest and Norton in it was the best. At the time we were the most under-rated pack outside Super League but we managed to change a few people's views, especially in 2001."

The following table shows the appearances record of the four props in the six years from 1998 to 2003 inclusive and indicates what a fine contribution they made.

Player	1998	1999	2000	2001	2002	2003	Total
Casey	0	28	24	22	4	0	78
Clegg	15	30	29	33	38	3	148
Guest	0	5	20	26	30	19	100
Norton	0	0	0	31	25	10	66

Guest returned to the club briefly, in 2006, playing five more games, to take his overall tally of appearances to 105.

Leo Casey arrived at the club as captain in 1999 and proved a real inspiration, leading from the front and by example. He continued to flourish under Mike Ford in the autumn of his superb career and, as a player at both Oldham clubs, will be remembered as a true Roughyed front-row warrior. Leo first came to the notice of the rugby league world when Featherstone Rovers paid £100,000 for his services to the old Oldham club. He wore the famous blue and white jersey with distinction as well as representing Swinton and Rochdale Hornets. Leo's rugby league career turned full circle when he rejoined Oldham St Anne's, his first club, after his professional days were over and represented the green and golds in the BARLA National Cup final against Wath Brow Hornets from Cumbria at Bloomfield Road in Blackpool.

John Hough praises Leo's contribution: "Leo was an absolute stalwart. I remember watching him play for the old club at Watersheddings but it was only when I played alongside him that I realised just how tough he was." Former team-mate Lee Doran says: "As a youngster, I played in a school match on a Saturday morning once, then rushed home to watch the BBC rugby league coverage in the afternoon. I vividly recall watching Leo play on television for Featherstone. Not many years later I was sharing a dressing room with him as his team-mate. It was something special. Leo was a man of few words, but when he spoke, everyone listened. We could go onto the field for a tough match and with a bruising 80 minutes ahead, but with Leo in the side, we all knew we'd be OK. He was a great pack leader and a man I looked up to greatly."

Jason Clegg was an absolute colossus from the day he made his competitive debut against Heworth in the first match of 1998 until he left the club at the end of 2003. He faced some experienced and tough prop-forwards in his Oldham career, such as Danny Sculthorpe and Andy Ireland of Rochdale Hornets and Tim Street and Dave Whittle of

Leigh, but stood tall against them all and appeared to relish the challenge he faced. To make 148 appearances shows the durability of the man. A fantastic effort by a real fans favourite. "I loved my time at Oldham. Being from Rochdale, well Wardle near Littleborough to be precise, I took a bit of stick about playing for the old enemy. My mum and dad did too, but we all had broad shoulders," he grins. "I was lucky because at my amateur club, Littleborough ARLFC, then at my first professional club Bradford, at Oldham and finally at Keighley, where I brought the curtain down on my career, I was with a lot of very good people who all helped to make my rugby league days a great part of my life."

Asked about a particular memory from his time at Oldham, Jason didn't hesitate to talk about the trip to Plymouth and the few days with the Royal Marines. "It was a fantastic experience for us all," he says. "We never knew what they were going to throw at us next, so it became known as *Operation Cilla Black – Surprise, Surprise*. We worked exceptionally hard during the day but enjoyed ourselves at night too, a Plymouth nightclub called Destiny's saw quite a bit of us that week. They were great days." John Hough says: "Cleggy had the best feet I've ever seen on a prop, and for a big lad he could really skittle a few players with his daunting runs." Lee Doran was a team-mate of Cleggy's for much of his time at the club. "Cleggy was a one-off, he brought so much to the team and to the club as a whole. He was a great lad to have around the place and in the dressing room. He was a real joker, breaking the ice more than once with the leading officials from the Royal Marines on that trip, when some of the other lads were like rabbits in headlights when these guys were barking out orders. But on the pitch he was our enforcer and a real powerhouse."

Danny Guest was used principally as an impact substitute at Oldham, with the majority of his 100 games coming off the bench. A huge man, Danny would benefit from opposition teams tiring late in games when his weight and power coming down the middle was a massive weapon in the team's arsenal. Guest was at Oldham Bears prior to the closure of that club and played in their last ever match at Headingley against Leeds Rhinos. He also played in the thrilling Law Cup win against Rochdale Hornets in 1998, but it was the following year before he joined the club permanently. A bad knee ligament injury put paid to his career at the end of 2003. "A tough up-and-down player, very quick for his size and an outstanding defender," is John Hough's tribute to Danny.

Paul Norton – 'Knocker' – was a terrific club-man, 'no edge' to him according to John Harbin and a real grafter. He had a problem with his upper spine and neck region for some time and soldiered on regardless until the injury proved too much and he had to retire at the age of 31.

Paul recalls: "I think the fact that I played in the front row was perhaps the reason my neck didn't hold up after my operation." He continued with a grin: "Maybe I had a screw loose playing the game the way I did, I don't know! Anyway, I was gutted having to retire in my prime but I wouldn't have changed my time in rugby league for anything. I loved it at Oldham, my team-mates were great lads, like brothers to me, and the fans made me feel on top of the world every time I played. We were one big barmy family. Oh yes, playing in another Grand Final, and winning, would have been something I would have loved to have done before I retired."

Asked whether his injury is still troubling him, 14 years later, he replied in typical 'Knocker' fashion: "Every now and then it does, but it could have been a lot worse. At least I can still train." Jason Clegg pays tribute to Norton: "What a great character he was, what a great lad." And John Hough once more: "Knocker' had one of the best and toughest tackling techniques I have ever seen and made many a bone-crunching tackle". And Doran once more: "Knocker' was a terrific signing by the club when he joined from Chorley Lynx. He wasn't a big name in the sport but he brought so much value to the team."

The club were delighted at the end of the year to see five of their players called up for international honours. Chris Morley, whose brother Adrian is regarded by many good judges as one of the finest British forwards of recent times, had a solid season in Oldham's second-row and was capped twice by Wales, against Russia in Aberavon, a match Wales won 74–4, and against England 'A' at Headingley. Four players, Lee Doran, Neil Roden, Phil Farrell and Martin McLoughlin were picked to represent Ireland and they all turned out in the European Nations Cup. Doran played at centre, Roden at scrum-half, Farrell in the second row and McLoughlin was a substitute as Ireland beat Scotland 24–22 in Glasgow. Doran was again at centre, Roden again at scrum-half and McLoughlin again a substitute as the Irish pushed France all the way at Dalymount Park in Dublin, before losing 26–18. "It is always an honour, for the club as well as for the lads themselves, when our players play international football," said Chris Hamilton.

Doran smiles when he remembers back to the day he heard he had been picked for Ireland, the birthplace of his grand-father. "Steve Molloy, our coach at Oldham, rang me at 7.30 one morning. I couldn't understand why he was ringing me so early and I thought it was a wind-up. But after a while I realised that 'Molly' was serious especially when he started congratulating me. I thoroughly enjoyed wearing the green and white shirt, as I know we all did. Three years later, after I had moved to Rochdale Hornets, we played a match in Russia, would you believe. It was freezing there, I still remember the cabbage soup we were given to keep us warm."

43

Welsh international, Chris Morley.
(Both photos courtesy Oldham Rugby League Heritage Trust).

Irish international Martin McLoughlin with Gavin Dodd
and Simon Svabic in support.

The versatile Jon Goddard, equally effective at centre or full-back.
(Photo courtesy Oldham Rugby League Heritage Trust).

As well as the five internationals in the Oldham camp, Jon Goddard's burgeoning reputation earned him a place as a substitute in the National League Under-21s side that took on the Super League Under-21s at Leigh. Then later in the year he was again named in the same squad, along with team-mate Craig McDowell, for a tournament called the La Perouse Challenge in France. The squad was coached by Whitehaven boss Steve McCormack and managed by Chris Hamilton.

All at Oldham were pleased also for their former player Ian Sinfield, then of Keighley Cougars, who was selected for a National League Two

45

representative side that took on the touring New Zealand 'A' team. Ian later returned to the Roughyeds in 2007.

2003 was a very busy year off the pitch at Oldham too. A new Social Club in Werneth was opened providing a base for fans and a venue for post-match refreshments and drinks for players. It was also used for club functions such as dinners, quiz nights, Junior Roughyed Christmas and Halloween parties and end-of-year team presentation nights. By the end of the year, the board of directors at the club was down to two, as Stewart Hardacre resigned his position due to business commitments elsewhere following the resignation of Melvyn Lord three years earlier.

The hope of everybody at the club was that 2004 would see further progress as Steve Molloy's tenure as player-coach continued into a third year. The boss had been rewarded for a fine job in 2003 with a new one-year deal up to the end of the 2004 season. The club made an audacious triple swoop on neighbours Rochdale Hornets by snapping up centre James Bunyan, Welsh international scrum-half Ian Watson and big prop Paul Southern. All three had played major roles in helping Hornets to a third place finish in National League One in 2003 while Bunyan, a former Super League player with Huddersfield Giants, had been a key member of their side in 2001 and 2002 when they also finished third each year. Watson, a great tactician, had played in Super League for Workington Town in 1996 and Salford City Reds in 1997 and 2002 before joining Hornets and later became a top-class coach with Salford Red Devils over a decade later.

Southern, vastly experienced, had played 112 games in the top flight for the Willows outfit between 1997 and 2002. Also, Lee Marsh and Nick Johnson, who had done well on loan in 2003, joined permanently from Salford and Bradford Bulls respectively. The five signings showed that Oldham meant business in 2004.

The season began once again with the Arriva Trains Cup and the early rounds of the Challenge Cup. In the former competition, results were promising with big wins, home and away, against a Rochdale side clearly missing their three star men and against Chorley Lynx and Swinton Lions. Winger Johnson scored try hat-tricks in consecutive games against Chorley and Rochdale to establish himself on Oldham's left wing and prove to everyone that he was a winger of real ability at this level. Two heavy defeats by a powerful Leigh Centurions side, however, kept everyone's feet firmly on the ground.

Luck was with the club in the Challenge Cup with two home ties against amateur opposition. Castleford Panthers could be proud of their tenacious display in holding Oldham to 16–8 at a rain-swept Boundary Park in the third round. Next up saw the first of three ties between 2004 and 2009 against Featherstone-based Sharlston Rovers, a team that included future Roughyeds star, Danny Grimshaw, at scrum-half in this first meeting in 2004 and again when the two teams met again a year later. The Yorkshire side did well, but Oldham came through 24–4 to set up a mouth-watering fifth round clash against Super League giants Warrington Wolves at Boundary Park. The visitors, including future Roughyed forwards Warren Stevens and Paul Noone, won 44–10, but Oldham did well for large parts of the game and were applauded off the pitch by fans at the end. "I recall the Warrington game fondly," says Dane Morgan. "It was probably the hardest game I played in for Oldham, but as a part-time team against full-time opposition, we competed extremely well. It was only late in the game that they skipped away with it."

Before the league season began in mid-April, a prodigal son made a surprise and emotional return to the club. Pat Rich's last appearance had been in the Grand Final against Widnes in 2001 after which he moved on. His return to the fold almost three years later was welcomed warmly by fans who remembered his solid defence and particularly his outstanding goalkicking. His second debut for the club came in an Arriva Trains Cup game against Rochdale and he followed this up by scoring a try and kicking five goals as Oldham cantered to a 42–15 win over Swinton in the same competition. It felt just like old times.

The league season began encouragingly with an excellent 50–24 win against a lacklustre Featherstone Rovers side at Boundary Park in which Bunyan revealed tremendous promise by romping in for four tries. However, he only played 14 times for the club before moving to Halifax in mid-season. It is rare that Rovers concede 50 points no matter who the opposition so Roughyed fans were on cloud nine that evening. Another fine win at Halifax followed and with an Arriva Trains Cup quarter-final away to Doncaster Dragons and a potentially exciting clash with Leigh Centurions at home on the horizon, it was a good time for all concerned.

Unfortunately despite two tries from Lee Marsh and six more Rich goals, Doncaster pinched a thriller, 32–28, so Oldham's cup run was over. Leigh were white hot in 2004 and thrashed the Roughyeds 60–20 at Boundary Park on their relentless march to Grand Final success and eventual entry into Super League for 2005. Dane Morgan has more reason than most to recall the Leigh match. "Unfortunately, I was red carded at a crucial time of the game. One of the Leigh forwards threw an uppercut at me as I was getting off him in the tackle. This wasn't seen by the referee, but my response certainly was. I had no arguments, I knew I had to go, but I regret it to this day because we were well beaten in the end." However, in the next home game, Jon Goddard scored a thrilling hat-trick from full-back as the old enemy, Hornets, were beaten for the third time in less than two months.

As early summer approached, the Boundary Park pitch needed to have reseeding work done on it so it was time to hit the road again for the team. After beating Rochdale on 23 May, they didn't turn out at Boundary Park again until the visit of Hull Kingston Rovers on 1 August. Nobody said it would be easy at Oldham.

So it was 'find a venue' time once more for the board. The next match was against Batley Bulldogs on 30 May, the Sunday of the Spring Bank Holiday weekend. What better way to spend a long weekend at that time of year than visiting the seaside and watching the Roughyeds at the same time? It seemed a perfectly good question so, with all other options closer to home drawing a blank, the board made a ground-breaking decision to contact Blackpool Football Club to investigate the possibility of taking the match to Bloomfield Road.

Chris Hamilton recalls: "There weren't too many rugby league, rugby union or football clubs in a rush to help us out so, bearing in mind it was a Bank Holiday and we didn't have much time – the last match at Boundary Park was only the previous Sunday – we thought it might be an interesting proposition for our fans to follow us to Blackpool that weekend. It turned out really well too, our 'home' crowd was only beaten by our two games against Leigh and a play-off tie against Featherstone all year. Subsequently, the Northern Rail Cup Final was held at Bloomfield Road from 2005 to 2012 and since 2015, the Summer Bash fixtures, including the iPro Sport League One Cup Final, have been held at the same venue. This all came about as a direct result of our match there against Batley in 2004. The RFL realised that playing matches in the seaside hot-spot of the north on a Bank Holiday weekend is a good idea. I'm sure Summer Bash will go from strength-to-strength and I'm glad that its origins were from us back in 2004."

For the record the Bulldogs rose to the occasion and won 44–20 after Oldham, with a weakened side, had raced into a 20–0 lead. Lee Marsh remembers it well: "It was a terrific stadium to play in. Although building work was going on at the ground – the stand was in a huge 'L' shape from one corner to the corner directly opposite – it was a really enjoyable experience for us all, apart from the result, of course."

Unfortunately, the Bloomfield Road experiment was a one-off and the club's next two 'home' games – against league leaders Whitehaven and Halifax – were played at the Victory Park ground of non-league football club Chorley. My memories of this ground are good ones, a long grassy bank down one side of the pitch which was perfect for watching the match on a warm summer's day. The Oldham players must have enjoyed it too because they played exceptionally well against Whitehaven to win 31–22 and then came from 14–6 down to beat Halifax 24–14 on a Saturday afternoon in mid-July.

Nick Johnson scoring against Hull Kingston Rovers at Boundary Park in 2004.
(Photo courtesy Oldham Rugby League Heritage Trust).

The squad was strengthened at this point with the signing of experienced Halifax utility man Jon Roper, a Cumbrian who had played 83 games in Super League for Warrington Wolves between 1996 and 2000 and another 13 for Castleford Tigers in 2001. Molloy earmarked him for left centre for the final stretch of the season, replacing Pat Rich who left the club for a second time after the Leigh game at Hilton Park on 25 July.

On returning to Boundary Park, another virtuoso display from Goddard helped to put Hull KR to the sword in searing heat. A 29–24 win owed much to the full-back's outstanding breaks from the back along with two more Lee Marsh tries, who whether he played stand-off or loose-forward, was proving a fine capture. "The Rovers game was a tough one," Lee recalls, "it was very hot and I remember thinking what a tough opponent the Papua New Guinean Makali Aizue was." Marsh continues: "I really enjoyed my year at Oldham, as much as at any of the other clubs I played at. I know we were not far away from being

49

one of the best clubs outside Super League that year. With a bit more luck we could have reached the Grand Final."

As the play-offs approached once more, fans were confident that the team would do well as they had in previous years. However it wasn't to be this time round as a below-par display against Featherstone at Boundary Park, a team who were clearly out for revenge following their drubbing at the same venue earlier in the year, saw Roughyeds crash out at the first hurdle. In a topsy-turvy game, in which the lead changed hands several times, Rovers' French international scrum-half, Maxime Greseque, was the difference with four goals, a drop-goal and an assured display with ball in hand. So sadly the play-off campaign, and the season, were over.

Dane Morgan was a tower of strength during his time at the club. "I had a fantastic two years at Oldham," he said. "Steve Molloy assembled a good team over the two years, we had a lot of good times and fine wins. It was great to play with a mix of young and experienced guys. Jon Goddard and Lee Doran were talented young players while Steve really led from the front. Paul Norton, in 2003, and Jon Roper, in 2004, were good honest professionals too. I loved the culture of playing in England. We played hard on the field and we celebrated hard after the game. Some of my greatest memories as a rugby league player were from my time at Oldham and all the great people involved with the club at the time."

So, despite a fine season from Goddard, consistently good showings from new boys Watson, Southern and Lee Marsh and a tremendous 26 tries from Nick Johnson, which was the highest number of tries in a season in the new club's short history, the team had, in the final analysis, failed to make an impact in the business end of the season when it mattered most. Sadly, for Steve Molloy, the writing was on the wall and, sure enough, his contract was not renewed for 2005. After two and a half years, the Molloy reign was over.

In the end of season European Nations Championship, the Ireland squad included Paul Southern as well as Lee Doran and Martin McLoughlin, Ian Watson was chief organiser for Wales and centre Iain Marsh was selected for Scotland. The Irish again did particularly well, defeating Wales 25–12 at Aberavon RFC and Scotland 43–10 at Navan RUFC in County Meath before slipping to a 36–12 defeat to a strong England side at Warrington.

5. An overseas invasion

On 9 October 1988, the biggest match in world rugby league, the World Cup Final, took place between New Zealand and Australia at Eden Park in Auckland. Playing full-back for the Kiwis that day was 22-year-old Gary Mercer, a young Bradford Northern player, who was looking to establish himself in the Kiwi side after moving to England to test himself in the old First Division a year earlier. Mercer went on to enjoy a superb career as a tough and combative player who was equally at home in the backs or forwards; always played above his weight and never failed to give 100 per cent commitment. On leaving Northern, he played for Warrington – including a Challenge Cup semi-final against the old Oldham club and the Wembley final against Wigan in 1990 – for Leeds, for Halifax and for Castleford in a glittering playing career that included 21 appearances for his national side. He was player-coach at Halifax in Super League between 1999 and 2001 and then took over the reins temporarily at Castleford after the sacking of Graham Steadman in 2004. Despite narrowly failing to keep Castleford in Super League that year – they were in deep trouble when he was appointed mid-season – it appeared he was a coach to be reckoned with and when the Yorkshire club decided not to retain him for 2005, Oldham swooped and appointed him as head coach late in 2004.

Following Mercer's appointment, Chris Hamilton said: "We believe all the characteristics Gary showed in his playing and coaching career to date will stand us in good stead." Mercer responded: "Oldham are a great club with a lot of history who have been through some turmoil over the years. They have been there or thereabouts recently and it will be my job to take them to the next step."

Steve Molloy's assistant, Andy Proctor, also left the club at the end of the 2004 season so there was a promotion for former player Keith Brennan, who had been coaching the club's Academy side and was now installed as Mercer's assistant. One of the advantages of appointing a man like Mercer, with his track record in the game and his considerable contacts worldwide, was that Oldham were now well placed to attract players from overseas, particularly from the southern hemisphere. Several established players left the club before Mercer's arrival, so it was imperative that he strengthened the squad ahead of the 2005 season. One of his contacts was former Kiwi team-mate Kevin Iro, the Wigan and New Zealand centre star and Mercer wasted no time in liaising with Iro about potential targets for Oldham. Although Iro represented New Zealand with distinction, he is, in fact, from the Cook Islands, a small group of islands in the Pacific Ocean rich in rugby league talent. He was keen to push the claims of several of his fellow islanders.

One of the signings Oldham made, on Iro's recommendation, was fiery forward Tere Glassie, who had already played at Boundary Park as part of the South Sydney Juniors team that played Oldham in 2000. Tere casts his mind back to early 2005: "Kevin Iro and Gary Mercer were close friends from their Kiwi days and when Kevin put some of our names forward, Gary was keen to act on his advice. I was delighted to sign for Oldham along with Dana Wilson and Carlos Mataora. I knew Dana and Carlos well before we linked up at Oldham. In fact, we had all played for the Cook Islands together and won the 2004 Pacific Cup in New Zealand. The experience and the publicity we gained from that tournament undoubtedly helped us to seal our moves to England. Three other Cook Islanders came to England at the same time: Byron Ford, who later had a loan spell at Oldham, Kane Epati who joined Hull Kingston Rovers and Adam Watene signed for Castleford. We were all confident in our ability to do well."

Dana Wilson was a huge prop-forward who proved to be very difficult to stop close to the line and Carlos Mataora was a tricky half-back or hooker. All three islanders proved to be extremely popular during their season at the club. Also arriving was the Australian-based New Zealander Marty Turner, recommended by former Wigan and New Zealand coach Frank Endacott, who proved to be a superb acquisition. Having spent time at Melbourne Storm and Brisbane Norths, Marty came with a reputation as a fine organiser, defender and goalkicker and lived up to all the expectations bestowed upon him.

Gareth Barber recalls: "Turner was a fantastic player, right up there with the best players I ever played with. His skill levels were excellent, he could easily have played in Super League. It was a pleasure to play in the same side as him." What made Turner's efforts so remarkable was that three years earlier he had spent time in intensive care in hospital after rupturing his spleen, fracturing ribs and suffering concussion in a car accident.

As well as the men from the other side of the world, the club made several other potentially exciting signings. Ricky Bibey, who had been playing at St Helens, and Simon Haughton, formerly of Wigan, were two of the biggest names. It appeared to be a real coup when both agreed to join the Roughyeds. Also, Damian Munro finally fulfilled a lifetime ambition by signing on the dotted line, centre or back-row forward, Mark Roberts, joined from Warrington and local lad, Alex Wilkinson, arrived after playing at Hull.

Bibey was a tough uncompromising prop-forward with games under his belt for both Wigan and Leigh, as well as Saints, when he joined Oldham. He is one of the few men to have won a Challenge Cup winners medal with both Wigan and Saints, being a substitute for Wigan in the 2002 final against Saints at Murrayfield in Edinburgh which the Cherry and Whites won 21–12 and again for Saints against Wigan in their 32–16 triumph in the Millennium Stadium in Cardiff two years later. He was also in the England 'A' squad that toured Tonga and Fiji in 2002.

Haughton was a real enigma. In his younger days he was a strong running second row forward and was capped by both England and Great Britain while at Central Park. He was also a substitute in Wigan's 1998 Super League Grand Final winning team against Leeds Rhinos at Old Trafford, a match incidentally which featured two future Roughyeds, Marcus St Hilaire and Graham Holroyd, in the Rhinos ranks. But as his former team-mate Kris Radlinski explains in his excellent autobiography, *Simply Rad*, Haughton's passion for rugby league was somewhat different to that of many of his peers. "Simon scored some of the best tries I have ever seen from a second-row forward. He was such a big man and incredibly fast, and in the early days of Super League he was unbelievable. His biggest problem, and I think he'll admit this, was that he didn't love rugby league – he simply found himself to be very good at it. He scored tries for fun when he was a youngster, which alerted Wigan, and when they signed him up so young, it seemed like the logical career path for him. He trained hard but he didn't have a strong affection for rugby league and I can't remember him ever watching any games as a spectator."

After leaving Wigan, Haughton played rugby union for Orrell RUFC before being persuaded to play league again by Oldham. He was quoted in the *Wigan Post* at the time: "I miss the contact and free-flowing play of league. I always knew I would return one day. I spoke to a few clubs, including Leigh, but it wasn't just about getting back into Super League. Oldham coach Gary Mercer is someone I played against and have a lot of respect for. He obviously has a lot of coaching ability too. I soon realised that they were an ambitious club and the club for me." Asked by the *Wigan Post* if Haughton was Oldham's biggest signing in their short history, Chris Hamilton said: "That's without a shadow of doubt, given Simon's credentials and achievements. When his name was first mentioned to us, from my point of view I thought it would be fantastic but that we would be very lucky if it came off. It just shows that hard work and determination can prevail."

The 2005 season began in mid-January when Leeds Rhinos Oldham-born prop-forward, and former player at the old club, Barrie McDermott, invited the Roughyeds to provide the opposition for his testimonial match at Headingley. It was an invitation the club were delighted to accept and an evening that everyone connected to the club will remember with affection. It was also a great night for Barrie, of course.

Left: Gavin Dodd, a product of the club's youth system and a fine wing, centre or full-back, had a great year in 2005.
(Photo courtesy Oldham Rugby League Heritage Trust).

Below: Cook Islander Tere Glassie, seen here with team mascot Reece Halstead at Batley in 2005.

Stand-off half Simon Svabic, impressive when switched to loose-forward
by Gary Mercer in 2005.
(Photo courtesy Oldham Rugby League Heritage Trust).

In mid-February, the season began in earnest with a match in the newly-named Northern Rail Cup against Blackpool Panthers – 2004 had been the final year for Chorley Lynx and the club had been re-born as Blackpool Panthers – and the return of a familiar face to Boundary Park. Lining up in the Panthers front-row that day was none other than Steve Molloy. In the first half, it appeared that Molloy and his new team-mates were on their way to a shock victory, leading 20–4 at the break. Fortunately for Oldham fans, debut tries from Glassie, Munro, and another new boy, Martin Elswood, saw the Roughyeds scrape home 22–20. It had been a nervy and unconvincing start to the Mercer reign. Things only got worse rather than better initially, however, as two defeats, home and away, to Swinton Lions followed. Despite Wilson, Mataora, Roberts and Wilkinson notching their first tries for the club in these two games, consecutive defeats to a side from National League Two did not augur well.

A Challenge Cup trip to Post Office Road on a Friday night in March to take on Sharlston Rovers for the second year running was billed as a potential cup upset by the media but, buoyed by a four try salvo from Haughton and a debut try off the bench from former Academy player, Andy Gorey, the Roughyeds blasted any thoughts of a cup shock out of the water with a comfortable 46–14 win to progress to the fourth round.

In this match, Haughton showed real glimpses of the undoubted quality he possessed and which he used to produce on a regular basis at the highest level. Sadly, his performances in an Oldham jersey only fleetingly reached those levels and, partly due to injury, he only played 14 games for the club, scoring seven tries. He was unstoppable against Sharlston Rovers though, and his display that evening remains my lasting memory of him as an Oldham player.

Gorey, 19 years old at the time, remembers the cup-tie well: "I had signed for my hometown club as a 16 year old, playing in the Academy under Shaun Gartland, son of the former Watersheddings coach Brian Gartland, and Shaun taught me a lot. We won an Academy Grand Final against Doncaster Dragons at Manor Park, the home of Oldham Rugby Union Club, but I dreamed of playing in the first team. I had trained for a few weeks with the first-team squad in early 2005 but when I got the call from Gary Mercer to say I was in the 17 against Sharlston, I was shaking with anticipation. On the night he pulled me to one side and told me to play my normal game, enjoy it and not let the home crowd intimidate me. I ended up scoring a try so I was delighted."

But in the Northern Rail Cup, two defeats to Rochdale Hornets meant early elimination from the competition, despite a second win against Blackpool. Gavin Dodd, who went on to have a superb season, scored a try hat-trick in defeat at Spotland, but the win over the Panthers in a match played at Preston Grasshoppers Rugby Union Club, meant little in the overall scheme of things. However, everybody's spirits were lifted considerably when the Roughyeds returned to Post Office Road to face Featherstone Rovers in the first National League One game of the season and put up a fine performance in pinching a 20–20 draw. Gorey again justified his selection with another try. Unfortunately it proved a false dawn as the next five matches, including defeat to a strong Castleford Tigers outfit, just relegated from Super League, and a home Challenge Cup tie against York City Knights, were lost.

I remember the Castleford match at Boundary Park for two reasons. Firstly, there was a huge turn-out of fans from Yorkshire, who packed into the Rochdale Road stand and gave their team wonderful support throughout the match. The other reason was the appearance of Cook Islander Adam Watene in the Castleford line-up. Watene joined the Tigers at the same time as Tere Glassie, Dana Wilson and Carlos Mataora joined Oldham and was well-known to the Oldham boys from their days back home. Adam helped Castleford back into Super League in 2005 before joining Bradford Bulls and then Wakefield Trinity Wildcats. Tragically he died from a suspected heart attack in October 2008 aged 31, while doing weight training in the gym at Belle Vue.

Speaking at the end of the year and looking back, Marty Turner described the first three months of the season as "the bad old days", a clue perhaps as to the improvement in the club's fortunes in the second half of the season. This began in early June when, just as in 2004, Boundary Park was unavailable due to reseeding of the pitch. So it was another new venue and more out-of-town games for the team to cope with. Sedgley Park Rugby Union Club were the willing landlords and three 'home' matches against Rochdale Hornets, Halifax and Featherstone Rovers were switched there prior to the return to Boundary Park for the Hull Kingston Rovers match on the last day in July. Sedgley Park was an archetypal rugby union venue with a clubhouse behind the posts at one end of the pitch, a huge playing area, deep in-goal areas, a small stand, terracing down the whole of one side and tall trees surrounding it. Supporters used the club car park at their own risk as it overlooked the pitch so a hefty penalty kick to touch could easily have smashed a windscreen. Oldham played several matches there in subsequent years and the venue was also used regularly by Swinton Lions at various times. It wasn't in Oldham and wasn't a typical rugby league venue, but it did provide a ground for the club to play at in the short term. For that the board were eternally grateful to the officials at Sedgley Park for their hospitality.

So it was then that on 5 June 2005, the team picked up its first league win of the season – and eased relegation worries in the process – in their first outing at their temporary home. It was a fantastic match too, a tremendous advert for rugby league, any rugby union officials or supporters watching could only have been impressed. A crucial Turner drop-goal plus six goals from the boot of the talented Kiwi helped the Roughyeds pip their derby rivals the Hornets, 25–24. A week later, Barrow Raiders were thrashed 40–22 at Craven Park and a slow climb away from the lower reaches of the league had begun.

Defeat by a strong Halifax side at Sedgley Park followed but then arguably the best display of the season, a cracking 38–20 win against Featherstone, put smiles on fans' faces once more. The *Manchester Evening News* described this win as follows: "A virtuoso display from stand-off Marty Turner gave Oldham their third win in four games and saw Featherstone coach Gary Price hand in his notice after the match. Seven goals and a try capped another fine performance from the New Zealander who is fast becoming one of the hottest properties in National League One. On a balmy day at Sedgley Park, Tere Glassie also impressed and scored Oldham's fourth try before his compatriot, Carlos Mataora, left two defenders in his wake in scoring under the posts." So the overseas contingent were coming good and it was no coincidence that the team had started winning as a result.

Damian Munro, meanwhile, was loving wearing the Oldham jersey at last. "Despite being approached on a number of occasions previously, I felt the time was right to join when I did," he said. "At last I was able to pull on the number two shirt that my dad had first worn in the 1970s and 1980s. It was a tough start to the season, we were a brand new team almost, learning how to play together. I recall one of the early season games against Rochdale Hornets in which we were losing at half-time and Gary Mercer really laid into us. I was hiding in the toilet. However, as a group we stuck at it, along with the ardent fans, and we ended up having a good second half to the season. One notable performance that I recall was against Hull Kingston Rovers at Boundary Park. We won convincingly and I was lucky enough to score a hat trick against the team that had won the Northern Rail Cup earlier in the season. I also remember pushing Castleford, who were full-time, all the way in the return match at Wheldon Road which showed how much we had progressed as a team. Although I could not match my dad's achievement in scoring a hat-trick of hat-tricks (three tries in three consecutive matches), at least I was proud to follow in his footsteps and play on the wing for Oldham."

The game against Hull KR that Damian mentioned was a great team display in the first outing back at Boundary Park after the summer recess. However in the next home game, against Batley Bulldogs, a handful of former Roughyeds favourites came back to haunt the club. Remarkably, the Batley team that day included Neil Roden, Dane Morgan, Mark Sibson, Martin McLoughlin, Iain Marsh and Darren Robinson. All had moved to Mount Pleasant after leaving Oldham and they all played as the Yorkshire side turned around a huge deficit, just as they had at Bloomfield Road a year earlier, to take away the two points. On this occasion, Oldham had raced into a 28–0 lead after 27 minutes only for it all to go painfully wrong later in the game, the visitors winning 34–32. Roden was, of course, to rejoin Oldham later after a short spell at Leigh and continue the wonderful service he had given prior to his move.

An excellent win at Rochdale preceded the Batley game and the season came to an end with a fine display against Barrow Raiders at Boundary Park, the Roughyeds winning 52–12 with Munro scoring a second hat-trick in five games, and a loss at Halifax. The Barrow game is best remembered in the Halstead family as being my dad's last ever home game covering the club for the *Oldham Chronicle* as he retired later in the year. He was awarded a guard of honour by the players of both teams on the pitch before the match. I know it is something he will never forget and was a fine gesture by the club to arrange it.

Unfortunately, the play-offs were out of reach for the Roughyeds in 2005, but as the *Gillette Rugby League Yearbook 2005-06* said: "Oldham's achievement in avoiding relegation ranks alongside those of many of the teams above them, after a hugely challenging campaign for the club. Coach Gary Mercer was well behind his rivals in terms of recruitment when he took over before the start of the season, and a poor Northern Rail Cup campaign appeared to signal a fall from grace for a club that was one game away from Super League just four years earlier."

Ominously, news of financial problems affecting the club began to make the headlines in 2005 although they did become the first rugby league club ever to have different shirt sponsors on their away kit than those on their home kit in the same season. "It was novel and original and obviously having two different shirt sponsors helped us financially," said Chris Hamilton. In spite of the financial difficulties, however, the team continued to be competitive all season. Mercer, with help from his assistant, Keith Brennan, and former Featherstone Rovers, Oldham, Bradford Northern and Great Britain forward, David Hobbs, who helped his old mate out on match days for a few weeks in mid-season, did well in these difficult circumstances.

Gareth Barber recalls: "Gary made me captain in 2005, so I owe him a lot for that. I loved captaining the side, as with goalkicking I like to think I thrived on the extra responsibility. Gary also played me at hooker for the first time in my life and I thoroughly enjoyed that too. Being able to get in to dummy-half and try to boss the show suited me down to the ground. Gary was good to me and for the team as a whole, no doubt about that." Tere Glassie agrees: "Gary Mercer was a passionate coach. He had been a very successful player and earned respect because of that. He was good to play for, part of him was still very much a player when he was coaching."

Mercer was offered a new deal by the board for 2006, but chose to reject it to pursue other avenues in his life. He has spent much of the time since leaving Oldham working in Scottish Rugby Union, as defence coach for Glasgow Warriors, as assistant coach of the Scotland Under–20s team and for the Scottish Rugby Academy. He also had a spell in 2014–15 as head coach of the Yorkshire Carnegie Rugby Union club based at Headingley.

At the end of the season, the *Oldham Chronicle* praised the contribution of Gavin Dodd, Marty Turner and Simon Svabic, who completed his third season in Roughyeds colours. "Dodd played in every game, scored more tries than anyone else, minimised his tendency to lean towards the outrageous and battled through the pain barrier to defy an ankle ligament injury over the last seven or eight weeks of the campaign. His mates call him 'The Space Man', but local lad Gavin had his rugby boots in 2005 very much on terra firma. Result? His best ever season for the club in his favourite position and, appropriately, with No.1 on his back." Dodd's fine season inevitably attracted the interest of other clubs and sure enough, he left at the end of 2005 to join Widnes Vikings. Jon Goddard's fine Oldham career also came to an end as he took up a one-year full-time deal with Hull Kingston Rovers.

The *Oldham Chronicle* continued: "After a relatively quiet start to his first stint in England, the likeable, unassuming Kiwi half-back Turner oozed class. An accomplished footballer, a brilliant defender and a goalkicker of genuine class, he was full value for money as the club's overseas quota import. Svabic also produced his best ever season in a Roughyeds jersey. Mercer pulled off a master-stroke when he switched him from stand-off to loose-forward. The position suited him, he suited the position. Lucky 13? It certainly was for Simon."

Asked about his year in England, Glassie grinned: "The novelty of seeing snow wore off pretty quickly when it all turned to black slush and the roads were covered in black ice. I loved living in the North of England though. Yes, it was cold, but I had a ball there. Oldham was a great introduction into life in the north, a town that is passionate about rugby league and their professional team. I was keen to stay in England so spent the next three years at Leigh Centurions, Castleford Tigers and Dewsbury Rams. My memories of my time at Oldham are all good ones. Of course, it is hard not to think about those times without being reminded of the loss of Dana but I spent plenty of good times with him and all the lads from Oldham."

Tere refers there to the sad loss of Dana Wilson who was tragically killed in a road accident in Cheshire in September 2011. He had left Oldham after the 2005 season and saw service at Leigh and Halifax, scoring the winning try for the Centurions in the 2006 Northern Rail Cup Final against Hull Kingston Rovers at Bloomfield Road. Everyone at Oldham was devastated when news of Dana's death filtered through. Glassie says: "Of the group of Cook Islanders who left our shores to come to England in 2005, two, Adam Watene and Dana, have unfortunately left us."

The coach of Leigh in 2006, the club that Tere and Dana signed for on leaving Oldham, was Tony Benson, who would coach the Roughyeds between 2009 and 2012. "Tony was a very good coach and is a very good person," said Glassie.

So with Gary Mercer deciding not to take up the offer of a new deal, the board were looking for a new coach again in 2006. The financial issues surrounding the club were such that it was always likely to be a long, hard year and that is unfortunately exactly how it panned out. The man the board turned to in late 2005 was a man who had enjoyed a fine career as a player and also as a coach, former Wigan and Halifax loose-forward John Pendlebury. Although Pendlebury served the Central Park club well as a player, he is perhaps best remembered for an incident in the 1987 Challenge Cup Final at Wembley where, playing for Halifax, he produced a wonderful match-winning challenge on St Helens' Kiwi centre Mark Elia just as the latter was crossing the try line late in the game. Elia looked a certain scorer as he lunged for the line with plenty of room in which to work, but remarkably Pendlebury appeared from nowhere and managed to dislodge the ball from Elia's grasp as he was in the act of touching down. Moments later the hooter sounded and Halifax had won. It was a similar challenge in many ways to the brilliant try-saving tackle that Hull FC hooker Danny Houghton produced on Warrington forward Ben Currie in the closing stages of the 2016 Cup Final.

Of course, Pendlebury's name went down in Halifax folklore and even more so 11 years later when, as coach, he guided them to third place in Super League and was named Super League Coach of the Year as a result. At Oldham, however, he was up against it from the outset as several players, including Gavin Dodd, Jon Goddard, Ricky Bibey and the four overseas men had all left the club and there just wasn't the money available to recruit players of the quality of previous years. Two players who did arrive were the Corcoran brothers, Ged and Wayne, and both were influential, along with long-serving John Hough, in a young side. Ged had been playing at Dewsbury Rams and later went on to be assistant coach to Mark Aston at Sheffield Eagles while Wayne was signed from Halifax. Wayne, a Rochdale lad, had been a member of the North West Counties tour to Australia in 2001 that my dad was media manager on and was a fine ball-playing back-row forward.

It is interesting to note that several of Corcoran's team-mates on that tour also played for Oldham later, namely James Coyle, David Allen, Adam Sharples, Andy Ballard, Gareth Hayes and Carl Forber. More about some of these players later.

Part of the agreement with Leeds Rhinos when Oldham travelled to Headingley in early 2005 for the Barrie McDermott testimonial was that Rhinos would send a team to play Oldham at Boundary Park as part of the pre-season preparations in 2006. It was a great evening witnessing many of the Super League team's young stars playing and the game had an added twist when Barrie made an appearance for both clubs, one half each.

Hardly had the Northern Rail Cup campaign began before the first body blow of what would be a tumultuous season arrived. Pendlebury resigned citing personal reasons and this was before the National League One season had even started. But the board acted quickly in appointing a successor, bringing in local man, Steve Deakin, a former assistant coach at Sheffield Eagles, London Broncos, Huddersfield Giants and Halifax who had been head coach at the French club Union Treiziste Catalane (UTC), the fore-runner to Catalans Dragons, until December 2005. Deakin was quoted as saying at the time: "I am privileged and proud to be coach of my home town team. When I got the call, I couldn't get in the car quick enough."

One of only three wins the team enjoyed in 2006 came in the third round of the Challenge Cup, against local amateurs Saddleworth Rangers at Boundary Park. On a snow-covered surface, Roughyeds won 34–10. A familiar face in the Rangers line-up that day was loose-forward, Emerson Jackman, who had played for Oldham in 1998 and 1999. So after beating Rangers and completing a Northern Rail Cup double over Keighley Cougars, the league season began in early April with a heavy home defeat to Hull Kingston Rovers.

Sadly this was the first of 18 straight league defeats. Arguably the best performance during this horrendously tough period came against Halifax at The Shay in June. Although trailing 28–0 at half-time, the introduction from the substitute's bench of young half-back Paul Ashton, son of former Watersheddings star Ray Ashton, turned the game on its head. 'Ashy' scored two tries and created two more with astute kicks to the corners to give real hope to the fans that a famous comeback win might be on the cards. Unfortunately the fightback fell short, the home side hanging on – just – to win 34–28. "It was a pleasure to play for Oldham, the team my dad had represented in the 1980s," said Paul recently. "I often watch recordings of him in action at Watersheddings. They were great days. My dad was well looked after by Oldham when he arrived at the club from amateur rugby league in Widnes in 1979 and the colts coach at the time, Brian Gartland, became a good family friend. In the Super League era, when Brian's son Steve was part of the squad, I was allowed to train with the Bears first-team as a 15 year old lad. I was a cheeky half-back and loved joining in at touch football with them. Martin Crompton was the captain at the time and I loved taking him on in training. Being cocky helped me a great deal to play scrum-half when I turned professional."

Sadly the mini-renaissance at Halifax didn't last long and a 62–0 drubbing by York City Knights at Sedgley Park, a 58–10 loss away to the newly-named Doncaster Lakers – a match in which Cook Islander Kane Epati scored a remarkable six tries - and two 70 point hammerings by Widnes Vikings merely rubbed salt into gaping wounds. It didn't help either that Gavin Dodd raced in for three tries in the game at Widnes. The Vikings had a prolific try-scorer in 2005 in Australian half-back Dennis Moran, and he helped himself to seven tries over the two games against Oldham that year with future Roughyed Mick Nanyn scoring five times over the same two games. It was certainly a tough time for all concerned at the club.

Looking back, Steve Deakin talks positively about the players he had at his disposal in 2006. "At no point did any of my players hoist the white flag or throw in the towel. We had several losses, of course, but they approached every game prepared to give of their best and always believed a win was imminent. I could tell when the players finished their pre-match warm-ups every week that they truly believed this was going to be their day. I like to think they were enjoying their rugby too, despite the results. My son-in-law, David Best, played for me that year and he has told me that the year was one of the most enjoyable of his professional career."

Youngster Andy Gorey was beginning to build on the exciting start he had enjoyed to his career the previous year. "I began to establish myself in the side in 2006 and although we were losing, it felt amazing representing Oldham. The individual highlight for me was in the Widnes game at Boundary Park. We were well beaten, but we never gave up, Widnes were on fire the whole game. I only remember them dropping the ball once, close to our line, and I picked it up and saw an open field in front of me. I pinned my ears back and set off. I knew I could run a bit but then I noticed that Dennis Moran was chasing me and trying to cut me off. That just made me run even harder. Luckily I managed to make it to the line and the fans of both teams applauded me all the way back to my own half. The fans spend their hard earned money supporting the club and as players we wanted to do all we could for them. I loved playing under Steve Deakin. I also scored two tries at Batley that year with a cracked sternum which prevented me from breathing properly which is something else I am very proud of. Playing for the Roughyeds was something I had always wanted to do and I thank everyone concerned for giving me the opportunity." Gorey finished 2006 as the club's leading try-scorer with 10.

Coach Deakin continues: "I had enjoyed a lot of success coaching in France – UTC won the French Championship in 2005 – but at Oldham it was very different, in 2006 anyway. As a coach, you do begin to question if what you are doing with the team is right, but I always believed it was. I know the players were always with me. I felt for them when defeat followed defeat."

The 2006 season also marked the end of Gareth Barber's and Phil Farrell's days at the club. It had been a roller-coaster ride for Gareth with many highs and a few lows. After a short spell at Rochdale Hornets, he joined Oldham Rugby Union Club at Manor Park and is still playing for them, and captaining them, to this day. "In a way, playing union felt like a fresh start for me. I enjoyed learning new skills and taking on fresh challenges. League and union are so different. I loved my days in league and now I enjoy union too." There is no doubt that Barber's rugby league career will be remembered fondly by Roughyeds supporters. Phil Farrell left to join neighbours Rochdale Hornets after amassing 125 appearances for the club. Most fans would agree that he was a consistent stand-out performer in his six years as a Roughyed, a cracking captain and a person in whom big brother Andy, and nephew Owen Farrell, the current England rugby union star, should be rightly proud.

As far as the financial troubles were concerned, much of the debt that was hanging over the club was paid off and that was to the immense credit of all concerned. 2006 was not a year to be looked back on with any great affection, but by the season's end there was light at the end of the tunnel and as supporters looked forward to life in National League Two in 2007, things could only get better.

Photo: 2006 top try-scorer Andy Gorey scoring against Leeds Rhinos in a pre-season friendly at Boundary Park. (Photo courtesy Andy Gorey)

6. Looking to bounce back

As the dust settled on the club's relegation season, and a year in the third tier of rugby league awaited the Roughyeds, there were two silver linings to the clouds for fans to take heart from. First, the darkest days of the 2006 financial crisis were now in the past following sterling work by the board in addressing the debt and by fans and others with the club at heart who held bucket collections at matches and raised funds in numerous other ways. Everybody had pulled together and the Roughyed spirit, so often evident on the pitch, showed up off it in droves as well. The second was that coach Steve Deakin had now had time to take stock, take a look at his squad and decide how best to strengthen it with the funds at his disposal. It was clear to him I'm sure, as it was to the fans, that the playing side of the club would need a large upheaval if the team was to be competitive in National League Two in 2007, let alone pushing up towards the top of the division.

What any team needs in a situation like this is a quality, experienced old hand at half-back to guide the team around the pitch and take control when the going gets tough. Who better then to carry out this role, at stand-off in this case, than old favourite Neil Roden? Neil had left the club at the end of 2004 to join Batley Bulldogs for 2005 before spending the following year with Leigh Centurions. "It was good to pull on the Oldham shirt again," says Neil. I definitely got the impression talking to him that he couldn't wait to get back, having been such a key figure at the club in his first spell between 2000 and 2004. "2007 proved to be a very good year for us. We improved steadily as the season went on and personally I think it was one of my best seasons. Steve Deakin was an excellent coach, very clever and a great bloke. I would say categorically that he ranks alongside Mike Ford as the best coach I ever played under. He certainly knew how to get the best out of me."

Roden wasn't the only club stalwart to return. Ian Sinfield had played in the 1998 Law Cup win and spent four years at the club before joining Rochdale Hornets and later Keighley Cougars and Swinton Lions. Jason Clegg signed for the Cougars just days before Sinfield moved to the Lions. "I couldn't believe it," says Cleggy, grinning. "One of the reasons I signed for Keighley was because my old mate, Sinny, was there. Then in no time at all, he had left. I had a word or two with him about that."

Ian recalls: "I thoroughly enjoyed the 2007 season back at Oldham. The second half of that year includes some of my best memories as a player. We went on an excellent winning run after recruiting some really good players. I was part and parcel of the set-up and it was great."

Others to join prior to the beginning of the season included prop-forward Jason Boults and hooker Simeon Hoyle from Halifax, winger and centre partners Gareth Langley and Craig Littler from St Helens, loose-forward Kris Smith from Swinton Lions, former Keighley Cougars prop Richard Mervill and two overseas players, French forward Said Tamghart and Australian loose-forward Geno Costin. In addition, full-back Paul O'Connor re-signed after making three appearances in 2006. It is fair to say that, without exception, all of these close-season acquisitions did well in 2007 and, in some cases, for considerably longer.

In terms of length of service to Oldham, only two players, Neil Roden and John Hough, topped the number of appearances made by Jason Boults. Taking into account that he played at open-side prop for the majority of his games, this illustrates what a great contribution to the cause the Yorkshireman made over the years. By the time he hung up his boots in the professional game – he demonstrated his love for rugby league and for the hard graft of being a front-row forward by re-joining his old amateur club Siddal in Halifax after leaving Oldham – he had amassed a terrific 193 games for the Roughyeds over eight seasons at an average of 24 plus games per season. Take a bow Jason.

Langley and Littler played just one game each in Super League for Saints, but joined Oldham with the good habits from having learnt their trade at one of the country's top clubs instilled into them. The one game they did play was a memorable one for them, however, as they both crossed the whitewash for tries as a weakened Saints team, depleted due to the upcoming Challenge Cup Final against Huddersfield Giants in 2006, pushed Catalans Dragons all the way in the South of France before losing 28–22. Both proved excellent captures by Steve Deakin with Langley, from either right wing or full-back, scoring 13 tries and kicking 35 goals in 30 appearances in 2007 and Littler scoring six tries in 27 appearances from right centre. Having played together at Knowsley Road, they knew each other's games inside out and formed an effective right-wing partnership, the best at the club since Anthony Gibbons and Joey Hayes in 2001.

Langley reflects: "The two of us played together at academy level, in reserve grade and in the one Super League match for Saints. I had no hesitation in signing for Oldham after meeting Chris Hamilton and Steve Deakin and was asked to try to persuade Craig to join me. He did, and our partnership was reignited."

Richard Mervill played in a terrific 31 matches in 2007 in the engine room of the front row and had a superb season. Ever reliable, strong and powerful, Mervill stayed at the club for three years and was a big influence in the pack throughout. A vastly under-rated player, he was much respected by his team-mates who appreciated the work he got through, on both attack and defence.

Said Tamghart became a massive crowd favourite, bringing a touch of Gallic flair to Boundary Park. He was the third Frenchman to play for the club following Laurent Minut and Emmanuel Peralta in 1999. With an international cap for Les Tricolores to his name before arriving at Oldham, it was clear that Said was a very good forward, who played well above his weight, ran strongly and defended well. Steve Deakin used him as a 'super-sub' in his two-year stint at the club, entering the fray, as Danny Guest used to, when the opposition were tiring. Said's power and strength was best used down the middle. Tamghart wore the Oldham jersey 63 times in 2007 and 2008 and remarkably only started three times, the remaining 60 appearances came off the bench.

Fans of the old club at Watersheddings remember with great affection two Australian loose-forwards, John Cogger and Stuart Raper, who performed admirably in the red and white in the 1980s and 1990s. In 2007, a compatriot of Cogger's and Raper's, who played in a very similar style, signed for the club, Geno Costin. The *Manchester Evening News* spoke to Geno early in his stint at Oldham: "I considered moving to London like many Australians coming to the UK do, but to be honest the big city did not appeal to me. I wanted to be somewhere totally different to home." Geno originated from a sleepy suburb of Brisbane and he continued: "Oldham seemed a great choice and I signed for the Roughyeds while still in Australia. I am loving the change of scenery here in the North of England."

Geno was a fine addition to the squad and scored eight tries in 25 appearances in 2007 as well as bringing a touch of Australian humour and banter to the dressing room. "Geno was a cracking lad, great for team morale," said Chris Hamilton.

Paul O'Connor became, like Jason Boults, another to end up with over 100 career games for Oldham on his rugby league CV. He began 2007 well, playing in the first 14 games, before he left the club temporarily to take up the option of a trip to Australia. It was a real blow to the team because, as he proved in later years at the club, he was a full-back with the heart of a lion, tremendously brave and courageous and a man every player would want alongside him in the trenches.

The Northern Rail Cup began in February 2007 with Oldham placed in Group 4 alongside Rochdale Hornets and Swinton Lions. As well as home and away games against the two local rivals, there were also two cross-group games against Dewsbury Rams. Frustratingly, only one of these six matches was won, the match at Swinton. Although Rochdale and Dewsbury were from National League One, it was not the start fans had been hoping for bearing in mind all the new arrivals. The third and fourth rounds of the Challenge Cup, however, provided far more hope. After beating amateurs East Hull at Hull Ionians RUFC 26–10, an intriguing trip to Cougar Park to face Keighley Cougars faced the team in round four.

Thus followed the best performance of the season to date in a cup tie which saw an 8–0 half-time deficit blown away in the second half as, playing down the slope, Roughyeds ran in five tries with Langley scoring twice, substitute Paul Ashton scoring a gem under the posts and then, in the final 10 minutes, loose-forward Kris Smith showing his undoubted talent by twice ghosting through the last remnants of defence to cap a great 26–16 victory. I was standing behind the posts at the bottom end of the ground in the second half that day and it was terrific to see the tries flowing in such an important cup tie. "I remember that match, and my try, well," said 'Ashy'. "My dad used to teach me as a youngster that pace off the mark was vital for a good half-back. I saw a gap from the base of the scrum and just went for it."

Kris Smith had been at Leeds Rhinos as a youngster and also played for Halifax and London Broncos before moving to Swinton Lions and on to Oldham. He was a fine player, but unfortunately only made 10 appearances for the club due to injury. His performance at Keighley that day proved what might have been for him as a rugby player if he had managed to stay fit, but he certainly hit the headlines in later life by marrying Australian singer Danni Minogue, becoming a male model and appearing on television, mainly in Australia.

Three days after the Keighley tie, on Wednesday evening, 4 April 2007, the National League Two season began for Oldham with a Boundary Park meeting with a Featherstone Rovers side who became a major rival as the season progressed. Playing in League Two for the second consecutive year, having failed to win promotion in 2006, Rovers were coached by former Watersheddings favourite David Hobbs. They had set their stall out to go up in 2007 by signing Super League trio Paul Handforth, Tommy Haughey and Jamie Field. All three turned out at Boundary Park as Rovers made their intentions clear with a 23–12 win. For Oldham, it was an inauspicious start, but a 40–20 win away to Blackpool Panthers in the second game got everyone smiling again.

It wasn't just the result by the seaside that day though that lifted the spirits. Making his debut after signing from Widnes Vikings was Kenyan wing sensation Lucas Onyango, a man who went on to become one of the most popular players to wear the Roughyeds jersey in the 20 years of its existence.

Lucas outlines his sporting background and how he became the first player from Africa to represent the club. "As a youngster in Kenya I played basketball and was involved in athletics. Lots of Kenyan athletes become good middle or long distance runners, but I was a sprinter. As for basketball, although I was 6 feet one other guys were taller than me. So at High School I started to play rugby. Of course it was rugby union, but I loved running with the ball as a winger. I played for a club called Mean Machine RUFC which was affiliated to the University of Nairobi. The club has a great history and has produced several Kenyan internationals. They gave me my chance and their style of play and character toughened me up and helped to turn me into the player I later became.

Then I was selected to represent my country at sevens in the Commonwealth Games in Manchester in 2002. It was a thrill playing at the City of Manchester Stadium, now, of course, known as the Etihad Stadium and the home of Manchester City Football Club. I had a sister living in London so after the Games I stayed and moved down there. The big city was too busy for me though, I was used to a much slower way of life in Kenya. So I moved up north and played club rugby union in Manchester. I had a trial at Sale Sharks, but England internationals Jason Robinson and Mark Cueto were there so I was up against it. However, I had seen rugby league on television and fancied giving it a go. Jason recommended it to me as well and said I had nothing to lose, I could always return to union if I didn't like it. As a former rugby league star with Wigan and Great Britain and rugby union World Cup winner with England, I reckoned his advice was worth listening to. So I signed for Widnes in 2005 while Kiwi Frank Endacott was coach. The former Cronulla Sharks star and Australian international David Peachey was at the club at the time and he helped me a lot in my development as a rugby league player. I scored six tries in eight appearances in 2006, but then got a knee injury which held me back for a while. Soon after I heard Oldham were interested in signing me and I met Chris Hamilton and Steve Deakin on the East Lancs Road for talks before signing in early 2007."

I feel sure that when the Vikings snapped up Onyango they saw tremendous potential in him as a flying winger, not dissimilar in style to a man who had graced the old Naughton Park pitch before moving on to Wigan, the great Martin Offiah. Lucas had searing pace, a great body swerve and the same high-stepping action used to evade would-be tacklers as that which Offiah had used to such great effect before him. Lucas grins when he hears his name mentioned in the same breath as Offiah's. "I think it's a very good comparison," he laughs. "We both came out of rugby union for a start and both played on the left wing for Widnes. I used to see all the photographs of him on the walls during their glory days in the late 1980s and 1990s and knew then what a hard act he was to follow." Onyango's debut for Oldham against Blackpool was rich in promise, with his first try for the club coming soon after half-time.

Another less heralded, but equally significant, signing was prop-forward, Tony Tonks, who arrived from Bradford Bulls and also made his debut at Blackpool. Tonks was a powerful and aggressive forward and became a key figure up front for the team in his only season at Oldham. Tonks remembers: "I had a great year at Oldham, really loved it. The other lads were cracking to be around and the fans were great too. However the coaching staff were brilliant. It was a wonderful environment to be in for me as I was a young lad at the time. I loved playing for Steve Deakin. He was a genuine guy who really knew his rugby. He made the best use of what he had and did a cracking job with players, making them realise how good they could be. He held a good young side together well."

Following a 32–20 home win over Keighley, another significant match in the club's season followed on Friday 4 May against the embryonic South Wales outfit, Celtic Crusaders. In their inaugural season a year earlier, the Crusaders, including a large contingent of Australian players, had, like Featherstone, narrowly failed to win promotion but were named by bookmakers as favourites to go up automatically in 2007. Their Australian coach, John Dixon, had a rich pedigree, having worked under the great Wayne Bennett at Brisbane Broncos and he was able to entice several fine players from his homeland, who certainly knew their way around a rugby pitch. Full-back Tony Duggan, centre Mark Dalle Court, half-back Jace Van Dijk and loose-forward, Damien Quinn, were excellent experienced players and it meant that Crusaders would take some stopping in National League Two.

On the first weekend of May, the RFL had introduced a new initiative for Super League clubs – the Magic Weekend. This has developed into a thriving and popular part of the Super League season, but in 2007 it was brand new and was played at the Millennium Stadium in Cardiff. As an encore, on the Friday evening before the main event on the Saturday and Sunday, Celtic Crusaders had pencilled in a home fixture at their ground in Bridgend with a view to tapping in to some of the Super League support already arriving in South Wales and the general excitement surrounding rugby league in those parts that weekend. Who better then to provide the opposition than Oldham?

It was a huge evening for Crusaders, made even bigger by the presence of Sky Sports television cameras, but make no mistake it was a big occasion for the Roughyeds too, and in no way did they intend to be cannon fodder for the Welsh side on their big night. A superb crowd of 3,441 attended to fully vindicate the Crusaders' decision to host the game on the Friday evening and at half-time, with the home side leading 22–6, it appeared that their players had warmed to the occasion also. Then, early in the second half, an incident occurred which appeared to irrevocably turn the game in Oldham's favour. Jason Boults and Luke Young, of Crusaders, were sent to the sin-bin for fighting after a mini-brawl and the incident fired up Oldham to such an extent that they then proceeded to score five tries in 25 minutes of scintillating catch-up rugby league. Tonks, Langley, Alex Wilkinson twice and Littler all crossed the Crusaders line and, added to Onyango's first-half effort, saw the game turned on its head. Oldham won 34–26, a fantastic result and a real turning point in the club's season.

Neil Roden played a key role in the win that night: "It was a great win and one of my favourite games in Oldham colours. Although we were underdogs, and trailing at half-time, Steve Deakin was really calm and told us that if we were a bit smarter, the rewards would come. As we went out for the second half, we all had a feeling we could turn it around. After the incident in which 'Boultsy' and Young were sin-binned our pack really stood up to theirs and gave us the belief that we needed to go on and win."

Following victory in Bridgend, the team extended their winning run in National League Two to seven matches with further wins in May and June against Barrow Raiders and York City Knights at home and London Skolars and Workington Town away. The only blip during this period was a heavy Sedgley Park defeat by Super League side Harlequins RLFC – formerly London Broncos – in the fifth round of the Challenge Cup. The Londoners were skippered that day by England international Rob Purdham, whose brother Garry, himself a rugby league player, was tragically killed in the infamous Cumbria shootings of June 2010.

The cup tie against Harlequins brought the curtain down on the Oldham playing career of John Hough. One of only two substitute appearances John made in 2007, it was his 228th and final competitive appearance in a Roughyeds jersey, just short of 10 years after he became the first player to sign on the dotted line for the new club. It was the end of an era. Throughout his time at Oldham, John had worn the badge with pride, never shirked anything, always given 100 per cent for the cause and, at his peak between 1999 and 2002, was undoubtedly as good as any Number 9 outside of Super League. The following is a breakdown by year of John's appearances, second only to Neil Roden in the 20 years of the new club.

1998	21
1999	30
2000	33
2001	27
2002	37
2003	27

2004	12
2005	20
2006	19
2007	2
Total	228

Left: John Hough and Joe McNicholas, team-mates between 1998 and 2003, together at a Penrith Panthers versus Canterbury Bulldogs NRL game in 2017.

Between 1 February 1999 and 16 April 2001, John made a staggering 83 consecutive appearances. Hough says: "I thoroughly enjoyed my years at Oldham. The first year, 1998, was very special with it being a brand new club at the time. 2001 was my favourite season when we reached the Northern Ford Premiership Grand Final against the odds. I wore the Oldham jersey one last time, in the Kevin Sinfield testimonial match against Leeds Rhinos in early 2008 and that was a nice way to finally hang up my boots as a player." John put all the expertise and experience he had gained while wearing the Oldham number 9 shirt to good use in 2009 when he took over the coaching of the club's reserve team and led them to Championship Grand Final success in 2011. Speaking from his home in Perth, Western Australia, he continued: "20 years on from when I signed for the club, I often look back fondly on my time at Oldham. The camaraderie I enjoyed with the rest of the lads is something I will cherish forever and, despite living on the other side of the world now, I still call many of them friends. I continue to follow the Roughyeds fortunes and wish them all the very best in the future."

The Barrow match at Boundary Park on 20 May saw the debut of exciting centre Adam Hughes, a class act, and worthy of playing at a higher level than League Two. Hughes marked his first appearance in Oldham colours with two tries and went on to become a key figure in the team as the season progressed, finishing with an impressive 22 tries in 16 appearances. Forward Adam Robinson also made his debut against Barrow as the board looked to strengthen the squad whenever the opportunity arose. Manchester businessman Bill Quinn had taken over as chairman in early 2007 to form a three-man board alongside Chris Hamilton and Sean Whitehead, with Chris continuing as chief executive. Sean left the board in 2009 and then in 2010 Bill moved on with Chris resuming the chairmanship. Neil Roden scooted in for a fine hat-trick against Barrow as the visitors, with six league wins from six at the time, were well beaten.

Performances were up and down over the next few weeks, however, with defeats at Featherstone, Keighley, Swinton and Barrow ensuring early season optimism was kept in check. The new signings continued to arrive with scrum-half James Coyle and hooker Matty Brooks joining the club. The sticky spell – only one win in five games – ended when

Hunslet Hawks came to Boundary Park on 22 July and with the irrepressible Hughes in imperious form, scoring four tries, the Roughyeds won 52–22 with Coyle also scoring in only his second appearance. Speaking of Hughes, Neil Roden said: "I struck up a good relationship with Adam on the left edge. He was a great try scorer and game changer." Lucas Onyango agrees: "Adam was definitely the best centre I had the pleasure of playing with, a great footballer, try scorer and try creator. He set up a lot of tries for me in my first season at Oldham as well as scoring plenty himself."

After the Hunslet game, a tricky trip to York City Knights followed and this match is best remembered for a late match-winning drop-goal from another new arrival, the much-travelled Rob Roberts or 'Two Bobs' as he became known to all at the club. With the scores locked at 14–14 and time ticking away, Roberts showed all his class and experience by taking it on himself, on debut, to stroke home the winning one-pointer to the jubilation of Oldham fans present. It was a huge moment in the team's late-season push to finish as high as possible in the league and keep the pressure on Celtic Crusaders and Featherstone at the top.

Two more home wins followed against Blackpool Panthers and Workington Town, the latter match seeing the first appearances of Cook Islander Byron Ford and Scottish international Gareth Morton, both signed on loan from Hull Kingston Rovers. Byron recalls how his move came to take place: "I had just come off an eight-week spell on the sidelines at Rovers with a broken hand. I played a couple of comeback games in the Under–20s team, but it didn't feel right playing against the youngsters. I needed to get fit again in first-team rugby. A move to Doncaster on loan had been discussed, but Steve Deakin called me to say that Oldham were interested and asked if we could meet. We did and 'Deaks' sold the club to me with talk of promotion from National League Two being his goal for the year. I had been promoted with Rovers the previous year after an exciting National League One Grand Final victory over Widnes Vikings at Warrington – a match, incidentally, in which Jon Goddard scored two tries – so the chance of experiencing another Grand Final with Oldham was too good to miss."

Ford was a big strong winger and, like Hughes, a great try scorer. Playing on the right flank against Town he scored two late tries to fully underline his potential and demonstrate what a key addition to the side he could be. His Hull KR team-mate Morton was an excellent goalkicker who appeared to have modelled his kicking technique on that of England rugby union star Jonny Wilkinson.

Two more away wins followed, against Gateshead Thunder and Swinton Lions, before the crunch return with Crusaders at Boundary Park. The Welsh team appeared to be champions elect and with the automatic promotion slot that went with it, they were in no mood to relinquish their place at the top of the league. However defeat at Oldham and they could still be caught by Featherstone. For the Roughyeds, victory was important to help to stave off Barrow's late push for third spot and the less difficult run in the play-offs that followed. It was a crucial and intriguing game, made more so by the memories of Oldham's fantastic comeback in Bridgend three and a half months earlier. Crusaders headed north that day – Thursday 30 August – for Sky Sports coverage once more and in front of a gate of 4,327, the best National League Two crowd of the season, the scene was set for a classic. The crowd that evening was swelled by a clever marketing ploy by the club in which fans were given free admission, but were asked to donate one pound to charity instead, with funds to be split between Dr Kershaw's Hospice and the Rugby League Benevolent Fund. The match lived up to its billing but it was the visitors who produced a quality performance when they needed it, winning 32–18. Two of their tries, however, appeared contentious and were awarded after being referred to the video referee. "I felt we were unlucky, to say the least, with both calls," reflects Steve Deakin. There was no debating a spectacular long-range try by full-back Tony Duggan though, with even Oldham supporters shaking their heads in disbelief at its quality. Winger Paul Ballard, later to play for Oldham and brother of another future Oldham winger Andy Ballard, scored twice that evening. It was the win that Crusaders craved and virtually wrapped up promotion for them.

For Oldham, it meant that even if they beat Swinton Lions and London Skolars at home in their last two league games, if Barrow won their last two, against Blackpool and Featherstone, both at home, Roughyeds would have to settle for fourth spot. That is exactly what happened as the Raiders thrashed Rovers 30-4 to seal third place. Now Oldham would have to do it tough in the play-offs if they were to reach the Grand Final.

Swinton came to Boundary Park for the second time in 12 days in the first play-off match having pushed Oldham all the way in the league encounter, eventually succumbing to a Byron Ford hat-trick and a 30–22 defeat. There was no mistake from Oldham second time around, however, Lucas Onyango and Rob Roberts both scoring twice in a fine 36–6 win. "I loved the big open spaces of Boundary Park," said Lucas, after ripping the Lions defence to shreds with his raw pace down the left wing. Workington were then disposed of 48–0 in the next match with full-back Gareth Langley scoring a hat-trick and Adam Hughes two tries. There was some exciting rugby being played by the team with the forwards dominating down the middle and the backs looking sharp and dangerous with Langley, Ford, Hughes and Onyango in particular, posing a huge threat out wide. Langley, primarily a winger, explains how his move to full-back came about. "I hadn't worn number 1 on my

74

Left: Gareth Langley in action against Workington Town at Derwent Park in 2007 (Courtesy Gareth Langley).

back since academy days at St Helens but 'Deaks' asked me to slot in there when Paul O'Connor left the club to go to Australia.

I was keen to help the team out so I agreed. I was pleased, on the whole, with how I coped with the positional switch."

So after winning the two fairly straightforward games well, the battle against the big two, Barrow and Featherstone, was still to come. The next fortnight was to be the acid test for the team, were they good enough to reach the Headingley Carnegie Grand Final and win it?

Barrow had won 10 of their last 13 league games prior to the play-offs including a 34–26 victory over Oldham in July and that terrific mauling of Featherstone in their final game. Rovers had extracted full revenge by beating the Cumbrians 36–20 at Post Office Road to book their place in the Grand Final so this meant a trip to Craven Park for Oldham in the final eliminator, or in other words, in a fascinating Grand Final shoot-out.

Oldham fans headed up the M6 in droves on the last day of September for what promised to be a magnificent win-at-all-costs play-off battle. Langley gives an insight into Oldham's preparations for the big game. "The squad travelled to Cumbria on the Saturday and stayed overnight. I asked for special dispensation to travel north on the Sunday morning because I was giving my cousin away at her wedding on the Saturday. 'Deaks' wouldn't allow it which I fully understood, he wanted the whole squad to be together the night before the game and on the morning of the game. So I travelled up on my own at about 9pm on the Saturday evening, arriving at about 11.30pm."

It turned into one of Oldham's best performances in the history of the new club and a day the fans will always remember. Barrow were destroyed in their own backyard by a Roughyeds side oozing confidence and playing some sublime football, and with the omnipotent presence of the menacing Hughes at centre. After a tight first quarter, the Raiders were blown away in the second, Hughes and James Coyle scoring two tries in six minutes and with four goals by Langley, having a stormer at

75

full-back, Oldham led 16–0 at half-time. Gareth grins as he recalls his kicking: "I had missed every kick I took when practicing on the pitch before the game and Barrow fans were barracking me. Thankfully, I kicked six from six when it mattered including one from the touchline. I gave the home crowd a wry smile as I ran back!"

The third quarter saw the home side desperately trying to claw their way back, with half-backs, Australian Pat Weisner and local boy Darren Holt, particularly dangerous. They managed to break Oldham's defensive stranglehold just once, but the Roughyeds quelled the storm and wrapped proceedings up with two further tries by Hughes in the final 10 minutes. The first came from a kick close to the line by Geno Costin but the second was Hughes all over. Breaking clear deep inside his own half, he raced clear and dived in under the posts in front of Oldham's travelling support. What a magnificent moment that was, one I will never forget. The final score of 28–6 was evidence enough, it appeared, that Oldham were the real deal in 2007 and that only Featherstone Rovers stood between them and a place back in National League One for 2008.

Neil Roden, as ever a key man in the side, said: "It was a cracking win at Barrow, a great performance and a great result." Tony Tonks recalls the match with delight: "Adam was fantastic that day," he said. "He was a great player, too good to be in National League Two. From a personal point of view, I had a running battle with Barrow prop Brett McDermott, one of the hardest props I have ever faced."

Although everyone connected to the club was ecstatic that evening, Byron Ford had picked up a hamstring injury which was to make him extremely doubtful for the Grand Final a week later. Ford had made a huge impact on the right wing and his loss would be a tough one to take. "It really was a race against time," recalls Byron. "I was injured in the 79th minute at Barrow when the match was already won. It was so frustrating. I was treated by the physios at my parent club, Hull KR, which I appreciated because their Super League season had ended but they worked on me all week. I remember lying on a bed getting treated for hours that week. I didn't train with the Oldham lads at all and had a fitness test the day before the game. It felt much better so I was passed fit." So Ford was named on the right flank as usual when the teams were announced to the crowd shortly before kick-off.

Gareth Langley again speaks about the eve of Grand Final preparations: "As with the Barrow match, we stayed overnight on the Saturday, in a hotel in the Leeds area. Rhinos star, Kevin Sinfield, presented us with our playing jerseys and we all stood up to say a few words. One or two of the lads, myself included, had everyone in stitches with some of the things that were said but it was great for team spirit.

Left: Loan signings Byron Ford and Gareth Morton at Boundary Park in 2007.

Steve Deakin had stressed all year that we needed to win promotion, not only for ourselves, but also for our fans who had stayed loyal to the club despite a tough year in 2006. He spoke about that again that evening. We were all in it together."

The match was the second of a triple header, sandwiched between the Rugby League Conference National Grand Final between Bramley Buffaloes and Featherstone Lions – won 42–30 by the Lions – and the National League One Grand Final between Castleford Tigers and Widnes Vikings – won 42–10 by the Tigers. Rovers supporters turned up in vast numbers, many of them wearing flat caps – hence the unofficial nickname of the 'Flat Cappers' – but Oldham fans were in confident mood too. Unfortunately, despite another cracking long-range try – this time an interception – from Hughes, the Roughyeds never really got going and the Yorkshire side dominated from start to finish. Sadly, Byron Ford was led disconsolately from the pitch early in the match, never to return. "I ended up tearing my hamstring when I had a run from a scrum. As I sat in the changing room I was shattered, distraught that I had let people down, my team-mates but especially 'Deaks'. It was a bitter pill to swallow. I still recall it with sadness and I would say without a doubt it was one of the reasons why I returned to Australia soon afterwards, definitely one of the biggest regrets of my life."

Ford's injury was only one of three picked up however, with Tony Tonks and Geno Costin also being forced to quit before half-time. Steve Deakin was adamant that the decision to play Ford was his, and his alone. "It was a Grand Final, and if ever there was a time to gamble on a player's fitness, then this would be it. The injuries cost us dearly with none of the three players able to return at any point in the match. It meant our options with substitutions were limited and we had players playing out of position while covering others. Despite this, Featherstone

77

only scored three tries and two of those came from kicks. They rarely opened us up."

Neil Roden recalls: "We went into the match very confident. The three early injuries hurt us, however, and we ended up second best unfortunately. Byron was a big loss because, along with James Coyle and Rob Roberts, he added a lot of quality to the side in the final third of the year."

Tony Tonks left the club after the Grand Final to join Featherstone: "We were unlucky with injury in the final. I was gutted for the coaching staff because they really deserved promotion. Featherstone came in for me as they prepared for life in National League One. My wife and I had just had our first child so I really wanted and needed to be playing closer to home in Yorkshire. But I thoroughly enjoyed my time at Oldham." Ian Sinfield, who started in the second row in all four play-off ties, but was forced to switch to the front-row in the Grand Final when Tonks was injured, added: "I think the Grand Final was a game too far, to be honest. We peaked at Barrow in the previous game." And Langley admitted his personal performance didn't meet his expectations that day. "I know I didn't play well, I struggled to keep hold of the ball and missed a relatively simple kick at goal. Looking back, I think nerves played a big part."

Stuart Dickens, the Rovers prop, had a terrific game up-front. "The build-up to the game was very tense," he said. "We had the upper hand over Oldham in the league but we knew they were a good side. There was a lot of pressure on us to gain promotion because we had missed out the year before. We had a superb following from our fans and right from the kick-off I was confident that if we played well and stuck to our game plan, we would win. I felt we were always in control without ever hitting top gear and our experience helped us to retain control. The main emotion after the game was relief because it was something we had worked two years for. The big games are difficult to enjoy because there is so much at stake but we certainly enjoyed ourselves afterwards."

Following the disappointment of Grand Final defeat, two players, Adam Hughes and Rob Roberts, had the honour of playing international rugby in the autumn, for Wales. Both players were called up three times, against a touring Papua New Guinea side in Bridgend, a match Wales won 50–10, and two qualifying matches for the 2008 World Cup. Scotland were pipped 18–16 in Glasgow but the Welsh were well beaten by a Lebanon side, with a strong Australian influence, 50–26, in the final game, at Widnes.

7. More Grand Final heartache

Having failed to gain promotion in 2007, the board and Steve Deakin were determined to strengthen the squad for 2008 in a bid to go one better and match Celtic Crusaders and Featherstone Rovers success in achieving their goal at the second time of asking. Barrow Raiders had snapped up Adam Hughes during the off-season so impressed were they by his self-destruction job on them in the final eliminator so it would take a big signing to replace him. Not many centres come much bigger than Widnes Vikings star Mick Nanyn and it was he the club turned to, to fill the void left by Hughes's departure. Nanyn, son of Oldhamer Mick Nanyn senior, who played for Wigan in the 1970s and 1980s and elder brother of young prop, Danny Nanyn, who made 20 appearances for Oldham between 2004 and 2006, had amassed a phenomenal 434 points for Widnes in 2007, with 28 tries and 161 goals in 29 appearances. Although the loss of Hughes was a serious body blow, there is no doubt that Nanyn was potentially a worthy successor.

The backs were further strengthened by the acquisition of three vastly experienced former Super League stars. Three-quarters Daryl Cardiss, Danny Halliwell and Marcus St Hilaire – known as 'Junior' to his team-mates – had spent several seasons in British rugby league's elite competition and the three signings proved that no stone was being left unturned as the club set out its stall to get out of National League Two.

The pack was similarly bolstered with two former Super League forwards in Simon Baldwin and Phil Joseph plus the ever-reliable Tommy Goulden, from Rochdale Hornets, a man who had been a thorn in Oldham sides over the previous two years. It was clear to see that a very good squad was being assembled.

Like Adam Hughes's spell at the club in 2007, Mick Nanyn's stint as an Oldham player only lasted one year. But as in his time at his previous clubs Swinton Lions, Rochdale Hornets and Widnes Vikings, his stay was a points-laden one with the powerful centre crashing in for 21 tries and kicking 139 goals in 2008, for a total points haul of 362, to leave him second only to Wigan Warriors winger Pat Richards in the top points-scorers list covering all three divisions and all competitions. Nanyn must have been an intimidating sight for would-be defenders as he ran at them, complete with headgear and with legs like tree trunks he was a very different centre to Hughes but equally effective. His goal-kicking was exceptional too and he rivals Pat Rich, Marty Turner and future captain Lewis Palfrey as being the best goalkicker to represent the new Oldham club in its 20-year existence. Many fans have discussed whether Hughes or Nanyn was the better centre during their relatively short spells at Oldham. It's a difficult question to answer as they were so different. My vote would go to Hughes though, as he was a classical centre in the old-fashioned style, a winger's centre, a great footballer and polished in everything he did. Nanyn's strength was just that – powerful and destructive when in possession, and his accumulation of points was outstanding. It really would have been something if both had played in the same team.

Daryl Cardiss was an accomplished winger, having played for Wigan Warriors, Halifax Blue Sox and Warrington Wolves between 1996 and 2004, but sadly for him, and the club, he missed a huge chunk of the season due to injury. He returned for the final run-in to the year, eventually making 14 appearances for the club, scoring two tries.

The much-travelled Danny Halliwell had played for five different clubs in Super League, Halifax Blue Sox, Wakefield Trinity Wildcats, Warrington Wolves, Leigh Centurions and Salford City Reds between 2000 and 2007 and arrived at Oldham after a second spell with Leigh. He had a cracking year in 2008 for the Roughyeds, playing in 34 matches, scoring 20 tries and turning in a record-breaking performance against Workington Town at Boundary Park in August. Since 2002, Gareth Barber had held the record for most points in a match with his 26 against Dewsbury Rams at Hurst Cross, but Halliwell scored 28 against Town with four tries and six goals, whilst deputising at left centre and as goal-kicker for the injured Nanyn.

Marcus St Hilaire had a terrific pedigree in the game, having turned out for Leeds Rhinos, Huddersfield Giants and Bradford Bulls in 12 seasons of top-class competition. In all he made 201 appearances in Super League between 1996 and 2007, scoring 73 tries. Here was a player of the highest calibre who was committing himself to the Roughyeds' cause. 'Junior' became a real favourite at the club, never failing to impress, whether playing at full-back, on the wing or at centre. A classy footballer and tough defender, he eventually played in 85 games for Oldham over four seasons, 2008 to 2011, scoring 31 tries.

Simon Baldwin played in Super League for Halifax Blue Sox, Sheffield Eagles and Salford City Reds before joining Oldham after spells in 2007 with Rochdale Hornets and Whitehaven. However his appearances were limited to just eight due to injury. Phil Joseph was a member of Huddersfield Giants Super League squad in 2004 before playing for Swinton Lions in 2005, Hull Kingston Rovers in 2006 and Halifax in 2007 before signing for the Roughyeds. He was a combative, uncompromising forward with a no-nonsense approach and played 55 times over two seasons, scoring 16 tries. Equally effective at hooker or loose-forward, he showed his versatility by twice appearing at stand-off half and twice at centre in Oldham colours. Tommy Goulden became a great favourite at the club with his strong running and terrific work-rate. With 15 tries in 30 appearances in 2008 and another 11 in 23 in

2009, he was a prolific try-scorer for a second-row forward and always appeared to raise his game in the bigger matches or when the going got tough.

As had been the case in 2005 when Barrie McDermott invited Oldham to Headingley to provide the opposition for his testimonial match, Rhinos star loose-forward Kevin Sinfield, another product of Oldham's terrific rugby league breeding ground, did the same in early 2008. So for the second time in four years, Roughyeds trod the famous Headingley turf and in so doing enabled the Rhinos faithful to pay tribute to one of their own. 'Sir Kev' was a legend at Leeds even then and in the years since his popularity and standing at the club, and in the game of rugby league as a whole, has grown to almost unprecedented levels. A real sporting hero, born and brought up in Oldham. Leeds again agreed to play Roughyeds the following year in a pre-season game, but unfortunately this one was postponed due to inclement weather.

Hopes were high among fans as the Northern Rail Cup swung into action once more. Oldham were in Group 4 with neighbours Rochdale Hornets, Salford City Reds and Swinton Lions. In a fantastic match at Boundary Park in the third game, the City Reds, from National League One, were stunned 18–14, the Roughyeds extracting full revenge for a heavy defeat at The Willows two weeks earlier. Three wins from four were picked up against Rochdale and Swinton so the club progressed into a quarter-final qualifying round tie against another National League One side, Whitehaven, at Boundary Park. In the meantime, however, the Challenge Cup and National League Two began.

For the first time in the 11 year history of the club, the Challenge Cup draw pitted them against a team representing one of the Armed Forces. The Army away was the tie awaiting the Roughyeds in round three and a long trip into north-east Hampshire and the famous army barracks in Aldershot. The match represented a relatively safe passage into the fourth round with Oldham winning 56-10, James Coyle scoring a hat-trick and his eighth try in only the sixth game of the season. The scrum-half had a great year in 2008, scoring 21 tries and finishing joint top try scorer with Mick Nanyn as well as creating several more with his classy distribution. Although the team came through the potential banana skin of the trip down south, most Oldham fans present were talking about the performance of Ben Seru, the Army's left-winger, who caused no end of problems for the Roughyeds defence. The Fijian's dazzling display had everyone on the edges of their seats and a few weeks later, Oldham made a sensational swoop to sign him. It appeared the winger had all the attributes to do well in rugby league, size, strength and speed, but sadly for everyone concerned, not least the player himself, he picked up a serious knee injury in a later round of the Challenge Cup against Wakefield Trinity Wildcats in June and never played again. Rugby league is a tough and unforgiving sport but Seru was desperately unlucky. Of course, the same could be said as well for Oldham.

The National League Two season began on Good Friday, 21 March, with a high-scoring thriller against Rochdale at Spotland and a 46–32 success. Two more big wins, against Hunslet Hawks and York City Knights, followed with plenty of points being scored and lots of exciting football being played. Next up came the Northern Rail Cup tie against Whitehaven and a hard-fought 16–6 victory to push Oldham into the quarter-final against Batley Bulldogs at Mount Pleasant in late May.

Following the first league defeat of the season at Keighley Cougars, the fourth round of the Challenge Cup beckoned and a trip to Swinton. Roughyeds had already won 52–10 there in the group stages of the Northern Rail Cup and triumphed again this time in a much tighter game, by 20–8. After two more home wins against Rochdale and Blackpool Panthers, the fifth round sent the team to Dewsbury Rams. In a terrific display of attacking football, the Rams were ripped apart with Tommy Goulden making the headlines with four tries and Mick Nanyn notching two tries and nine goals for a personal points haul of 26. Oldham now found themselves in the quarter-finals of both the Northern Rail Cup and the Challenge Cup, heady times, indeed, for the fans. It wasn't mentioned by too many people around the club but it was a fact that the team were now within two wins of Wembley Stadium and the Challenge Cup Final.

Unfortunately, it was too good to last, of course, and a disappointing 24-16 loss at Batley Bulldogs in the Northern Rail Cup last-eight was followed a week later by a 46-4 loss at Super League outfit Wakefield Trinity Wildcats in the big one. This was the match that Ben Seru made his one and only appearance for the club. Despite an early try from Lucas Onyango, on the opposite flank to Seru, that gave Oldham the lead and had supporters believing that anything was possible, reality was soon restored and the Wildcats hit back to lead 20–4 at half-time and ran in five more tries after the break. Despite the two cup defeats, however, the team was kicking along nicely and the two cup runs had given supporters a huge lift after the Grand Final setback of 2007 and also gave the club a boost financially.

A midweek trip to a revitalised Gateshead Thunder in a re-arranged fixture due to Oldham's cup commitments came just three days after the Challenge Cup exit and this match was destined to become the most controversial and talked about one of the season. Thunder, having struggled in 2007, enjoyed a new lease of life in 2008 under the tutelage of flamboyant Australian coach, Dave Woods.

Top: Prop Jason Boults, a mainstay of the Oldham front-row between 2007 and 2014 (David Murgatroyd).

Middle: Marcus St Hilaire, with Lucas Onyango in support (David Murgatroyd).

Bottom: Coach Steve Deakin twice led Oldham to Grand Finals.

They surprised everyone by racing to automatic promotion with some quality performances and results. Bolstered by a quartet of talented Australians, they had great back-up from local born products such as Kevin Neighbour and Neil Thorman, brother of Chris Thorman who had been a member of Huddersfield Giants Northern Ford Premiership title-winning side of 2002.

In 2007, the RFL had changed the usual points system of two for a win, one for a draw and nothing for a loss and replaced it with three for a win, two for a draw, one for a defeat by twelve points or fewer – a bonus point – and nothing for a defeat by more than twelve points. This new points system was to have a huge impact on Oldham's season in 2008, and especially so in the fixture on Tyneside on Wednesday evening, 4 June. Steve Deakin explains: "Gateshead were a good side and we knew it was a tough ask to win there. However, we didn't expect to be the victims of a refereeing decision that still irks me to this day. The home goal-kicker, Dan Russell, was allowed to re-take a crucial kick at goal, having missed it once, because some of our lads had moved in front of the goal-line as he kicked it. I have no issue with the fact that they did so, but how often do you see a kicker allowed to re-take an unsuccessful conversion for this reason? Rarely, if ever, have I seen it happen, before or since. We eventually lost the match, 32–18, thereby missing out on a bonus point, which we would have had if we had lost by 12 points, rather than 14. The significance of this was that three months later, Barrow Raiders pipped us on points-difference for the second automatic promotion place which would have been ours had we earned a bonus point at Gateshead."

In charge of the match was Oldham-born Robert Hicks, at the time a young referee, having achieved his Grade One refereeing status just two years earlier. Over the next decade, Hicks would become one of the leading officials in the British game. He was a touch-judge at Challenge Cup finals in 2010, 2011 and 2014, at Super League Grand Finals in 2013 and 2014 and at the Four Nations final in 2014. He then refereed the Super League Grand Final in 2016 and, as he told me recently, achieved a major ambition by refereeing the England versus Australia Four Nations encounter at the London Stadium in 2016. He was then named as the First Utility Super League Referee of the Year in 2016. In 2008, however, the less salubrious surroundings of Gateshead's International Athletics Stadium, in front of a sparse crowd of 444, saw Hicks in charge of Oldham's visit.

Hicks described his role in the controversial incident that Oldham maintain played a large part in costing them automatic promotion. "Gateshead had scored a try – one of five they scored on the night – and as their goalkicker, Dan Russell, prepared to take the angled conversion, I told the Oldham players to stay behind the goal-line until the kick had been taken, as I always did when kickers were preparing to attempt to convert a try. In rugby union, players are allowed to run out in a bid to distract the kicker, but this isn't the case in rugby league. In fact, the Rugby Football League had issued an edict to referees to be particularly wary of this around that time. However some of the Oldham players ignored what I had said – they may have claimed they hadn't heard my instruction, but they should have been aware of the rule anyway – and encroached over the goal-line as Russell was about to take the kick. The kick was unsuccessful and I, therefore, made the decision to allow him to re-take it. I had actually warned the Oldham lads three times. Subsequently, Russell was successful with the re-taken kick."

He continued: "Oldham felt I was being harsh and pedantic allowing the kick to be re-taken. But I maintain to this day that the decision I made was the correct one and this was, in fact, confirmed for me by my refereeing assessor who was sitting in the stand. As an Oldham lad, I used to watch the old club at Watersheddings with my granddad and I also supported the new club up to 2001, after which my refereeing duties took over. I was at the 2001 Northern Ford Premiership Grand Final against Widnes Vikings and at the 2007 National League Two Grand Final against Featherstone Rovers. I was touch-judge that day at the National League One Grand Final that followed, but watched the Oldham game first with interest. Obviously as a referee I cannot support any one team anymore, but I certainly wish Oldham well in the future."

Two games after the disappointment in the North-East, Oldham thrashed Hunslet Hawks 66–10 at the South Leeds Stadium, with points-machine, Mick Nanyn, helping himself to 26 points – this time with one try and eleven goals – for the second time in 2008. Further comfortable wins followed against London Skolars and Blackpool Panthers, the latter game featuring another Neil Roden hat-trick, before the eagerly-awaited re-match with Gateshead, played at Sedgley Park, on 29 June. Thunder arrived having won each of their previous nine league games, including the controversial home win over Oldham three and a half weeks earlier. There was to be no repeat for them, however, with Roughyeds turning on the style and powering to an impressive 40-16 victory, one of only three league defeats suffered by the visitors all season. One of Oldham's stand-out performers that day was full-back Paul O'Connor, returned from his Australian adventure, and fully established again at No.1. 'POC' raced in for a splendid hat-trick against Thunder and finished 2008 with 17 tries in 35 appearances. He would go on to be a mainstay of the side in the next two years and a huge influence on the team in 2009 and 2010.

That month, June 2008, saw club chairman Bill Quinn taking part in a charity boxing event organised by the Steve Prescott Foundation to raise funds for cancer charities. Prescott, the former St Helens, Hull FC and Wakefield Trinity Wildcats full-back, had been diagnosed with a rare form of cancer in 2006 and had established his Foundation to raise funds a year later. Steve lost a tremendously brave battle with the disease in 2013, but not before he had written his very moving autobiography, *One in a Million*. The book, written with the help of journalist Mike Critchley, describes the boxing event as follows: "Former rugby league players were enlisted to fight at the Reebok Stadium in Bolton. Getting them to don the gloves was tougher than the organisers expected but eventually some of Steve's former team-mates and opponents agreed to undertake ten strenuous weeks of training to take part in the contest. All the boxers were assessed and matched up to the same-standard opponent to create competitive fights and were policed by former World Champion, Steve Collins, who was instructed to stop any fight at the first sign of anyone getting hurt. Among the bouts were Steve Hampson v Anthony Sullivan; former Super League referee Karl Kirkpatrick v Jason Donohue; and Maea David v Esene Faimalo. Brad Hepi lost to Oldham chairman, Bill Quinn, who had boxed as an amateur, and Alan Hunte, Garry Schofield, Warren Jowitt and Tim Street also took part."

Just a few weeks later, on Thursday 17 July, the Oldham club made its own contribution to charity fund raising when the Boundary Park clash against Doncaster, televised live by Sky Sports, saw the team boasting a catching all pink strip. The *Oldham Chronicle* reported as follows on the evening of the match: "The concept of wearing the pink strip provides an illustration of support for the club's fund-raising initiatives. Dr Kershaw's Hospice and the Genesis Appeal, for research into the prevention of breast cancer, will benefit on the night from the minimum charity submission of one pound from each spectator. No admission fee will be charged due to help from sponsors meeting the costs of staging the fixture. No professional men's rugby league team in the United Kingdom has ever worn a pink strip for charity before and officials had to gain special permission from the Rugby Football League for their pink plan." Following on from the club's similar initiative at the Celtic Crusaders match a year earlier, it again emphasised how the club appreciated the work that cancer charities do. A fine crowd of 2,806 attended, the highest National League Two crowd of the season, just as the crowd figure at the Crusaders game had been in 2007. The match was won 36–16 with two more tries from Tommy Goulden. "Tommy was an absolute machine!" said Gareth Langley.

Doncaster, however, were to become a major thorn in the Roughyeds side as the season drew to its conclusion. Under new ownership, and with rugby league legend Ellery Hanley as head coach, they had reached the Northern Rail Cup Final earlier in the year, losing to Salford City Reds, before launching a major bid for National League Two play-off glory. Future Castleford Tigers and England scrum-half star Luke Gale was a dynamic and exciting influence on their side in 2008, going on to beat his club's tries in a season record with 30 and being named National League Two Young Player of the Year. They gained almost immediate revenge for their defeat at Boundary Park by winning the return league fixture 18–10, before returning to Oldham for the first round of the play-off series in mid-September. Unfortunately, Roughyeds were off-colour on the day and the visitors, brilliantly led by Gale, who scored two tries and kicked six goals, booked their place in the Grand Final with a fine display of attacking football, winning 32–20.

For Oldham, the defeat was a setback but they got a second bite at the cherry with another home game, a week later, against Rochdale Hornets. Turning in a much improved performance and with Langley and Goulden both scoring twice, Roughyeds ended their neighbour's hopes with an ultimately convincing 38–14 win. "It was always good getting one over on the old enemy," smiled Langley.

So, for the second consecutive year, Steve Deakin had led his troops to the Grand Final, this time to be held at Warrington's Halliwell Jones Stadium. Disappointingly, for team and player, Neil Roden had picked up an injury against Hornets and was forced to sit out the big game. Unbeknown to anyone in the Oldham camp, Ellery Hanley had told the Doncaster players just before kick-off that he was to leave the club after the game and this bolt from the blue appeared to inspire his side. Oldham dominated the game for long periods, however, but were unable to turn pressure into points, particularly in the first half. Only one try was scored – by substitute, Ian Hodson, a player who had re-signed for the club in June after giving excellent service in 2005, 2006 and 2007 – and although 6–2 in front at the break, the general feeling among fans was that the lead could, and should, have been a more substantial one. Those worst fears were confirmed in the second half when Doncaster scored three tries, one of them, by the nemesis Gale, a controversial one as he appeared to ground the ball short of the try line. Despite a Mick Nanyn score out wide for Oldham, the third Doncaster try, by substitute Kyle Briggs, seven minutes from time, was the final nail in the Roughyeds' coffin.

A distraught Steve Deakin said after the match: "I was more disappointed by this defeat than by any other in my coaching career. Some big incidents went against us and cost us dearly, but we self-destructed. The Grand Final was there for us to take and we failed to take it." Giving a view from the victorious Doncaster camp, second-row forward Craig Lawton, later to sign for Oldham, said: "Ellery Hanley was a very professional coach, he prepared us extremely well for games, none more so than the Grand Final. We were totally focused on the job in hand and we had to be because Oldham had given us some tough games that year. Luke Gale was brilliant for us. We also had two other excellent half-backs, Kyle Wood and Kyle Briggs. Unfortunately, I dislocated my shoulder midway through the first half so I won't forget the match in a hurry."

Following the second failed promotion attempt, Steve Deakin was not offered a new contract by Oldham so his stay at the club was brought to an end after almost three years. There is no doubt that his astute coaching helped to produce a team that played some exciting football during his tenure, but in the final analysis he had failed to deliver the promotion the board craved, and they decided it was time to start afresh in 2009.

Speaking in 2017, Deakin said: "I want to go on record as saying how much I enjoyed my time at Oldham. I am naturally disappointed that I was unable to take the team to the next level, and to get so close twice was gruelling. I had some fine players with me during my time at the club, guys who made the headlines regularly but also several unsung heroes whose role in a rugby league team is so crucial. Also it would be remiss of me not to say 'hats off' to Chris Hamilton, who has stuck by the club from day one in 1997 and is still going strong now, 20 years later. His tremendous loyalty to the club should be acknowledged and applauded."

There was consolation of some kind after the Grand Final in 2008 for Mick Nanyn, who was named in the Scotland squad to take part in the World Cup, held that year in Australia. The Scots finished second in a three team group, behind Fiji but ahead of France, with Nanyn being a substitute against the French and starting at right-centre in his team's thrilling 18-16 win over the Fijians. They were then involved in a play-off for seventh spot but lost to Tonga with Nanyn again at right-centre. It is interesting to note that the Ireland World Cup squad included five players who turned out for Oldham at some point during their careers. Although not at the club at the time of the tournament, Shayne McMenemy, Lee Doran and Ged Corcoran, plus two players who would sign for Oldham later, Wayne Kerr and Stevie Gibbons, all made the trip Down Under.

8. Mixed emotions

As mentioned in Chapter 5, the head coach of Leigh Centurions in 2006 was the well-respected New Zealander Tony Benson, formerly coach of the renowned Junior Kiwis team and a man who led his new English outfit to Northern Rail Cup Final success that year. Tony spent just one year at Hilton Park before a new avenue in his rugby league coaching life opened up for him in 2007, in the unlikeliest of places. The Emerald Isle beckoned and Benson moved across the Irish Sea to try to identify and develop Irish based talent ahead of the 2008 World Cup in Australia.

He took charge of the Ireland 'A' side in the Home Nations Championship and later was in charge of an emerging Ireland squad – the Irish Wolfhounds – on their development tour of his homeland, New Zealand. In 2008, he moved to the bright lights of London to take charge of a London Skolars team, desperately trying to establish themselves in England's sports-mad capital city. Eventually commuting from his home in the North-West of England proved too much for him and a move closer to home for the 2009 season was what he was looking for. It just so happened that Oldham were in the market for a new coach at this time and Benson was eventually appointed as the Roughyeds Head Coach late in 2008.

Speaking at the time, Benson told the *Manchester Evening News:* "For me it's an absolute honour to be coach of such a fine club, particularly with the history that Oldham's got. I understand what's expected of me, especially with the last couple of years we've had. It's a very difficult job to reach a Grand Final, so to do it twice is pretty magnificent really. I'm confident that if we can pull together – and by that, I mean players, supporters, the reserve players and the staff at Oldham – then we can make a real go of this."

Seven of the 17 players who took to the field in the Grand Final against Doncaster left the club at the end of the season in 2008, so Benson was immediately able to make signings and attempt to build his own squad. This he did and several of the newcomers were vastly experienced and with proven Super League pedigree. Full-back Paul Reilly joined after playing for Huddersfield Giants and Wakefield Trinity Wildcats, former Sheffield Eagles, Halifax Blue Sox, London Broncos and Huddersfield Giants winger Lee Greenwood arrived as did local lad Paul Highton, a front-row warhorse from his days at Halifax Blue Sox and Salford City Reds. Flying winger Andy Ballard moved from Salford City Reds, young half-back Thomas Coyle, brother of James, from Wigan Warriors, fire-house prop Jamie I'Anson from Celtic Crusaders, back-row forward Dave Allen, formerly of Wigan Warriors and Widnes Vikings and another back-row forward Craig Robinson, brother of Adam, from Rochdale Hornets. Despite these eye-catching additions, however, the new boss's most intriguing close-season signings appeared to be two young Irishmen, prop Wayne Kerr and hooker Stevie Gibbons. Both of these Irish-born and Irish-developed players had impressed Benson during his days in Ireland and both had followed him to London Skolars and then again to the Roughyeds.

Paul Reilly was always one of my favourite opposition players when he lined up in a Giants jersey, reminding me very much of my boyhood idol, the great Martin Murphy of Watersheddings fame. Tough as teak, abrasive, skilful and a great last line of defence, Reilly made 158 Super League appearances in the claret and gold, played in the 2006 Challenge Cup Final against St Helens at Twickenham and played twice for England in the European Nations Championship of 2004, scoring two tries and winning the man of the match award in his country's 36–12 victory over Ireland in the final at Warrington. "I still have the recording of this match at home," grinned Paul. "I came to Oldham at the end of my career. I knew Marcus St Hilaire from my days at Huddersfield and Chris Hamilton sold the club to me. It made my decision to join an easy one. I had a neck injury when I signed unfortunately and it curtailed my appearances. When I did play the injury was always in the back of my mind. I thoroughly enjoyed my time at Oldham though and Tony Benson invited me to assist with the coaching, which I loved doing. I would have liked to extend my stay at the club but I had difficulty getting time off work to fit in the hours required for training sessions. I still look out for their results with interest to this day."

Lee Greenwood, another Roughyeds newcomer, played for England in the same tournament, scoring twice in a 98–4 rout of Russia in Moscow. Greenwood arrived at Oldham with 81 top-flight appearances behind him and a highly respectable 39 tries. Both players brought considerable experience and expertise to the back-line.

Andy Ballard took over the goal-kicking mantle from the departed Mick Nanyn and went on a points-scoring bonanza in the first two-thirds of the season, twice breaking the Roughyeds points in a match record. The 28 points that Danny Halliwell picked up against Workington Town a year earlier was surpassed, ironically against the same opposition, in a 66–14 Boundary Park romp in March and then having broken the record with 30 points, Ballard contrived to smash his own new record just over a month later. A remarkable 34 points came the way of the prolific wingman with two tries and a phenomenal 13 goals in an away day classic from the Roughyeds, winning 78–10 away to London Skolars in May. "I was aware that I had broken my own record against Skolars," smiled Andy, when I reminded him of his feat recently. "It seems a very long time ago now, but it felt good at the time." It really was a year of personal points records in 2009 because, after Ballard had moved on to Barrow Raiders in July, young forward Chris Baines equalled the 34 points by bagging four tries and kicking nine goals in a thrilling 54–30 play-off victory over Hunslet Hawks in September. More about Baines later.

James Coyle had been a top performer in 2008 and the Coyle influence grew even stronger early in 2009 when younger brother Thomas joined his elder sibling at the club. Both Coyle boys had made a handful of appearances in the Wigan Warriors first team, following in the footsteps of their father and grandfather, both called Bernard, who had donned the cherry and white jersey in the 1970s and 1940s respectively. "I am two and a half years younger than James, so we had only ever played together briefly, in the Wigan Academy team," explained Thomas. The two brothers would share the Oldham half-back duties, however, for several games in 2009, partly because the evergreen Neil Roden was out injured for part of the year, but also because it did appear watching them together, that they shared a certain telepathy on the pitch. Both were quality players, of that there was little doubt and real fans' favourites whilst at Oldham. Thomas would unfortunately, however, play a pivotal role in ending Oldham Grand Final dreams once more, five years later, whilst playing for Hunslet Hawks. More of that later.

Bearing in mind that Paul O'Connor, Lucas Onyango, Marcus St Hilaire, Danny Halliwell and Roden were all still at the club, and playing well, the backs were shaping up nicely despite the departures of Gareth Langley, Daryl Cardiss and Nanyn before the season started.

Paul Highton was a youngster at Waterhead ARLFC before turning professional for Halifax Blue Sox and then two years later beginning a long and illustrious association with Salford. He played for the Yorkshire outfit in the first two years of Super League, 1996 and 1997, before moving to the Willows in 1998 and going on to play nearly 200 Super League games for the club. The Roughyeds needed front-row strengthening as Adam Robinson and Said Tamghart left the club in late 2008 and in acquiring the services of the vastly-experienced Highton, the board knew they were replacing like with like. Joining Highton were two more props, less experienced but with youth on their side, former Leeds Rhinos Academy player Jamie I'Anson and Irishman Wayne Kerr. I'Anson had a fine season in Oldham colours in 2009, playing in all but three matches in all competitions but then surprised everyone at the club at the end of the year by temporarily quitting rugby league to take on a new sporting challenge in his life – cage fighting! More of this later.

As for the two Dubliners, Kerr and Stevie Gibbons, it was a real opportunity for them to flourish in rugby league following their spell under Tony Benson in London and their early careers in Ireland. Kerr was a huge man, very physical and fast for a prop and he certainly took some stopping when in full flight. He stayed at Oldham for two years, eventually playing in 51 games and scoring 10 tries. Gibbons's stay was a shorter one, unfortunately, playing only seven times in 2009 before moving on.

The redoubtable Dave Allen was a classy back-row forward who had grown up at Wigan Warriors and joined Oldham after a spell at Widnes Vikings. It is interesting to note that three of the youngsters on the North-West Counties tour to Australia in 2001 that my dad was part of, Allen, James Coyle and Ballard, were all at Oldham together in 2009. As a rugby league supporter it is good to see that talented teenagers who are picked for representative sides in their youth eventually go on to make their mark in the professional game as adults.

So as the 2009 season began, it wasn't only the backs that were looking in fine fettle, the pack was too. As well as the newcomers, Jason Boults, Richard Mervill, Tommy Goulden, Phil Joseph and Rob Roberts were all still at the club. Also young forwards Chris Baines, who had been at the club since 2006 and who went on to enjoy his best season in Oldham colours in 2009, and Luke Menzies, who had joined initially on loan from Hull Kingston Rovers in 2008, both did well.

The Northern Rail Cup was revamped into two pools, with teams playing four matches with the top four in each pool progressing to the quarter-finals. Oldham enjoyed a fine NRC campaign, winning three of the four games to finish second behind Halifax in Pool 1. The Tony Benson era got off to the best possible start with a stunning 22–20 victory away to eventual cup winners Widnes Vikings in mid-February. Andy Ballard showed immediately how important he would become for the side by contributing 18 points, with a try and seven goals, as a Vikings team, including Gavin Dodd and Lee Doran, were humbled in front of their own fans. For Widnes, it was a wake-up call ahead of a long season, but for Oldham it was a terrific tonic and the springboard for qualification from the pool stages. A 54–4 rout of Rochdale Hornets at Boundary Park followed with four players, Ballard, Halliwell, James Coyle and Goulden all scoring two tries before a 32–14 win at Hunslet saw the Roughyeds into the quarter-finals, despite an earlier 34–22 loss to a Sheffield Eagles side including Ged Corcoran and Matty Brooks among their ranks. Paul Reilly crossed for three tries against the Hawks with Jamie I'Anson notching his first two tries for the club against the Eagles. A comfortable 26–8 Challenge Cup third round victory over Sharlston Rovers – again – meant that Oldham could enter the newly-named Championship One season with a great deal of confidence.

Of the first 10 games of the league season seven were won, several in convincing fashion, with lots of points scored. Lee Greenwood and Wayne Kerr both scored twice in a 36–18 home win over Blackpool Panthers, Marcus St Hilaire bagged a brace as Hunslet were beaten for the second time in 2009 and Dave Allen and 'Junior' again each crossed twice, with Ballard scoring three, as Swinton were beaten 44–26. The run also included two large wins against Workington Town and London Skolars in which Ballard twice broke records. Against Town, James Coyle notched three tries while the Coyle brothers and Neil Roden all scored twice as the Oldham half-backs blitzed the Skolars in London.

The team's Challenge Cup story in 2009, however, was a mixed one. The fourth round draw pitted Roughyeds against French opposition for the first time and Lezignan became the second French rugby league team to grace Boundary Park following in the footsteps of Paris St Germain, who had twice travelled to Oldham, in 1996 and 1997, to face Oldham Bears in Super League. In an incredible game of high octane rugby league and fantastic attacking play – although both defences left much to be desired – Oldham won 60–30, an amazing aggregate of 90 points in one match. Lucas Onyango scored three times with St Hilaire and Ballard crossing the whitewash twice. The backs were certainly on fire in the first half of 2009. Unfortunately, the fifth round saw Oldham crash out in desperately disappointing fashion, losing 34–16 to Championship side Gateshead Thunder at the Northern Echo Arena in Darlington, in the first professional rugby league match ever played in County Durham.

This cup exit was followed a month later by another one, Featherstone Rovers knocking Oldham out of the Northern Rail Cup at the quarter-final stage, with a 32–18 win in a tie televised live by Sky. The game was played at Leigh Sports Village as Boundary Park was unavailable at the time thus adding another venue to Oldham's list of grounds they have called 'home' at least once.

Another below-par display came at York in late June. In a match played on a Thursday evening and again in front of Sky cameras, the home side triumphed 20–18 to keep the pressure on runaway leaders Dewsbury Rams in the Championship One table. The Rams had a phenomenal year in 2009, becoming only the second team ever to finish their league campaign with a 100 per cent record, following the achievements of a fine Hull FC side in the old Second Division in 1978–79. Keighley Cougars and the City Knights were following close behind and it was a battle royal for the Roughyeds to stay in touch as the play-offs beckoned. A Paul O'Connor hat-trick was the highlight of a 60–6 win at Workington, but consecutive defeats by Keighley and Dewsbury in July had fans getting restless and beginning to worry that the team was starting to under-achieve.

In July news of more financial worries began to circulate at the club. To make matters worse, Andy Ballard, Danny Halliwell, James Coyle, Rob Roberts and Dave Allen all joined Barrow Raiders, either on loan or permanently, in an audacious swoop by the Cumbrians. It was a mass exodus from Oldham and one that helped to galvanise the Raiders to an extent that they surpassed all expectations, a year after winning promotion from the third tier, by not only reaching the Championship Grand Final, but winning it. With a side including all five former Oldham stars, Barrow smashed Halifax 26–18 in the final at Warrington.

As for Oldham, the five players leaving left a gaping hole in the side and despite Boundary Park wins over Rochdale Hornets and London Skolars, the latter in yet another live Sky televised game, the final three games before the play-offs saw just two points picked up, from a 30–30 draw at Blackpool Panthers. The signs were not overly good as the play-offs commenced. During this period, however, several players put their hands up and performed admirably. Experienced men like Reilly, St Hilaire, Neil Roden and Goulden came to the fore whilst younger players like Thomas Coyle, appearing to thrive at half-back following his brother's exit, Chris Baines and Luke Menzies excelled.

Also, the club conditioner, Martin Roden, cousin of Neil, picked up his playing career again. Martin explains: "I arrived at the club as conditioner soon after Tony Benson had been appointed and enjoyed working with a talented squad of players and putting them through a gruelling pre-season. There were some experienced players and I set out to make pre-season as demanding as any of the lads had ever been through. I had played briefly for Tony at Leigh Centurions in 2006 and jumped at the chance to get my boots on again, which I had fancied doing all along anyway. After several lads moved to Barrow, the opportunity presented itself. Playing with Neil again was a big bonus for me. We had come up through the ranks together, starting at Wigan St Patricks ARLFC as juniors before both signing for Wigan. Eventually Neil moved to Oldham and I signed for Leigh." Martin played in the last ten games of the season in 2009, scoring four tries and became a regular in the team between 2010 and 2012 as well as taking on the role of assistant coach to Benson ultimately.

Two excellent home wins, 31–26 against Swinton Lions and 54–30 against Hunslet Hawks – in the match that Baines equalled Ballard's points in a match record – pushed Oldham into a Grand Final eliminator against the fancied York City Knights at the Huntington Stadium. The emergence of Baines into a forward to be reckoned with at this level was a remarkable one. The former Warrington Wolves Academy player appeared 65 times in Oldham colours between 2006 and 2008, often as a substitute, but it was in 2009 that his chance to take centre stage arrived, particularly after the five players had departed. Not only did it present Baines with the chance to stake a claim for a regular starting spot in the team but he was also given the added responsibility of taking over from Ballard as first-choice goalkicker.

Chris explains: "Goalkicking was something I had done as a junior but never as a professional. I hadn't needed to because there had always been established kickers at the club, men like Mick Nanyn and Andy Ballard. Then all of a sudden, we found ourselves without one mid-season. Paul O'Connor said he would give it a go but he wasn't comfortable doing it. I said that I had kicked in my younger days so I started practicing again."

Baines kicked for the first time in the draw at Blackpool prior to the play-offs and landed a crucial goal late on to earn Roughyeds a share of the spoils. Seven more goals in the last two league games, against York and Hunslet, were followed by five in the win over Swinton in the first sudden-death game. But it was the Hunslet re-match at Boundary Park in the play-offs when it really all came good for him. Not only did he land nine successful goals, but he also raced in for four tries to equal Ballard's record of 34 points. It was a fantastic individual performance and came at the perfect time, helping to push the team to within one win of another Grand Final.

Over the years, the team had treated fans to several outstanding displays away from home in sudden-death play-off rugby. Late-season victories on opponents grounds include Doncaster Dragons in 2000, Leigh Centurions and Rochdale Hornets in 2001, Hull Kingston Rovers and Hornets again in 2002, Featherstone Rovers in 2003 (this was actually the final league match of the season but was effectively sudden-death as explained in Chapter 4) and Barrow Raiders in 2007. The match at York turned into another of these great Roughyeds play-off displays, one which stands out in the memory for years to come. Fans knew it would be tough because the City Knights had finished five points clear of Oldham in the Championship One table and had completed a league double, winning 37–24 at Boundary Park in the penultimate league match after their earlier win at home in front of the Sky cameras.

It was made even tougher when Marcus St Hilaire, a huge calming influence on the side, was a late withdrawal through injury leaving a huge void at left centre. Enter young Ben Heaton, 19 years old, a product of the club's youth system, and with just one substitute appearance in the first team to his name. 'Junior's boots were huge ones to fill, but did Heaton look nervous? Not in the slightest. After just five minutes, Big Ben scored the first try of the match, then soon after made a searing break out of defence which led directly to another. For one so young and with so little experience, it was a stunning start to the match. With veteran full-back Paul Reilly turning back the clock with a brilliant two-try display, the first before half-time and the second just after, and Chris Baines and Tommy Goulden also crossing, the Roughyeds had raced into an unassailable 30–4 lead after 42 minutes.

"I smashed my nose at York that day," remembers Reilly. "I must have looked a sight with a huge plaster over my face. So although I tend not to remember too many individual games in my career, I certainly remember that one." Two tries from Kiwi half-back, Matt Ashe, a late-season addition to the squad, and another one by Lucas Onyango, saw the Roughyeds home 44–14 in a brilliant team display. So for the third consecutive year, and for the first time under Tony Benson, fans had a Grand Final to look forward to. The team had bounced back extremely well from the mid-season upheaval and fully deserved their place in the final against Keighley Cougars. Surely it would be third time lucky?

The Grand Final, played on 4 October 2009, was a particularly poignant occasion for Chris Hamilton. Three months earlier he had been awarded the prestigious title of President of the Rugby Football League. In July, the *Oldham Chronicle* reported Chris's appointment as follows: "Loyalty, dedication, long service and a steely determination to keep professional rugby league alive in Oldham were rewarded when Christopher Hamilton was installed as President of the Rugby Football League. A founder member of Oldham Rugby League Club (1997) Ltd, the club's Chief Executive and former Chairman is the first official of the club ever to wear the RFL's presidential chain of office. 'The appointment is a great honour for me, but also for the Oldham club,' said 46-year-old Mr Hamilton. 'Plenty of illustrious people have had the role before me and I hope I can follow their example while also offering my own persona as I represent the RFL at various functions throughout my year of office. When I helped to establish the new Oldham club back in 1997 I never thought it would lead to anything like this. Motivation has only ever been a desire to keep professional rugby league alive in Oldham, and that is still the case. Along the way, there have been lots of ups and downs and plenty of blood, sweat and tears, but we are still in there battling despite the many and mountainous obstacles to progress, and that is very gratifying. There have been lots of changes in the game, and we now have a fabulous product. On and off the field, rugby league has come on in leaps and bounds. Sadly, not enough people watch the sport and that is an issue clubs need to address, particularly those lower down than Super League.'

He is Oldham's reigning Man of the Year, not only for his work with the Roughyeds, but also for his public-spirited achievements in raising thousands of pounds for breast-cancer and breast-care charities by a series of sponsored physical and mental challenges. Mr Hamilton's first official duty as RFL President will be at the Northern Rail Nines and the

Northern Rail Cup final at Blackpool this weekend. Next week, with his partner Gillian, he will represent the RFL at a Buckingham Palace garden party – his second visit to the Palace on RFL duties in eight years. Later in the year he will be on official duty at the Carnegie Challenge Cup final at Wembley and also at the Four Nations tournament. Only two Oldham officials, going back to 1897, have ever held similar positions and they were both honoured as chairmen of the Rugby League Council - G.F. Hutchins from 1938 to 1940 and Frank Ridgeway in the 1958–59 season."

So as Chris took his seat at the Halliwell Jones Stadium for the Oldham versus Keighley Cougars Grand Final, fervently hoping in his heart that the Roughyeds would finally put the Grand Final hoodoo to bed, he also knew that he would be tasked with presenting the cup to the winning captain at the end of the game. "I knew how disappointed I get when we lose any match, let alone a Grand Final," Chris told me recently. "So it certainly crossed my mind beforehand that I would have to do my utmost to disguise my feelings of despair if Keighley did happen to win."

The match itself was a thriller for the neutral supporter, but for the hundreds of Oldham fans it was yet another major disappointment. Despite holding a narrow 6–4 lead at half-time – they were twice denied by video referee decisions in the first half – it all went wrong after the break when Keighley, with half-backs Danny Jones and Jon Presley bossing the show, built up a commanding 28–12 lead. Credit Roughyeds with a stirring late comeback which resulted in tries to Marcus St Hilaire, Luke Menzies, his second of the match, and Wayne Kerr but it was too little too late sadly, and the Cougars held on by the skin of their teeth to win 28–26. Chris Baines had been tremendous in the closing stages of the season and had played well in the Grand Final too, making a superb break that led directly to Kerr charging 40 metres to score Oldham's final try two minutes from time. However, Baines missed a crucial goalkick at the height of Oldham's great comeback and the miss ultimately denied the team the opportunity to take the match into extra time.

"Thanks for reminding me about that!" said Chris recently with a grin, when it was mentioned to him. "It was one of those kicks that I was expected to kick as well, half way between the posts and the touch-line. They often become the hard ones though, because everyone expects you to kick it."

Martin Roden had made the hooker's job his own towards the end of the year and recalls the moments immediately after the hooter had sounded to confirm the Cougars victory. "I collapsed in tears on the pitch. I was wounded beyond belief. Chris Hamilton came over to try to console me, but it was so tough to take."

Chris Baines had his best season in 2009. (Photo courtesy Chris Baines).

Luke Menzies, playing in his final match for the club, had a stormer off the bench, perhaps his best match in Oldham colours, capped by his two tries. "I had played in the Grand Final against Doncaster in 2008 as well, as had several other lads, so to lose two in a row was heart-wrenching. The loss to Keighley was particularly agonising because we got so close. It was my last match before moving on. I met some very good people at Oldham and have some great memories." Menzies played for Dewsbury, Batley, Hunslet, Swinton and Salford after leaving the club and was one of the first batch of players signed up by the new Toronto Wolfpack team, based in Canada, ahead of the 2017 season.

Chris Baines also left the club after the Grand Final, ironically signing for Keighley. Here he pays tribute to the late Danny Jones, who died of a cardiac arrest while representing his beloved Cougars in a match away to London Skolars in 2015. Jones had been instrumental in helping his team across the line at Warrington with two tries and a man-of-the-match performance and Chris became a team-mate of his following his move. "Danny was the type of player that could make something happen from nothing. His rugby brain was brilliant and I was one of the lucky ones to play on the same team as him, as well as against him. Away from the pitch he was the life and soul of the party. He could make a joke out of any situation. He was the entertainer and the person that everyone wanted to be around. A really great guy."

Baines continued: "I would like to add that I loved my time at Oldham. 2009 was my stand out season and my only regret is that we failed to clinch promotion. It's a great club with a brilliant and loyal set of fans. I believe they deserve to be a Championship club and hopefully in time they will establish themselves at that level. Chris Hamilton deserves that, because he has been there from the start."

In the end of season European Cup competition, Marcus St Hilaire and Wayne Kerr both represented Ireland. 'Junior' played at right-centre against Wales and Lebanon, scoring a try against the Welsh, and Kerr played three times, against Serbia, Wales and Lebanon. The Irish squad also included two players, James Coyle and Stevie Gibbons, who had started the season with the club.

9. Whitebank Stadium – a home at last

By the end of 2009, Oldham RLFC (1997) Ltd had completed 12 full seasons as a professional rugby league club. At no time during those years had they played home games at a ground that they could justifiably call 'home'. Boundary Park is in Oldham, of course, but it is home to Oldham Athletic, not Oldham Rugby League Club. Spotland Stadium is in Rochdale, Hurst Cross in Ashton, Bower Fold in Stalybridge, Bloomfield Road in Blackpool, Victory Park in Chorley, Sedgley Park in Whitefield and Leigh Sports Village in Leigh. How amazing it would be if the club could be based in Oldham, at a venue that could be called 'home' was the feeling shared by everyone with the club at heart. In 2010, this dream of many finally came true.

As 2009 drew to a close, the club heard that Boundary Park would no longer be available to them in the foreseeable future. It was a huge blow. As the ground had been the only one in Oldham that the club had ever played at, what did the future hold if playing there was no longer an option? Something needed to be done, and quickly, otherwise the very existence of the club may well have been under threat.

Admittedly, Sedgley Park was available in the short term but everyone understood that being forced to play there over a period of time could well have been the death knell for the club. So, despite the team's terrific start to the season – seven straight wins from the beginning of the Championship One programme – the best piece of news to come out of the club in the first half of 2010 came when Chris Hamilton announced that it would be moving to the Whitebank Stadium in the Limehurst Village area of town in early May. Formerly home to amateur football club Oldham Town FC, who had gone out of business and in 2009 re-launched as Oldham Borough FC, the ground would become the rugby club's permanent home, with the opening match to be played against York City Knights on 9 May. It was wonderful news. At last, it seemed, the club's nomadic existence was over.

Although the Northern Rail Cup campaign ended with just one win – a Sedgley Park victory over Rochdale Hornets – and three losses, a club record 80–6 win over the South Wales amateur team, Blackwood Bulldogs, in the third round of the Challenge Cup, and then that splendid run of seven straight league wins, had fans feeling upbeat once more. New signings for 2010 included centre Mick Fogerty, a prolific try-scorer during spells at Keighley Cougars and Rochdale Hornets, winger John Gillam, formerly of Blackpool Panthers and Rochdale Hornets, utility back Mark Brocklehurst from Rochdale Hornets, hooker Danny Whitmore from Salford City Reds, big prop Dave Ellison from London Skolars, young second-row forward Joe Chandler from Leeds Rhinos and loose-forward Valu Bentley, a New Zealander who had been playing in France.

Of these, Fogerty, Gillam, Brocklehurst and Whitmore were all Oldham born, as was young forward Chris Clarke, who graduated from the club's academy team to enjoy a fine first season in the first team. It has always been good, and always will be, to see local born players wearing Roughyeds colours and performing well. Brocklehurst said: "I watched the old club at Watersheddings and then the new club at Boundary Park and it was always an ambition of mine to play for my hometown team. It was with great pride and pleasure when I finally achieved that." Whitmore agrees: "I thoroughly enjoyed my time at Oldham. I came from Salford and 2010 was my first year playing regular first-team football. Oldham is a great club with great fans who immediately made me feel welcome. The team was the closest knit group I've ever been involved with. All the boys got on famously, often socialising together. There was a great vibe amongst us, we all bonded together well, so important in a tough team sport."

Valu Bentley came from a successful rugby league playing family. Although born to a New Zealand Maori mother and Samoan father, he and his siblings, Kane, Andrew, Hamish and Jayne-Marie were brought up in France. Their dad was a rugby league player and Valu played alongside him and an uncle as a fifteen-years-old lad for a club called La Reole. Valu recalls: "La Reole was my hometown and I made my debut for them, at 15, against Carcassonne. All my family and friends were there but I remember it so fondly because I was playing alongside my dad. I will never forget that game, it will stay with me forever.

A couple of years later I signed for the French champions, Villeneuve-sur-Lot. We won both the French league championship and the Lord Derby Cup four times in five years between 1999 and 2003. Later I played alongside Kane and Andrew at Marseille. They were both fine players and represented the French national team on numerous occasions, including at the 2013 World Cup. Both are part of the Toulouse Olympique squad in the English Championship in 2017. Jayne-Marie played women's rugby league and she captained the French national side, leading her team to a World Cup, also in 2013. My youngest brother, Hamish, chose to play rugby union. It was an exciting move for me when I joined Oldham in 2010 and I would like to thank Tony Benson for giving me the opportunity to play for the Roughyeds. I stayed for three years and made some very good friends and memories. I learnt a lot from Tony as a coach and also as a man. Over the years we became very good friends and remain so to this day. Oldham Rugby League Club will always have a special place in my heart and I maintain an interest in their progress to this day."

Others who made their bow in 2009 became regulars in 2010 such as Matt Ashe and Ben Heaton. As mentioned previously, Jamie I'Anson had a big year in 2009, but quit rugby league to take up cage fighting. Nevertheless Oldham refused to accept he could not be tempted back. The *Guardian* ran a story about Jamie early in 2010. It read: "Oldham are to unleash cage fighter Jamie I'Anson on their Championship One rivals. The 22 year old prop, formerly of Leeds Rhinos, quit rugby league at the end of last season to take up the no-holds-barred mix of boxing, wrestling and martial arts, but has now signed a new short-term deal with the Roughyeds. I'Anson says he is meaner and leaner after training for his new sport and losing 21 pounds in weight. 'I am pleased to be back' said I'Anson. 'Tony Benson has never been off the phone so I have agreed a deal which will allow me to divide my week between rugby and training for cage fighting. I developed an interest in it when I was in Thailand in 2007 and I have fancied having a serious go at it ever since.' ... Chris Hamilton said: 'We wore Jamie down to sign again because we know he will give us everything he has got. We are delighted to have him back."

The new-look squad soon settled down and looked good very quickly. Lucas Onyango raced in for a splendid hat-trick against Swinton Lions in the opening league match, won 38–20 by Oldham, and this was followed by hat-tricks to Chandler and Brocklehurst as an outclassed Blackwood were thrashed in the Challenge Cup. A fine 29–16 win away to eventual champions Hunslet Hawks followed with scrum-half Matt Ashe scoring two tries and kicking four goals in a man-of-the-match performance. This win followed a defeat on the same ground, the South Leeds Stadium, in the Northern Rail Cup only four weeks earlier so augured particularly well for the season ahead.

At Easter, the team produced two more fine displays, beating Rochdale Hornets 22–16 at Spotland on Good Friday and then seeing off Workington Town 16–14 at Sedgley Park on Easter Monday. Ashe was really fulfilling the promise he had shown towards the end of 2009, having taken over the goal-kicking responsibilities from Chris Baines, and kicked another three goals, as well as scoring a crucial try, at Rochdale. Mick Fogerty was outstanding against Town, scoring two crucial tries in a very tight game.

John Gillam, a big powerful threat on the left wing, scored four tries in a 64–10 romp over Gateshead Thunder and on the May Day Bank Holiday Monday, Doncaster were well beaten 46–26 at the Keepmoat Stadium to ensure the team remained undefeated in the league prior to the long-awaited first outing at Whitebank Stadium.

On Friday 7 May, before the York match, the *Oldham Chronicle* commented: "Oldham enter an exciting new era when they take to their new Whitebank Stadium home on Sunday.

Whitebank Stadium, new home to the Roughyeds from May 2010

Left: Oldham born Danny Whitmore at dummy-half

Below: Ben Heaton races clear to score against Doncaster at the Keepmoat Stadium in 2010

(All photos David Murgatroyd).

The eloquent Valu Bentley and Lucas Onyango
at a club awards evening.

Paul O'Connor with the individual honours he achieved in 2010.
(Both photos David Murgatroyd).

As the visit of York City Knights approaches, club chairman Chris Hamilton is delighted that the hard work put into bringing Whitebank up to scratch has paid off. 'We are urging people to come out and support us for this historic game, which we will be playing on our own ground in the borough of Oldham,' said Hamilton, referring to the nomadic journey the club has undertaken since day one. 'I never thought I would be saying that. Five of our next six matches are at home and they give us the opportunity to cement the great work the team and coaching staff have put in to get us seven league wins out of seven. I would like to thank all the volunteers, club staff and companies who have been prepared to get their hands dirty and roll up their sleeves in order to help us get the match on. This is the starting point and work will be ongoing at the ground. But just to get to this point is fantastic and we will use it as a launch pad to take the club forward.'"

The match itself, against the City Knights, was the first of a quartet of enthralling clashes with the men from the Minster City in 2010.

Oldham versus York City Knights, Match 1, 9 May 2010.
York arrived at Whitebank having won four of their eight league matches to date, but from the off were clearly determined to spoil the Roughyeds' big day. Full-back Danny Ratcliffe had the honour of scoring the first try at Oldham's new home in only the fourth minute with prop Wayne Kerr scoring the Roughyeds first try at the new ground just three minutes later. The first half was tremendously exciting, real end-to-end rugby with winger Dennis Tuffour, second-row Steve Lewis and centre Lee Waterman scoring further tries for the visitors with wingers John Gillam and Lucas Onyango replying for Oldham.

Trailing 24–16 at half-time, Tony Benson needed to rally his troops during the break. Converted tries from Paul O'Connor and Mick Fogerty edged Oldham ahead but York refused to lie down and future Hull FC and Warrington Wolves winger Tom Lineham scored just after the hour to set up a frantic final quarter. The harsh dismissal of Kerr for a high tackle on Tuffour helped the Roughyeds' cause not one bit but, despite this, a second score from the impeccable O'Connor appeared to win the match for the home side. Unfortunately, the dangerous Tuffour broke Oldham hearts with a stunning late winner, racing the length of the field and leaving defenders in his wake to score by the posts. It was a cruel end to the match for 12-man Oldham. However, the two teams would meet three more times before the year was out.

The *Oldham Chronicle* reported on the match and the occasion: "The going was too tough for the Roughyeds as Tony Benson's men fell to a first defeat of their Championship One season. On an emotional day for all connected with the club, the Whitebank Stadium was spruced up superbly by an army of volunteers and 1,110 fans watched a tense

104

clash. But though Oldham managed to hang in for almost the full 80 minutes despite never quite hitting their straps – the loss of main playmaker Neil Roden before the game through injury was a major one – the final word went to York winger Dennis Tuffour. With a minute to go, the Knights man streaked home under the posts to settle the contest after both sides had tried and failed to break the deadlock with drop goals. The winning try came against 12 men, Oldham losing Wayne Kerr seven minutes after the restart in what appeared to be a harsh decision by referee Peter Brooke. A man down, Oldham battled on and, on another day, may well have sneaked home. It wasn't to be, but the Whitebank Stadium will no doubt be the scene of plenty of triumphs in the future."

And more from the *Oldham Chronicle* the following evening, Tuesday 11 May: "Chris Hamilton has put out an upbeat message to fans in the aftermath of the historic day at the Whitebank Stadium where the rugby league team played on its own ground for the first time in 13 years. 'I thought it went pretty well,' he said. 'This was the first time we have organised the full match-day process. We will debrief and there will be areas we can improve on. We will certainly have the opportunity because we have a lot of matches at Whitebank coming up, starting with the visit of London Skolars this Sunday. I thank everyone who turned up for the York game; volunteers, without whose help the game would not have taken place; and club staff for extra work in unpaid hours. A lot of people showed their appreciation of everything that has been done at the ground, and we are grateful to them for that.'

While Oldham lost 34–28 on the day, Hamilton feels that the result's significance paled when placed in the context of the achievement of getting Whitebank up and running — not to mention the terrific start to the season which sees the team top of the table after eight matches. 'The defeat was disappointing,' he admitted. 'We would have loved to claim another victory, but the occasion was all about much more than a game. It was a massive milestone in the club's history. Nobody was more gutted than the players but this was the first of five out of six games at home and I hope everyone will be back next week. If, last November, somebody had told us we would win seven of our first eight league games, be top of Championship One, and be playing on our own ground in Oldham we would have referred them to hospital for treatment. So we must not be greedy or too disappointed because we were beaten by York. The RFL were represented at the game by Emma Rosewarne, who was taking stock of what went on and making notes. No doubt there will be some things we need to look at, but that's only to be expected.'"

Following the last-gasp defeat by York, the Roughyeds followed up with a 46–12 victory over London Skolars at Whitebank the following

Sunday. The *Oldham Chronicle* provided a Whitebank update in the week leading up to a crucial top-of-the-table clash with Hunslet Hawks a week later: "As the Roughyeds prepare for the visit of Hunslet Hawks on Sunday in a game of huge significance at the top end of Championship One, work is carrying on apace at the club's new home ... Chris Hamilton is urging the Oldham public for continued help in improving the venue. 'It was never going to be 100-per-cent perfect, which is why we stressed the message that we would like people to bear with us and work with us - it is a new experience for us, too,' said Hamilton, following on from the club's first two home matches against York City Knights and London Skolars at the new ground. 'We are working very hard and taking on board a lot of feedback and have already improved one or two areas as a result of that. Those improvements are not necessarily visible to the general public. Last week, we did a lot of work in the home dressing room, as we also did for the officials. We also put a safety board up in the stand, as a temporary measure. Some of the work we are doing because it has to be done in order to tick boxes with the Rugby Football League. And some of the work is on a 'wish-list', if you like, in order to improve the match-day experience for spectators. ... The players have passed comment on the transformation that has taken place here in the space of just a few weeks,' Hamilton said. 'It is fantastic for them all that we have now got somewhere we can call home. It means so much to everyone, from players to the kit-man, coaches and staff.'"

The Hawks were a powerful side in 2010 and deservedly won automatic promotion at the end of the season. They were on fire at Whitebank, giving Oldham a lesson in clinical finishing, and scored 11 tries, including one by future Roughyed Danny Grimshaw, in a 60–6 win. It was a rude awakening for Tony Benson's side after their encouraging start to the year. However, it is a measure of a team how they respond to such a setback and Benson's boys did so in style, embarking on another winning run of six league games.

At the heart of the team's fine form in this period was young Cumbrian half-back, Gregg McNally, who had been signed on loan from Huddersfield Giants. McNally was a class act at scrum-half and with the experienced Neil Roden still going strong alongside him at half-back, the team were led around the pitch superbly with the rest of the side responding well to McNally's and Roden's lead. In many other years, the fine form may well have earned them automatic promotion but Hunslet's excellent season pushed Roughyeds into second place in the Championship One table, meaning another dose of excruciating play-off tension awaited the fans. It also meant that the teams immediately below Oldham in the table, particularly York City Knights and Blackpool

106

Panthers, knew they were in with a realistic chance of promotion despite finishing several points behind the Roughyeds.

Blackpool Panthers, under the leadership of former Oldham Bears scrum-half Martin Crompton, had a fine year after signing several good experienced players including former Roughyeds Paul Anderson, David Best, Danny Halliwell, Damian Munro, Mark Roberts and Simon Svabic. They beat a hapless Gateshead Thunder 132–0 in May in one of the most incredible points-scoring sprees of all time, with 14 different players scoring tries. Oldham, however, were in no mood to let the Panthers dominate them and produced two of their best performances of the year, home and away, against Crompton's outfit. A 40–26 win at Whitebank was followed by a thrilling 24–22 win away from home, with a fantastic three-try salvo from Paul O'Connor stunning the fancied Panthers. This win confirmed to fans that Oldham were capable of going all the way in 2010. Unfortunately, one of the best displays of the year was followed by the worst, a week later, when, against all the odds South Wales Scorpions came to Whitebank and surprised even themselves probably by winning 42–24 and ending any lingering hopes Oldham had of going up automatically. It proved to be a minor blip for Oldham, however, and the final three league games ended in victory, the first of which was the re-match with York at the Huntington Stadium.

Kiwi coach Tony Benson, in charge between 2009 and 2012.
(Photo David Murgatroyd).

107

York City Knights versus Oldham, Match 2, 8 August 2010.
Valu Bentley describes what turned into quite a day for the Oldham players. "We were running late for the kick-off because there had been an accident on the motorway which held us up. It was clear that we were going to struggle to arrive at the ground on time. We had to get strapped up and changed on the team coach but none of us were fazed by the sudden change of plan. We finally arrived 20 minutes before kick-off, dropped our bags in the changing rooms and ran out for the quickest and least structured warm-up I've ever been involved in. We then went out and beat York on their own territory! I recall after the match sitting in the changing rooms, looking at the boys and thinking, wow, did all that really just happen!" Well, Valu, it really did happen! Despite two tries by winger Wayne Reittie, a man who would prove to be a thorn in Oldham sides for several years, the superb Roughyeds replied with tries through John Gillam with two, Neil Roden, Paul O'Connor and Lucas Onyango with Matt Ashe kicking six goals from six attempts. Revenge was certainly sweet for the visitors that day.

Following the York win, Rochdale Hornets and London Skolars were beaten in the final two league games, with a rare Jason Boults try scoring bonanza – three in one game – against Hornets really setting the fans talking. The Skolars match was played in the capital city on the Friday evening before the Challenge Cup Final between Leeds Rhinos and Warrington Wolves at Wembley Stadium the following day and drew an excellent crowd of 1,375, over twice the Skolars' average league attendance for the year. The win also provided Oldham with a fantastic 100 percent winning record in league matches played away from home in 2010. For the record, the team's results on opponents' grounds were as follows:
Swinton Lions won 38–20
Hunslet Hawks won 29–16
Rochdale Hornets won 22–16
South Wales Scorpions won 22–16
Doncaster won 46–26
Workington Town won 28–16
Gateshead Thunder won 68–10
Blackpool Panthers won 24–22
York City Knights won 33–18
London Skolars won 48–18

So as the play-offs approached, Oldham were in confident mood having finished a whopping thirteen points ahead of York, their nearest challengers.

Oldham versus York City Knights, Match 3, 12 September 2010.

The attendance at the opening match at Whitebank in May was 1,110 and most fans felt confident that would be beaten for York's second visit to the ground in four months. With memories of their smash and grab raid on their last visit still fresh in their minds, the visitors arrived in confident mood. Things hadn't gone perfectly for them since the game in May, however, and they arrived this time with a new coach in the shape of Australian Dave Woods, the man who had masterminded Castleford Tigers' promotion in 2005 and Gateshead Thunder's in 2008. He was a canny and crafty coach who rarely settled for second best. Former Huddersfield Giants stand-off star Chris Thorman had been a key performer in the Knights side all year, but hadn't played at Whitebank in May. He was an experienced, influential player and Oldham knew they would need to stop him if they were to progress to the Grand Final. The first half was nip and tuck, York scored three tries to Oldham's two, by Joe Chandler and Danny Whitmore, and were leading 18–16 at the break. With use of the Whitebank slope to come in the second half, however, Oldham were not worried. Further tries by Kerr, Chandler, Bentley and Clarke finally sunk the gallant visitors, despite two late tries by Waterman and Thorman, which meant Oldham fans were biting their fingernails right to the finish. A final score of 41–32 was a huge one for the Roughyeds and saw them into yet another Grand Final.

Bentley remembers his crucial try in the 71st minute with great affection: "Gregg McNally chipped the ball over the defensive line, regathered and drew the full-back. I was pushing up on his outside and Gregg sent me clear. I ran faster than I had ever run in my life to make the 15 metres to the line and score. I threw myself into the fans and the happiness and emotions were out of this world. The rest of the boys joined me in celebrating with the fans. As I walked back up the hill before the restart, the fans were shouting 'Oldham, Oldham' and applauding loudly. Then I saw my young son in the crowd. He gave me a big thumbs up and that was the icing on the cake. I loved seeing my number one fans, my two sons Valu Tane and Junior while I was playing. Knowing they were watching always made me play that bit harder."

In front of a ground record crowd of 1,275, the first play-off hurdle had been overcome. York got a second chance, in the final eliminator, and on this showing, Blackpool Panthers, their opponents, would have to play very well to beat them. York were a good side and with Woods at the helm and Thorman orchestrating them on the pitch, they were definitely not out of it yet.

So the first season at Whitebank Stadium was over, the York play-off game being the last one at the stadium in 2010. Neil Roden acknowledged that the ground did tend to assist Oldham at times: "As a team we soon got used to playing at Whitebank and it suited us. Opposition teams never seemed too keen on the place and we used that to our advantage. We tried our utmost to turn it into a fortress, a place where we would feel comfortable and win a lot more games than we lost. We did that, not just in 2010, but in subsequent years also."

Lucas Onyango thoroughly enjoyed the Whitebank experience: "It was our new home," he said. "It was our job to make it home from home and we soon did that. It was certainly different to playing at Boundary Park, however. As a winger, what I enjoyed was playing down the slope. It was similar in that respect to Mount Pleasant at Batley. It was particularly good playing down the slope in the second half of matches when the big forwards were beginning to tire. It created a bit of room and I benefitted a few times from that and was able to score a few tries." Valu Bentley recalled: "I loved playing at Whitebank. It was a fantastic feeling being so close to the fans and listening to their singing and chanting. We could hear almost every word that was being said!"

As was expected, York beat Blackpool 38–18 to set up a fourth meeting with Oldham in 2010 in the Grand Final, meaning Roughyeds would meet a fourth different club from East of the Pennines in consecutive years following on from Featherstone Rovers in 2007, Doncaster in 2008 and Keighley Cougars in 2009.

Oldham versus York City Knights, Match 4, 26 September 2010.

As Oldham had finished the Championship One season well ahead of York, surely anything but a victory for Benson's boys would have been a travesty of justice. Oldham had beaten them twice, away from home in the league and at Whitebank in the play-offs and would have won the home league encounter too if it hadn't been for Dennis Tuffour's shock late try. True, the City Knights were a different animal under Dave Woods but where, oh where, did it all go so horribly wrong for Oldham in the game that mattered most? League form is no indicator of what might happen in a Grand Final and there have been several examples over the years of teams beating higher-placed opponents in sudden-death matches. The defeat that day at the Halliwell Jones Stadium though was a major setback. Neil Roden reflected on an underwhelming display from the Roughyeds: "Of all the Grand Final defeats we suffered, this one was the biggest disappointment of all. Apart from Hunslet Hawks, who were promoted automatically, we had been the best team all year but just didn't perform on the day." In a totally abject display, Oldham only crossed the York line once, Mick Fogerty replying to an early try from Wayne Reittie. Sadly that was as good as it got with York scoring further tries by James Haynes, Chris Thorman and Steve Lewis to win convincingly. Thorman was a stand-out man-of-the-match, dictating proceedings as we always feared he might, and dropping a late goal to cap the win for his team. It was a dejected and disillusioned set of Oldham fans that made their way home that evening and a sad end to what had been a fine year prior to the Grand Final.

The defeat also proved to be the last appearance in the excellent Oldham career of full-back Paul O'Connor. Paul had been a magnificent last line of defence for the team since first arriving at the club from Widnes in 2006. Such was his impact on the team he won a clean sweep of trophies in the end-of-season awards night in 2010, winning the player-of-the-year prize, chosen by coach Tony Benson, the players' player of the year award and also the supporters player of the year. The *Oldham Chronicle* quoted Paul as follows: "It was very humbling to receive three trophies and especially so to be voted player of the year by supporters and by my team-mates. Fans pay money to come and watch us play and their support is valued and appreciated by the players. I was embarrassed to listen to some of the nice things they said about me. Valu Bentley explained to everyone why my peers in the dressing room voted for me and what he said put a lump in my throat. But this is a team game and it's all about doing it for your mates."

2010 was a sad year for the sport of rugby league as a whole. On 2 June, one of the worst criminal acts involving firearms in British history occurred in Cumbria when a crazed lone gunman shot dead 12 people and injured several more, before killing himself. One of the people murdered was former Whitehaven and Workington Town player Garry Purdham, brother of Rob Purdham of Harlequins RLFC who had been capped five times by England. Garry still played our great game, turning out regularly for Egremont Rangers, a top Cumbrian amateur team. Garry's funeral took place on 10 June and was attended in an official capacity by Chris Hamilton, the President of the RFL at the time. Shaking his head Chris said: "It was such a shocking event. Garry was very well known locally, not just as a rugby league player but as a member of the local community. He was shot dead while cutting hedges down on the side of a road. When I look back on my year in office, there is no doubt that this was the saddest and most emotional event that I attended."

Four months later, on 3 October, a Garry Purdham Memorial Game was held at Whitehaven's Recreation Ground between Cumbria and England. The match, fittingly, finished in an 18–18 draw with Oldham's on-loan half-back Gregg McNally appearing as a substitute for Cumbria and kicking two goals.

In the end of season European Cup competition, Oldham's list of international representatives grew longer, and this time not just on the playing front. Head coach Tony Benson was proud to be named as assistant to Ireland coach Andy Kelly for the tournament. In addition, four players, McNally, John Gillam, Matt Ashe and Wayne Kerr were all part of the Ireland squad and played in all three of their games. Gillam scored two tries and McNally a try and a goal against France in Avignon, McNally scored two tries and five goals against Wales in Neath and Gillam scored two tries and McNally three goals against Scotland in Dublin. Although the Irish lost all three games, it was a highly successful tournament for the Oldham quartet.

10. A tough division to escape from

So it was back to square one for the club in their bid to get out of Championship One. The defeat by York City Knights in the Grand Final was a tough one to take, but Tony Benson knew the only way to go was to attempt to improve the squad, continue to work hard and do all in his power to ensure 2011 was a successful season. The *Oldham Chronicle* spoke to Tony while he was in Avignon with the Ireland side who were preparing for their European Cup clash with France in the autumn of 2010. "We have some unfinished business in 2011," said the Oldham boss. "We were all distraught on finals day, but that is behind us now and we have to move on. Once I knew for certain the club wanted to keep me I was never going anywhere else. I love the place. I just enjoy being there. It is a great club to work for. I have said it before and I will say it again; it was a privilege to be involved with Roughyeds and all that was going on at the club this year, highlighted by our move into the Whitebank Stadium. I am already looking forward to getting back into the old routine and getting stuck into the Oldham job again in about a month's time."

There were many reasons to be cheerful when looking back on 2010 as a whole, not least that Whitebank Stadium was now a home base for the club in Oldham, how well the team had settled down there, and appeared to enjoy playing there. As fans looked ahead to 2011, it was reassuring for them to know that for the first time, a full season of home games would be played at Whitebank, and that, surely, would prove to be a huge advantage for the team. In 2010, of course, the first third of the season saw the team still playing at Sedgley Park with the first match at Whitebank not until 9 May. This time, as the squad undertook pre-season training, they could look forward to a full year at their new home.

As ever the squad needed a revamp and Benson turned to a man who had played 119 Super League games for Warrington Wolves, as well as seven on loan at Harlequins RLFC, between 2000 and 2006 to lead his new-look pack. Paul Noone was an influential, strong-running, tough-tackling second-row forward, who also played for Widnes Vikings and Barrow Raiders, and would prove invaluable to a young side in 2011. He went on to make 27 appearances out of a maximum 27, was consistently good and helped to bring the best out of less experienced colleagues. Three other players with experience in Super League joined the club as well: former Wigan Warriors forward Andy Isherwood, former Salford City Reds hooker John Clough and scrum-half Carl Forber were the men Benson put his faith in to add some quality to the team.

113

Isherwood, in fact, was returning to Oldham because he played in three pre-season games for the club in 2005 before leaving the sport altogether for two years. "I didn't do myself justice last time. I am keen to return and make amends," he said at the time. Having played for Leigh Centurions, Widnes Vikings, Rochdale Hornets and Swinton Lions as well as Wigan, the club knew they were signing a much-travelled forward who would provide strength, power, experience and mental toughness to the pack.

Clough, the elder brother of future St Helens and Huddersfield Giants Super League forward Paul Clough, made 17 appearances in the top division for Salford between 2004 and 2006 and became an important pivotal figure in the Roughyeds pack in 2011. Forber had made his bow in first team rugby league with St Helens in 2004 and Leigh Centurions in 2005 before spending several years with Workington Town. He returned to Derwent Park later in his career, becoming a firm favourite there. Carl was yet another player to have been part of the 2001 North-West Counties tour to Australia previously referred to.

Centre Mark McCully, formerly of Rochdale Hornets, Workington Town and Blackpool Panthers, and prop Luke Stenchion from Dewsbury Rams also arrived at Whitebank and brought with them plenty of Championship experience. Young St Helens prop-forward Liam Gilchrist and five Oldham-born players with big points to prove, winger Shaun Robinson, utility players Matthew Fogarty and Ben Wood, centre Jack Bradbury and scrum-half Mick Diveney, also signed. So the nucleus of a good squad was assembled with a healthy mix of youth and experience.

Since the new club was formed in late 1997, it had never been able to stage the traditional Law Cup pre-season clash with old rivals Rochdale Hornets at its own ground. Spotland had been the venue for the majority of the games played with the odd one at Boundary Park. That all changed on the first weekend of 2011 when Whitebank staged a Law Cup game for the first time. On a dank, grey early January day, Oldham defied the conditions, as well as the opposition, to win comfortably and enable skipper Neil Roden to lift the trophy in front of his own fans.

The Northern Rail Cup began well with a 28–22 victory over Hunslet Hawks at Whitebank with centre Jack Bradbury, formerly a youngster at St Helens, scoring two tries and scrum-half Mick Diveney weighing in with a try and four goals. The new boys had made a good start. Unfortunately, that was as good as it got in the NRC, with defeats by Halifax and Swinton Lions away from home and a narrow 14–4 loss to Whitehaven at Whitebank ensuring the Roughyeds made an early exit from the competition. Lucas Onyango scored two tries in defeat at The

Shay. "Even though we lost I remember my two tries well that day. I don't usually recall individual tries or matches too well, Neil Roden is the man for that. But on this occasion I do because one was from long-range which I particularly enjoyed. I scored a few like that in my first couple of years at Oldham, but not quite so many in 2011. It felt good."

A 28–16 Challenge Cup victory against Yorkshire amateurs, Hunslet Warriors, followed the Whitehaven defeat. This was a match in which Roughyeds never hit top gear, but enormous credit goes to Warriors for their brave display. They were never out of contention until the final hooter and can be proud of their effort. However, the win extended Oldham's winning run against amateur opposition, stretching back to their first ever competitive match against Heworth in January 1998, a run that at the time of writing remains intact to this day.

The Championship One season also began well with a thumping 66–12 win over Gateshead Thunder at Whitebank, with Mark Brocklehurst scoring four tries, Andy Isherwood three and Valu Bentley and Matthew Fogarty two each. Brocklehurst, in his second year at the club, started the season with a bang. His four tries against Thunder took him to eight in just six games: "One of my fondest memories of playing for Oldham was crossing the whitewash several times in 2011. It was a great feeling playing and scoring for my hometown team," said Mark. In fact, Brocklehurst finished 2011 as the club's leading try scorer with 17 in all competitions, four ahead of his nearest challenger, Ben Heaton.

The next three league games were lost to quell some of the early season optimism amongst fans. Two fine Whitebank wins, 52–26 against London Skolars and 38–6 against Rochdale Hornets, however, pointed to better times ahead. Diveney enjoyed a fine display against Skolars, helping himself to two tries and six goals for a personal haul of 20 points, with Shaun Robinson notching his first brace for the club and Onyango also scoring twice. The Hornets game saw Carl Forber's debut, and he contributed a try and five goals in a solid team performance.

A second defeat of the year to Whitehaven, this one in Cumbria, tended to highlight a bit of inconsistency in the team, with four wins and four losses from the first eight league games. It is interesting to note that Whitehaven included in their team, in all three games against the Roughyeds in 2011, two very popular Oldham players from different eras. In their pack was former Oldham Bears Super League forward, Howard Hill, in the autumn of his career, and at stand-off was future Oldham captain Lewis Palfrey, who became an influential figure at the club between 2013 and 2016.

As the team prepared to face Doncaster at Whitebank in early May, a flurry of excitement had enveloped the dressing room as the Roughyeds had been drawn to face Super League giants Hull FC at the Kingston Communications (KC) Stadium in the Challenge Cup fourth round the following weekend. It promised to be a fantastic day for the club, win or lose, and the team dispatched their South Yorkshire visitors 46–24, Ben Wood scoring twice, to ensure they headed along the M62 and down Clive Sullivan Way the following Saturday in buoyant mood.

Chris Hamilton said at the time in the *Oldham Chronicle:* "It is a good draw for us. We could not have played a Super League club at Whitebank, so if we were going to be drawn with one it was obviously beneficial to be drawn away. Like all clubs in our position we wanted a tie that would give us a good chance of progressing or one with the potential to make us a bit of money and I think we have got the latter, given how well supported Hull FC are. They have international players right across the park, and we will be taking them on in a magnificent stadium. It will be a day to remember for everyone."

Unfortunately, as the big game loomed it transpired that Oldham were going to be missing 10 of their most experienced players through injury or suspension. The *Oldham Chronicle* previewed the game, which was played on Saturday afternoon 7 May: "Among the replacements for the missing players are full-back Steven Nield and stand-off Jamie Dallimore, both stepping up from the reserves for the first time, and back-row forward Michael Ward, who made his senior debut in last Sunday's 46–24 win against Doncaster. 'It will be a fantastic opportunity for a lot of our young players and every one of them will be intent on walking off the KC Stadium at the end of the tie with head held high,' said coach Tony Benson. 'Nield and Dallimore have been playing well in the reserves, while Ward did exceptionally well in his first taste of senior rugby last Sunday. Winger Shaun Robinson and his centre Matthew Fogarty, who is only 18, are back after injury and are really looking forward to highlighting their first year at senior level with appearances on the big stage. I am really looking forward to seeing how all these young guys do, and how they adapt to playing against high-calibre opponents in a stadium like the KC. It will be a huge experience for them.'"

As expected, the Super League big boys overwhelmed Benson's young side, winning 82–0. However, the Oldham players were able to walk tall as they left the pitch to polite applause from the Hull faithful, every one of them having given of their very best and never once having given up. It simply was a case of men against boys. The *Oldham Chronicle* reported as follows: "A Hurricane flew over the KC Stadium on a day in which Oldham's Challenge Cup campaign was emphatically blown to pieces. The World War Two fighter plane provided a terrific sight, marking as it did the anniversary of the two worst nights of the Blitz of 1941. The city of Hull took a real pounding, with more than 300 bombs dropped by the Germans 70 years ago. At least the Roughyeds' heavy loss was confined to the sporting field. It was hardly unexpected

116

that Hull FC would rack up a big score. Coach Richard Agar had opted to field a very strong line-up in a bid to maintain the continuity which has seen the Airlie Birds rise into the Super League play-off positions with a series of impressive recent displays. And as far as Oldham coach Tony Benson was concerned, with 11 men missing through injury, suspension and unavailability — Danny Whitmore dropped out on the eve of the tie — damage limitation was the name of the game, with more realistic challenges lying ahead in Championship One." Oldham lad Jordan Turner, formerly of Salford City Reds and later to play for St Helens, Canberra Raiders in Australia and Huddersfield Giants, scored a hat-trick for Hull and their highly respected current head coach Lee Radford, then their club captain, was another try-scorer.

It was one extreme to the other for the beleaguered Roughyeds because just a week after playing at the KC Stadium in the Challenge Cup, the team ran out at the far humbler surroundings of Virginia Park in Caerphilly, South Wales, to take on the Scorpions in Championship One. Despite welcoming back seven of the missing 11 players from the trip to Humberside, Roughyeds slipped to a second successive defeat to the Welshmen following their unexpected victory at Whitebank in late 2010. Further defeats at Swinton and Doncaster followed as the effects of taking on the full-time professionals of Hull FC in their own backyard took its toll.

However Benson soon had his boys buzzing again and they finished the league season extremely well, winning seven of the final nine games. The run began when South Wales came to Whitebank for the return match and Roughyeds finally broke the Scorpions hoodoo with young half-back Jamie Dallimore, a star of the club's reserve team, stealing the show with two tries, a drop-goal and man-of-the-match performance in only his second senior outing.

Benson strengthened his squad around this time by bringing in two youngsters from Leeds Rhinos on loan. Callum Casey, son of former Roughyeds prop-forward Leo Casey, a loose-forward, and second-row man Danny Bravo arrived from Headingley in a bid to gain first-team experience at Oldham. Both played in each of Oldham's last nine matches of the season and both proved useful additions to the squad.

Since Rochdale lad Ben Heaton burst onto the Roughyeds first team scene with that virtuoso performance against York City Knights in the 2009 play-off series, the young full-back or centre had regularly impressed and was beginning to attract the attention of leading Championship clubs with some fine displays in the red and white. A win against Whitehaven – including Howard Hill and Lewis Palfrey – at Whitebank in July saw Heaton at his best. The full-back regularly pulverised the Cumbrians with long breaks out of defence, scored two tries and walked away with the man-of-the-match award.

117

Left: Captain Neil Roden with the Law Cup after victory over Hornets at Whitebank in 2011.

Below: Carl Forber in Oldham colours in 2011.

(Both photos David Murgatroyd).

Left: Valu Bentley
scoring against
Gateshead
Thunder in 2011
(Photo: David
Murgatroyd).

Former Oldham forward Dana Wilson, tragically killed in a road accident in
September 2011, attempting to evade a Valu Bentley tackle while playing for
Swinton against the Roughyeds in May 2011. (Courtesy of Valu Bentley).

It was at this point that fans began to realise that the club would struggle to hold on to their prized asset beyond the end of the season. He was a fine player at Championship One level and would almost certainly be performing in the higher league in 2012 it seemed.

The geographical nature of Championship One, with some clubs based away from the traditional rugby league heartlands, meant that Oldham's next match was played in the shadow of one of the most iconic rugby grounds in the world – Twickenham. The London Skolars had switched their home fixture against Roughyeds to the Twickenham Stoop ground, famous home of the renowned Harlequins RUFC and, in 2011, of Harlequins RLFC also, and within shouting distance of 'Twickers' itself. Unfortunately, the plush surroundings seemed to inspire the home side who won 36–34 to inflict Oldham's first defeat in four games.

A 36–14 win over Keighley Cougars was arguably the team's best display of the season, because the Yorkshire outfit were eventually promoted to the Championship via the play-offs, along with Swinton Lions who went up automatically. Heaton raced in for two more tries with Neil Roden belying his years in another tip-top display. Further wins over Rochdale Hornets at Spotland – a great 38–16 mauling of the derby rivals – and 24–20 over Workington Town ensured Oldham earned a play-off spot despite their frustrating inconsistency at times throughout the year. Heaton scored 10 tries in the final nine league games to give the side a real attacking threat from deep and a rematch against Hornets at Spotland in the first knock-out match gave the team a good opportunity to make progress as it chased a place in its fifth consecutive Championship One Grand Final.

Sadly it was not to be this time. The home side played exceptionally well and fully deserved their 39–18 win. It was a disappointing display from the Roughyeds and a sad end to the year. For the first time since 2006, the season had finished early with no run to a Grand Final to enjoy. An emotional farewell to a fans favourite took place at Spotland that day. The Roughyeds career of Marcus St Hilaire came to an end when he was led from the field of play injured. The Oldham fans applauded him off warmly, realising that this was almost certainly his rugby league swansong. He had been a fine player in his career before arriving at Oldham and never once let his high standards slip while wearing a Roughyeds jersey.

When I say the fans had no Grand Final to enjoy in 2011, however, it is not strictly true. The club's reserve team, coached by former hooker John Hough, with former half-back Paul Ashton as his assistant, performed splendidly to reach the Championship Final against Widnes Vikings at Whitebank. John explains: "I began coaching the reserves in 2009 and we had a three year plan to win the league and start pushing

120

as many players through to the first team as we could. The 2011 Grand Final was one of my proudest moments. I am pleased to see a lot of players from that squad still playing professionally in 2017, whether at Oldham or elsewhere." Watched by a crowd that topped some first-team crowds that year, Oldham won 29–24 and received the trophy to much acclaim from their fans from former Wigan, Castleford, England and Great Britain star Barrie-Jon Mather. The reserves included several players who went on to become first-team regulars such as Jamie Dallimore, Michael Ward, David Cookson, Alex Thompson, Phil Joy, Danny Langtree, Kenny Hughes and Steven Nield. It is interesting to note that the Widnes team included two young forwards, Josh Crowley and Liam Thompson, both of whom joined Oldham just over a year later.

As Oldham fans had feared from midway through the season, Ben Heaton's time at the club ended after the play-off defeat. Championship side Halifax made their move after the season was over and Ben moved to The Shay with Oldham's best wishes. He scored 20 tries in 49 games for the club, including 13 in 19 games in 2011, when his reputation began to soar. He went on to give splendid service to Halifax in each of the next six seasons.

On the international scene, Oldham's two on-loan men, Callum Casey and Danny Bravo, ensured the club were once again represented in the autumn matches. Casey was a member of the Ireland squad for the series with France and Scotland and also a warm-up match for a Wales team preparing to do battle with the world's best, England, Australia and New Zealand, in the Four Nations. Callum was loose-forward in two of the three games and a substitute in the third. Bravo, meanwhile, took his rugby league talents across the Atlantic Ocean and represented Jamaica in two qualifying matches for the 2013 World Cup, both played in New Jersey, USA. Danny was in the second-row for Jamaica, a team comprised almost entirely of UK based professionals, against the USA and South Africa. Although they beat the South African team, defeat to the hosts meant it was they, the USA, who qualified for the World Cup.

The success of Oldham's youth policy and reserve team set-up under John Hough and Paul Ashton began to pay dividends for the first team in 2012. Four stars of the club's second string – Dallimore, Ward, Cookson and Alex Thompson – became regulars in Tony Benson's senior side while two more – Joy and Langtree – were given a taste of the action. Dallimore was an exciting attacking scrum-half who played off the cuff and was capable of cutting an opposition defence to ribbons in the blink of an eye. He was also a fine goalkicker and became the team's regular marksman in his first full season. He finished the year with an impressive 78 goals, to go with his eight tries. This left him joint fourth in the Championship One points-scoring charts. 'Dally' made an immediate impression, scoring two tries and kicking six goals for a personal haul of 20 points in only the second game of the year, a 36–36 draw against South Wales Scorpions in the Northern Rail Cup. That, unfortunately, was the only point the team gained in the NRC in 2012, a heavy home defeat to an excellent Featherstone Rovers side followed by further losses to Dewsbury Rams and Keighley Cougars. A John Gillam hat-trick against the Rams at Whitebank was the main highlight of the four games and as the Championship One season began, it was clear that the team had a lot of work to do.

When Michael Ward made his first tentative steps into the first-team against Doncaster in 2011, fans present at Whitebank that day were witnessing the debut of a player who would become one of the most popular to wear the red and white jersey in the 20 years of the club's existence. A week after his debut, 'Wardy' played in the Challenge Cup tie at Hull and my lasting memory of that match is of him intercepting a stray Hull pass deep inside his own half and running unchallenged in a straight line into Hull territory. On a day when very little went right for Oldham, it was a moment to remember. In 2012, 'Wardy' made 18 appearances, including seven off the bench, and scored six tries. His story is an interesting one. He first signed for Oldham as a 16-year-old in 2007, playing in the reserves, initially on the wing, but also at centre or anywhere in the pack. He had played rugby union for Oldham RUFC as a schoolboy as well as rugby league, but it was in the 13-a-side code that he saw his future, and Oldham fans are most grateful that he did. By the end of 2017, Michael had worn the Roughyeds first-team jersey 155 times, and complete with headgear, was a major influence in the side as a barnstorming prop-forward, usually introduced from the bench, and never failing to cause opposition defences problems with his rampaging runs.

David Cookson, a Rochdale lad, was a big centre with pace and power. Like Dallimore and Ward, he fully deserved his elevation to the first team, and made 18 appearances, scoring five tries, in 2012. He was tough as teak and this was never more emphasised than when he played in the 2014 Grand Final against Hunslet Hawks in headgear after receiving a nasty gash to the head in a crucial play-off tie at York two weeks earlier. After the game at York he was photographed with four surgical staples in his head and a huge grin on his face after Oldham had sealed victory.

Former Warrington Wolves youngster Alex Thompson was the fourth member of the quartet of 2011 reserves to make their mark in the first team in 2012. He was a fine loose-forward prospect and made 19 appearances, including 11 as a substitute, and looked every inch a player of real ability at Championship One level. His 12 tries made him the highest forward try-scorer at the club that year.

The loss of Ben Heaton meant that the club were in the market for a new full-back as the season approached. Oldham lad Miles Greenwood had been a star performer for Leigh Centurions and Halifax and the club turned to him. There is little doubt that Greenwood was a worthy successor to Heaton in the number one shirt and proved it by racing in for 20 tries in 25 games to finish way ahead at the top of the club's try-scoring chart. Taking just league games into account, he finished joint fourth in the Championship One leading try-scorers. Although Miles only played one year at Oldham, moving back into the Championship with Batley Bulldogs at the end of the year and later back to Halifax and then Rochdale Hornets, he made a lasting impression as an exciting attacker.

Another player to arrive from The Shay was second-row forward Paul Smith. With 69 games in Super League for Huddersfield Giants between 2004 and 2006 behind him, Smith joined Paul Noone and Valu Bentley in a back-row full of experience.

The team's fortunes picked up dramatically once the Northern Rail Cup was out of the way, with the first three league matches, against Workington Town at Derwent Park and Gateshead Thunder and Barrow Raiders at Whitebank all won. The Rugby Football League had decided that four clubs would be automatically promoted from Championship One in 2012 due to a re-structuring of the competitions, with the play-offs, for once, being used only to decide on a champion, not to fill a final promotion position. Consequently, it was imperative that the team finished in the top four. It did, however, provide the best opportunity yet for the club to finally achieve their goal of regaining their place in the Championship, lost in 2006.

Sandwiched between the three opening wins was a potentially difficult Challenge Cup third round tie against Egremont Rangers, played on a Friday evening in late March. The match was switched from Rangers' small ground to Whitehaven's Recreation Ground, and with a fervent home crowd behind them, Egremont were fancied by many to pull off a cup shock. Credit the Roughyeds then for quelling the Cumbrians' fire with a 22–14 win and a place in the fourth round assured. The draw set up a Whitebank clash with Barrow Raiders and in a superb game, Oldham turned in a heart-warming performance to win 26–14. The victory ensured the team a place in the last 16 for the first time in four years. Again the draw presented the club with a home tie, but when Super League giants St Helens were drawn out next, it was immediately apparent that the tie would have to be switched from Whitebank. As it was the board had little choice but to announce that the match would be played at Saints' plush new Langtree Park stadium.

123

Left: Marcus St Hilaire leaving the pitch at Spotland in his final appearance in rugby league. Right: Former Warrington Wolves forward Paul Noone walking out at Whitebank, thumbs-up for the camera.

The club's reserve team celebrate after winning the 2011 Grand Final against Widnes Vikings at Whitebank.
(All photos by David Murgatroyd).

John Gillam looking to out-pace the Keighley Cougars cover
in a 2012 Northern Rail Cup match.

Chris Clarke taking on the St Helens defence at Langtree Park
in the 2012 Challenge Cup match.

(Both photos David Murgatroyd).

Following many decades at their spiritual home, Knowsley Road, and one year ground-sharing with Widnes Vikings, Saints had moved into their new stadium at the beginning of the year. The match against Oldham was only their seventh at Langtree Park. Earlier in the season they had beaten Leeds Rhinos 46–6 there in Super League and only a week before the cup-tie, beat Widnes 62–0. It was clear that Oldham were going to have their work cut out.

In the meantime, however, a well-known face in rugby league circles appeared in the Oldham line-up away to London Skolars only five days before the cup-tie. Vastly experienced stand-off half Graham Holroyd joined the club for a short spell in mid-season. With over 300 senior appearances to his name, of which 143 were in Super League with Leeds Rhinos, Halifax and Salford City Reds, the Yorkshireman had also operated extensively in the Championship for Doncaster, Halifax and Swinton Lions before joining Oldham. In the event, he only turned out five times for the club and was ineligible for the Saints match because he signed after the cup deadline.

The match at Langtree Park was played on Friday evening, 27 April 2012, after Oldham's part-time professionals had been working in their full-time employment all day. No surprise then that Saints won comfortably, 76–0, but Oldham, missing regulars Neil Roden, Lucas Onyango, John Clough, Paul Noone and Paul Smith, put in a brave and spirited performance. Saints' fielded England internationals Paul Wellens, at full-back, and James Roby at hooker and New Zealand stars Francis Meli, who scored a hat-trick, on the left wing and Lance Hohaia at stand-off. The gulf in class was there for all to see and puts the result into perspective.

As was the case after the Hull cup-tie in 2011, however, the match against the full-time professionals took its toll on Oldham's part-timers and, sadly, the next seven league matches were all lost. Included in this run were two matches, home and away, against North Wales Crusaders, the Welshmen winning 36–32 at Whitebank and 30–28 at the Racecourse in Wrexham. A try scorer for Crusaders in both games was winger Adam Clay, destined to play for the Roughyeds with considerable success between 2014 and 2017. On the opposite flank to Clay, and also a try scorer in the match at Whitebank, was Rob Massam, later to join Rochdale Hornets and who would figure directly opposite Clay, his former Crusaders team-mate, in the 2017 Oldham versus Hornets derby at Bloomfield Road, Blackpool in Summer Bash.

The disappointing run of losses finally came to an end with a 25–24 home win over London Skolars with Greenwood scoring twice and Neil Roden banging over a crucial, match-winning drop-goal. Alex Thompson scored twice in a 44–12 win in South Wales, but then a heavy defeat at Barrow in early August had huge ramifications for boss

Benson. The match at Craven Park was his last in charge, his dismissal confirmed by the club in the week leading up to the next match against Doncaster at Whitebank. By this time it had become evident that the promotion dream had died once more as four teams, Doncaster, Barrow Raiders, Workington Town and Whitehaven had pulled clear at the top of the league and would all be promoted.

It had turned into a disappointing campaign for Oldham and Benson paid the price, his former conditioner and current assistant coach, Martin Roden, taking charge in a caretaker capacity until the end of the season. The final two league games were won, the highlights being a Thompson hat-trick, another 20 point haul from Dallimore, two tries from Mark Brocklehurst and a first senior try for young prop Phil Joy in a 56–12 win at Gateshead that finished the league season.

The team still had a chance to aim for a Grand Final appearance in the play-offs but that came to nothing, when they lost 34–29 at Workington in the first game. On another day they may have won, but luck was against them when Town scored a late try to pinch it. Former Roughyed Carl Forber landed five goals for the hosts with Paul Smith doubling his try tally for the year with a hat-trick for Oldham. Young forward, Jamie Acton, a Londoner, had a cracking game after missing several games through injury. He impressed Town officials with his dynamic, aggressive approach so much that they signed him for the following year. In 2017, Jamie's rise continued when he became a regular Super League player, in the colours of newly-promoted Leigh Centurions. Like Jamie I'Anson before him, Acton also participated in cage-fighting when not playing rugby league.

Although the first-team had a disappointing year, the reserves did exceptionally well again, despite the graduation of young players from the class of 2011 into the senior side. John Hough had taken up a role on the coaching staff at Huddersfield Giants in late 2011 so his assistant, Paul Ashton, took over ahead of the 2012 season. 'Ashy' recalls: "John brought me in initially to help out with the team's attacking formations. I became his assistant and then after John moved on I was delighted to step into his shoes. We had some good lads in the team and we reached a second Grand Final in two years. We lost to a crack Featherstone Rovers side, away from home, who remained unbeaten all year. I would like to say a special thank you to Mark Brocklehurst, who had been a member of the first team squad all year, but who helped me out on the coaching side at the back end of the campaign and played a few games for me too. 'Brocky' is a good friend of mine and his assistance proved invaluable."

Brocklehurst said: "Helping 'Ashy' out with the reserve team for a few weeks and then seeing them reach a second consecutive Grand Final, with limited resources, was very satisfying."

Left: Lucas Onyango, with a huge grin, on the way to scoring against Barrow Raiders at Whitebank in 2012.

Right: Full-back Miles Greenwood, 20 tries in 25 games in 2012.

(Both photos David Murgatroyd).

Tony Benson had overseen a period in which the club had moved into Whitebank Stadium in 2010, reached two first-team Grand Finals – 2009 and 2010 –, won a reserve-team Grand Final in 2011 and reached another in 2012, and developed a youth policy of which it could be proud. Ultimately, however, the failure to get out of Championship One had cost him his job.

Benson was not out of the professional game for long, however, taking over as head coach at Oxford RLFC, who were admitted to Championship One, along with other new boys Hemel Stags and Gloucestershire All Golds, in time for the 2013 season. He also took several of his Oldham players with him, his assistant coach Martin Roden, Lucas Onyango, Shaun Robinson, Brett Robinson, Alex Thompson, Chris Clarke, John Clough, Dave Ellison, Valu Bentley and reserve team half-back Tommy Connick. Martin Roden wanted to remain at the club as head coach but it was time for Oldham to explore new avenues in their quest to achieve their long-term goal of regaining their rightful place in rugby league's second tier. "I loved every minute of the four years I spent at Oldham," concluded Martin. "The people in and around the club are fantastic."

11. Welcome to a Bulls legend

In the early years of Super League, and stretching well into the new millennium, Bradford Bulls were a powerhouse of the game in this country. The club was one of the main protagonists in ensuring the switch to summer rugby league and a brave new world for our sport in Great Britain was a success. They, more than anyone else, epitomised how a switch to summer, allied to a successful team on the pitch and an excellent marketing drive off it, could draw huge crowds to matches.

Under the command of Australian Matthew Elliott and then their former hooker, Brian Noble, Bradford enjoyed a golden period in their history. They reached many big finals, won plenty of silverware and attracted some of world rugby league's best players to Odsal Stadium.

In among this galaxy of stars, however, was a man, born and reared on rugby league in the heartlands of the game in northern England, a rough, tough, powerful and uncompromising centre threequarter who took no prisoners and played the game the only way he knew how – with intensity, total commitment and a hunger to succeed. Scott Naylor had started his rugby league career at Wigan and then spent five years at Salford between 1993 and 1998. He scored two tries in the Willows outfit's stunning Challenge Cup victory against his former team in 1996, which brought an end to Wigan's unprecedented run of eight straight Challenge Cup triumphs. He played for Salford in Super League in 1997 and 1998, and then made the move across the Pennines to join the Bulls at their peak. Over the next five years, he was a permanent fixture at right-centre in their star studded line-up and his achievements in the game make impressive reading.

In 1999, his first season with the club, he was in the Bulls team that lost 8–6 to St Helens at Old Trafford in the Super League Grand Final. A year later he played at Murrayfield as Bradford won the Challenge Cup for the first time since 1949, beating Leeds Rhinos 24–18. Marcus St Hilaire was a substitute for Leeds that day. In 2001, Bulls had a fantastic year, winning the Super League crown this time, with a 37–6 mauling of Wigan Warriors in the Grand Final. They fully deserved to end that year with a trophy because they had also reached the Challenge Cup Final, losing 13–6 to St Helens at Twickenham. Naylor played at centre in both finals.

Bradford's victory in the Grand Final thrust them into the big-time even further when they met, and beat, the Australian NRL champions, Newcastle Knights, 41–26, in the World Club Championship at Huddersfield's McAlpine Stadium in early 2002. The Bulls were officially the best club side in the world and Naylor was very much part of the set-up. Later that year, they again reached Old Trafford, but their old enemy St Helens proved too strong once more, winning 19–18 with a last-gasp drop-goal from Sean Long. Naylor scored a try for Bulls that day. Then in 2003, Scott's last year with the Odsal club, they again lifted the Challenge Cup with a thrilling 22–20 win over Leeds Rhinos at the Millennium Stadium in Cardiff.

Naylor played four times for England during his days at Bradford, all during the 2000 World Cup. He started at centre against Australia at Twickenham in the opening match of the tournament, a game the visitors won 22–2. He was a try-scorer in a game against Fiji at Headingley, won 66–10 by England. In the quarter-final, he was a substitute against Ireland, also at Headingley and was back in the starting line-up for England's disappointing collapse against New Zealand in the semi-final at the Reebok Stadium in Bolton.

On leaving Odsal, he returned to Salford in 2004 for a short spell before retiring as a player later that year. He went into coaching and spent several years at The Willows, working with the club's Under–20s team and also assisting head coach Shaun McRae. After leaving Salford, he landed the head coach role at Leigh Rugby Union Club, but rugby league was always his first love, and in late 2012 he jumped at the chance to move back into league when the head coach role at Oldham was offered to him.

Chris Hamilton told the *Oldham Chronicle:* "I spoke to Shaun McRae at length about Scott and Shaun gave him a huge rap. Scott is hungry to get back into rugby league and has a burning desire to do well. He is a rugby league man through and through and has been looking for an opportunity like this for some time. He is driven, committed and dedicated. These were the characteristics that epitomised him as a player and I am confident that he will be no different in his first rugby league appointment as a head coach."

Naylor said: "I am looking forward to the challenge and no stone will be left unturned. There will be targets set by myself and the team, but for the time being we are looking to improve on last year."

Lee Spencer, or 'Spanner' as he was known throughout the game, a member of the Salford City Reds coaching staff for nine years, was appointed as Naylor's second-in-command. The boss said: "I jumped at the chance to approach 'Spanner' as soon as I knew he was available. I didn't want anyone else to beat me to him. He is quality - as a coach and as a person. He gives 100 percent in everything he does. He lives and sleeps the game and he pulled off a fantastic achievement last year when he guided Salford Under–20s to second in the league against top quality opposition from Super League's leading clubs. I am really looking forward to working with him again as together we face the challenge of leading Oldham to better and brighter things."

Not long after Naylor's and Spencer's appointments, the club announced it was to engage in an official link with Super League club Salford City Reds. Chris Hamilton told the *Oldham Chronicle:* "We are looking forward to working with Salford as we move in to a new era. The partnership is a hugely positive move for Roughyeds. It will provide us with new opportunities and not only in terms of players. We will be able to tap into the full-time club's strength and conditioning programmes, their medical expertise and their sales, marketing and commercial activities. Salford, like us, are keen to see their players at Oldham on a relatively long-term basis, as this will assist both clubs in their planning."

Steve Simms, the City Reds Director of Football, said: "Oldham is a forward looking club, based in a strong rugby league area. Both clubs will be able to look at players who might ordinarily not have forced their way to the front so quickly."

The link-up with the City Reds, allied to the fact that the club's new coaching team had worked at The Willows previously, immediately paid dividends on the playing front. Former Salford youngsters Lewis Palfrey, who was made captain of the team, Richard Lepori, Adam Files, Mark Hobson and Callum Marriott were snapped up as a new squad rebuilding programme got under way. Palfrey had played for Whitehaven and Batley Bulldogs since leaving the City Reds, Lepori had played in the Castleford Tigers academy side and Hobson had turned out for Rochdale Hornets but Files and Marriott came straight from Salford. Marriott was the son of the late Karl Marriott, the former Hornets forward.

Danny Whitmore, another Salford old boy, who had joined Batley after his earlier spell with the Roughyeds, rejoined the club on loan from the Yorkshire outfit. He commented: "Scott Naylor had coached me for three years at The Willows where I was playing alongside Lewis Palfrey. I played twice for Oldham at the beginning of 2013 and it felt great playing alongside Lewis and some other lads I knew from Salford days. Unfortunately, I broke an arm in the second of those games and the injury ruined my season. I re-signed the following year and played a few games, but then moved to Australia. I turned out for the Illawarra Cutters, who are a feeder club for the NRL side St George Illawarra Dragons."

Other players to sign included wingers Mo Agoro from Leeds Rhinos and Dale Bloomfield from Rochdale Hornets, young Widnes Vikings forwards, Josh Crowley and Liam Thompson and utility player Sam Gee, formerly with Warrington Wolves, Wigan Warriors, London Skolars and Whitehaven and grandson of Wigan legend Ken Gee. In addition to the new kids on the block, the club's excellent youth policy continued to come up trumps with full-back Steven Nield, prop Phil Joy, hooker

131

Kenny Hughes and second-row forward Danny Langtree making their breakthrough as first-team regulars in 2013.

Palfrey said at the time of his appointment as skipper: "I have captained the Salford academy and reserve teams but this will carry a lot more responsibility. I can't wait to lead out the team." Speaking in 2017, Lewis said: "I was surprised, but delighted, to be offered the captaincy in 2013. I didn't need asking twice to accept, I said 'yes' straight away. I was only 22, but had known Scott Naylor a long time. There was a huge overhaul of players from the previous year, it was like the 'changing of the guard'. Much of that first year was about getting to know each other and gelling as a team."

Naylor clearly placed plenty of emphasis on youth and as such, it appeared as though the career of long-serving Neil Roden was about to come to an end. Captain Palfrey was earmarked to wear the number six jersey so it didn't augur well for Roden. Neil said: "I didn't play much in 2013 – six games in total – and I could have left and gone on loan. However I spoke to Scott and became part of the coaching team which I enjoyed." So Neil followed in the footsteps of his former team-mate, John Hough, by taking on a coaching role at the club, in his case as coach of the Under–20s team, replacing Phil Costin. He had been a wonderful servant to the club as a player, playing elsewhere in only 2005 and 2006, and it was good to see him given an opportunity to pass on his years of experience to the young boys coming through. He was also awarded a well-deserved testimonial in 2014.

The following is a breakdown by year of Neil's 295 appearances and 113 tries for Oldham. Nobody has represented the new club more often, nobody has scored more tries or drop-goals and he was club captain for four of his 12 seasons at the club.

Neil Roden	Appearances	Tries
2000	19	6
2001	34	16
2002	36	20
2003	27	7
2004	22	16
2007	34	10
2008	33	12
2009	23	7
2010	21	4
2011	23	8
2012	17	4
2013	6	3
Total	295	113

Danny Langtree going for the line at Whitebank in 2013.

Winger Mo Agoro in spectacular try scoring action at Whitebank in 2014.
(Both photos David Murgatroyd).

Left: George Tyson racing in to score at Whitebank in 2014.
Above: David Cookson's war wounds after Oldham's win at York in the 2014 play-offs.

Dale Bloomfield scoring in the corner in the play-off victory at Hunslet in 2014.

(All photos David Murgatroyd).

The first game in charge for Naylor and Spencer was the Law Cup match at Spotland against Rochdale Hornets. It proved to be a winning start for the new look team as Roughyeds scraped home 22–20. Loose-forward Mark Hobson had just left Hornets after four years to join Oldham. "I enjoyed my time at Spotland," said Mark, "so it was satisfying to go back there and win. It felt great making my debut for Oldham against my former club, in a derby match and in front of several family members and friends from my Rochdale days. Winning the trophy really capped the day off well." So in their first outing, new captain Palfrey and his vice-captain, Gee, lifted the cup together to the delight of Oldham fans.

The team's first fixture in what would turn out to be the last ever Northern Rail Cup was against North Wales Crusaders at The Racecourse. The new agreement with Salford was immediately put to use with four players from the Willows turning out for Oldham under the new dual-registration procedure. Scott Naylor told the *Oldham Chronicle:* "Dual-registration is here to stay and most clubs are using it to their advantage. Salford coach Phil Veivers will tell us each week who is available to us and then 'Spanner' and I will decide what we should do with Oldham's best interests in mind. The system will seem strange at first because it is something new, but once people get used to it, it will become the norm. Salford are keen to help us to achieve our goals and aspirations and that has got to be good for our club."

The four players in question, relatively unknown youngsters Niall Evalds, Jon Ford, Will Hope and Jordan Walne all became familiar faces over the next few years. Evalds and Walne became regular members of Salford's Super League squad while Ford and Hope both eventually joined Oldham as contracted players. Unfortunately, the Roughyeds were well beaten by a strong Crusaders team and the defeat proved costly. Despite three subsequent wins in the competition, against Rochdale Hornets and Gateshead Thunder at Whitebank and away to South Wales Scorpions, the team failed to make it to the next round with only the group winners qualifying.

In the Thunder match, the new second-row pairing of Danny Langtree and Josh Crowley gave a hint of things to come with five tries between them, two by 'Langers' and three by Josh.

Hornets had been beaten twice already, but they exacted revenge by returning to Whitebank in the first Championship One fixture and won 28–18 to get their 2013 league season off to a flyer. That defeat, plus two more disappointing losses, a 36–10 Challenge Cup beating at Hunslet and an 18–16 home reversal against new club Oxford meant everyone's feet were kept firmly on the ground in the first third of the season. The RFL had taken its expansionist policy to a new level by admitting three new clubs, Oxford RLFC, Hemel Stags and

Gloucestershire All Golds into Championship One ahead of the new season. As described earlier, the Oxford head coach was Tony Benson and remarkably, the visitors' team to Whitebank on 28 April included 11 former Roughyeds in their starting 13. It really was an old boys' reunion. For the record, the 11 were Lucas Onyango, Shaun Robinson, Danny Halliwell, Tommy Connick, Brett Robinson, Chris Clarke, John Clough, Dave Ellison, Alex Thompson, Valu Bentley and Martin Roden.

It was a huge match for Oxford, for obvious reasons, and they deserved the win on the day. Lucas recalls: "It was a big one for us and we played really well. Oldham gained their revenge on us in the reverse fixture in Oxford later in the year though. In that match I scored a try in the first minute but then, sadly for me, I picked up an anterior cruciate ligament injury. It was a bad one and I was never to play professional rugby league again." For Oldham, the Whitebank defeat was the low point of the season, the only way was up from there.

That is exactly how things turned out, with the team suffering only one more league defeat – away to North Wales Crusaders – all season. After the loss to Oxford, the team won 11 and drew one of their final 13 league games. The highlight was a cracking 28–10 victory over eventual champions Crusaders in the return fixture. In front of a Whitebank season best crowd of 1,209, bolstered by a large, and very noisy, contingent of North Walians, the Roughyeds turned in a great performance with centre Jon Ford scoring a hat-trick and confirming once more what a fine try-scorer he was.

Ford scored 21 tries in 15 appearances in 2013, while at the club on either dual-registration or on loan from Salford. His left wing partner, Dale Bloomfield, scored 11 tries, including a hat-trick at Hemel in May, many of which were created by Ford. Bloomfield was quick to praise the contribution of his centre: "Jon made a lot of my tries in 2013, and in 2014 too. He was very tall and was able to use his height and his evasive skills to get outside his opposite centre on a regular basis, thus giving him the opportunity to send me clear. Every winger needs a good centre inside him, and Jon was certainly that."

Ford praised his winger too: "I played a lot with Dale during his two years at the club so we got to know how each other played and it certainly helped with our partnership. I would like to add that although I was on dual-registration at Oldham initially, and not everybody in the game was convinced about the concept back then, I was always made very welcome by the other lads and the coaches. I loved playing for Oldham and jumped at the opportunity to link up with them every time one came along."

As well as his three tries against Crusaders, Ford crossed the line four times at South Wales Scorpions, three times against Gateshead Thunder – in a match played at Filtrona Park, the home of South Shields

136

Football Club – and three more tries in a final play-off eliminator against London Skolars in September. It was a great effort by the Salford man and saw him top the Championship One try-scorers list for the year. "I enjoyed 2013 very much," Jon recalled. "It was my first season since leaving the Academy at Salford and my first crack at first team rugby. I was pleased with how it went."

Hooker Adam Files, on season long loan from Salford, also had a great try-scoring year. An ever-present with 24 appearances, he proved very elusive from dummy-half, especially close to the line, and scored a terrific 15 tries, to leave himself joint fourth in the Championship One try charts, a great effort for a number nine, particularly as he was often used as a substitute. Full-back Richard Lepori, destined to become a great favourite at the club over the next four years, added 12 more tries to finish joint sixth. Captain Palfrey kicked 87 goals to finish top of the Championship One goalkicking charts and second in the points list. The new boys were certainly beginning to make their mark.

In the pack, young guns Phil Joy and Danny Langtree, came on leaps and bounds under Naylor's tutelage. Joy, a huge unit, caught the eye of the boss straight away as a prop-forward of huge potential and played in 22 games out of a maximum of 24 in his first full season. Langtree, similarly, made a huge contribution alongside Josh Crowley in the second-row, playing 23 times, and loose-forward Hobson brought a touch of experience to the back of the pack with 22 appearances. Crowley had a superb first season, not missing a match all year and proved a real find following his move from Widnes.

Despite a one point loss to Rochdale Hornets in the first play-off game, a 64–8 mauling of London Skolars in the second pushed the team into yet another Grand Final, their fifth in seven years and the first under Naylor, in his first season at the helm. For the first time also, their opponents were the old enemy Hornets. It promised to be a showdown rich in passion, both on the pitch and in the stands. The match was held at Leigh Sports Village on 29 September, 2013. There was a powder-keg atmosphere as the old adversaries prepared to lock horns yet again, but this time where the stakes were so much higher than usual. Including the Law Cup game at the beginning of the year, the two teams had already met five times in 2013, Oldham winning three and Hornets two. But clearly the Grand Final was the biggest game of them all. Roughyeds had finished a whopping nine points ahead of Rochdale in the final league table, but as we knew from 2010, and the Grand Final loss to York City Knights, that counted for absolutely nothing on the big day.

Unfortunately, Oldham's Grand Final curse struck again. Hornets won 32–18 to give Oldham-born, former Roughyeds hooker or scrum-half, Chris Hough – cousin of John Hough – a fitting farewell to his career in the professional ranks.

Lewis Palfrey recalled: "It was a desperately disappointing defeat. I think the occasion got to us because we were well below our best. Some of our lads were in their first season out of Academy rugby and Rochdale had some real experience in their team. They also included Joe Greenwood, a terrific young forward, on dual-registration from St Helens. Joe went on to play regularly for Saints and now, in 2017, is playing in the NRL for Gold Coast Titans. Looking back though, it was a great experience for us and benefitted us no end in the next two years in our bid to finally win promotion."

The Rochdale team included former Roughyeds star Gareth Langley on the right wing: "I signed for Hornets in 2013 knowing I would be facing Oldham a few times that year. I made my debut for them in the Law Cup and took some light-hearted banter from the Oldham fans. I had a pint after the game with them though, there were definitely no hard feelings. I had followed Oldham's fortunes, and cheered them on, since leaving the club because I loved my time there. The Grand Final was a great game because, in my opinion, both teams played some cracking football. We had some good experienced players like Wayne English, Paul Crook and Steve Roper. I guess one team had to win and one had to lose. That is rugby league, and why we all love the game."

Oldham's try scorers were Jon Ford, Kenny Hughes and David Cookson with Palfrey kicking three goals. Ford said: "I wasn't 100% fit after dislocating my elbow not long before. It was very disappointing to lose nonetheless." Dale Bloomfield added: "The defeat was tough to take, especially with it being against my old club." Mark Hobson agreed: "The defeat still sits with me to this day. It was a blow I didn't see coming and didn't think we would have to take. It is not often you get the chance to play in a Grand Final against your old club and against old mates. I loved my time at Oldham. They were a great group of lads and Scott and 'Spanner' made a good coaching team. They were very thorough and demanded a great work ethic. Scott was clever with his coaching, both tactically and in getting the best out of his troops. He rarely had to shout to get his message across. 'Spanner' was the most enthusiastic coach I ever worked under. As a pair, they instilled a lot of mental toughness into the group. I am sure that benefitted them greatly when they did eventually get in to the Championship. I was delighted for them when they finally won promotion in 2015."

All year Richard Lepori had been hoping to win a place in the Italy squad to take part in the World Cup in the autumn of 2013. 'Lippy' takes up the story of his international dream: "I am half-Italian with a middle name of Antonio! I have an Italian father and English mother. My dad left his homeland to move to the UK in his 20s and stayed, in fact all my family on his side still live in Italy. My mum is from Cumbria, which is perhaps why I have turned out pale and full of freckles. I made my debut for Italy against Germany and also played against Serbia in 2013, but didn't make the squad for the World Cup.

Although I was disappointed to miss out, I was an inexperienced Championship One player after all, so on reflection I can understand why I wasn't picked."

Four years on, and the next World Cup to be held in the southern hemisphere in late 2017, is another goal for the dynamic full-back. "I played in several of the team's qualifiers for the 2017 World Cup, which I hadn't done four years earlier. I am really hopeful of earning a place in the squad second time round, it would be a dream to represent the country of my father's birth in a World Cup."

The 2013 Northern Rail Cup Final between Leigh Centurions and Sheffield Eagles at The Shay in Halifax was the last match played in the competition as it was disbanded ahead of the 2014 season. To compensate for the loss of matches and consequently income for clubs in the newly named Kingstone Press Championship One, the RFL asked clubs to play four opponents three times instead of twice. There were only nine clubs in the division due to a re-structuring of the three divisions and so the extra games provided Oldham with 20 league outings rather than just 16. So the Roughyeds found themselves facing Hemel Stags, London Skolars, Gloucestershire All Golds and Gateshead Thunder three times in league clashes. With all due respect to those four clubs, they were not particularly mouth-watering clashes and the potential effect on crowd figures was worrying.

On the playing front, two young forwards from Salford were brought in on season-long loan, 'blond bomber' George Tyson and prop Alex Davidson. Adam Files, who was at the club on a similar arrangement in 2013, became a contracted Oldham player in 2014.

The league season began in early March with a match that few people present will ever forget, but not for the rugby on show that day. Roughyeds made the long trek to Maesteg to take on the South Wales Scorpions in what they hoped would be an opportunity to get their season off to a flying start. Well they did bring home the three points for the win but that fails to tell the story of a traumatic day. The weather conditions were dreadful before the match kicked off and worsened considerably as the game wore on. The *Oldham Chronicle* reported as follows: "Oldham led 18-4 with eight minutes left when referee Adam Gill pulled the players off in appalling freezing rain, a pitch that held water and bitterly-cold winds. Oldham winger Dale Bloomfield and Scorpions' skipper Phil Carleton had already been taken to the warmth of the dressing rooms suffering from hypothermia-like symptoms.

Others on both teams complained of similar symptoms as the icy blast battered the hilltop Maesteg ground."

The *Oldham Chronicle* continued: "Roughyeds' coach Scott Naylor, who played most of his career when rugby league was a winter sport, said: 'They were the worst conditions I have ever seen on a rugby field. The referee told me at half-time of his concerns for player-safety. Later on it got completely out of hand.' Club chairman Chris Hamilton said that in the 17 years of the current Oldham club, no player had suffered hypothermia before: 'Heavy rain was non-stop from about an hour before kick-off and throughout the game. The wind picked up in the second half and from then on it was difficult to get across to people who weren't there just how severe it was.' Chris Thair, chief operations officer for Wales Rugby League, confirmed that Scorpions supported the referee's decision and were happy for the result to stand."

One of Oldham's try scorers in Maesteg was young full-back Steven Nield. He had made his first-team debut in the Challenge Cup tie at Hull in 2011 but it wasn't until 2014 that he made the full-back berth his own. This was partly due to the fine form shown by Richard Lepori in 2013 but a year on and 'Lippy' was no longer on the scene, having decided to spend the year in Australia. Lepori would be back at Oldham to resume his career with the club, but in 2014 Nield was to prove a more than capable replacement in the number one shirt.

So Oldham's league campaign was off to a winning start. However, a frustrating 20-20 home draw with Hemel followed in a match that saw Liam Thompson suffer a terrible facial injury in an accidental clash of heads with Kenny Hughes. Thompson received three fractures around his eye socket and cheekbone and was sidelined for over three months. Injuries of this nature serve as a reminder of just what a tough and physically demanding sport rugby league is. In the third round of the Challenge Cup, the team were drawn to play Egremont Rangers in Cumbria for the second time in three years. On the previous occasion, under Tony Benson in 2012, the tie was staged at the Recreation Ground in Whitehaven. This time the game was played at the less intimidating Copeland Stadium, a ground with an athletics track and a rugby pitch in the middle. Two tries each from Nield and Josh Crowley helped Oldham to a relatively comfortable win. Following a tight 18-16 victory over London Skolars in the capital, Roughyeds played their third Challenge Cup tie on the ground of a Super League outfit in four years when they travelled to Odsal Stadium to take on Bradford Bulls in the fourth round. The match inevitably followed a similar pattern to the games against Hull in 2011 and St Helens in 2012 with the full-time Bulls winning 60-6. Again, however, it was a gallant effort by the Roughyeds.

Celebrations after Steve Roper's try at Headingley
in the 2014 Grand Final.

Scott Naylor and Chris Hamilton at
the club end-of-season awards night.

(Both photos David Murgatroyd).

A Bloomfield hat-trick – his first of three in the league in 2014 – helped to see off Gateshead Thunder at Whitebank before the first major test of the team's title credentials followed, with a trip to Hunslet Hawks in mid-April. The Hawks and York City Knights had been relegated from the Championship the previous year and were tipped by many to go straight back up. Lewis Palfrey summed up the situation as follows: "Hunslet particularly spent a lot of money on players in 2014 and were rightly favourites to go up. They had a lot of experience in their team, players like prop Richard Moore, and others with substantial and recent experience in the second tier. We were always going to have to be at our very best to get on top of them."

Unlike in previous years, there was no automatic promotion this time round, with a top-five play-off series at the end of the year determining which team would be promoted. Clearly this made it doubly difficult for Oldham to achieve their goal of promotion in 2014. The signs looked ominous when Hunslet, brilliantly led by Danny Grimshaw, won convincingly 38-12 at the South Leeds Stadium. One of Oldham's try scorers was Mo Agoro, firmly established as the team's first choice right winger and, like Bloomfield, now in his second year at the club. The try Mo scored at Hunslet was the first of 14 that he accumulated over a period of ten successive matches, a run in which he crossed the line at least once in each game. It was a terrific burst of form by the likeable winger.

Four straight wins were to follow, the first of which – a 48-28 Whitebank victory over Oxford – saw the 2014 debut of Huddersfield Giants Oldham-born prop-forward Nathan Mason on loan. Mason had enjoyed a similar spell at the club the previous year, but in 2014 he exerted a huge influence on the side, playing 16 times, each one as a substitute. A thrilling 31-30 home win over York was next up, in which Bloomfield scored his second hat-trick of the year. The score doesn't tell the full story of a remarkable match in which Oldham led 27-0 but then resurgent York raced in to a 30-27 lead, only for Nield to win it for Oldham with a late match-clinching try. The third of these wins, a 30-22 success in Cheltenham against Gloucestershire All Golds, marked the debut of a man who would play a pivotal role in the team over the next two years, Steve Roper. The half-back had been a member of the Rochdale Hornets team in the previous year's Grand Final and joined Oldham, initially on loan. He proved to be a fine steadying influence, alongside Palfrey, on the team in the second half of the season and was also a fine stand-in goal-kicker when the captain wasn't playing.

A shock defeat at Hemel - the second time the Stags had avoided defeat against Oldham in 2014 – was followed by another four-match winning run. Some big scores were posted too, a 58-2 win against South Wales, 32-14 at Gateshead, 38-22 at Oxford and 46-6 in the reverse fixture against the All Golds. Agoro scored three of his fabulous fourteen tries against the Welshmen and Bloomfield completed his hat-trick of hat-tricks against the All Golds. Dale finished 2014 with 21 tries from 21 appearances to top the Kingstone Press Championship One try-scoring charts, whilst Mo scored 18 tries from 18 appearances. It was good to see the team playing such expansive football, thus enabling the two wingers to make hay while the sun shone. Dale said: "2014 was the better of my two years at Oldham. I got plenty of opportunities to score tries which is what a winger always enjoys doing. I was pleased with my tries to games ratio. The three hat-tricks were all scored at Whitebank. We played some good stuff there and became very tough to beat on our own ground. I enjoyed playing there. I loved my time at Oldham. We had a tight group and a good team. I also made mates for life. Scott and 'Spanner' complemented each other well. Scott was a good coach, tough, but good."

As the final third of the season beckoned, Oldham were in a three-way battle with Hunslet and York to finish top of the table, a spot which would provide the least difficult route to the Grand Final. The squad was further strengthened by the capture of two players who would become real favourites at the club, winger Adam Clay and hooker or half-back Gareth Owen. Clay had played previously for Leigh Centurions, North Wales Crusaders and Barrow Raiders after beginning his career at Salford, while Owen was yet another from the Salford academy, who had gone on to play 21 Super League games for the club. He also spent time on loan at Sheffield Eagles. Owen was delighted to join his hometown team. He said: "I grew up as an Oldham fan, watching them play at Boundary Park. I had wanted to play for Roughyeds since being a young lad. I vividly recall sitting in the stand watching Lucas Onyango race down the wing for Oldham and the run to the Grand Final in 2007 when Byron Ford was a player I particularly enjoyed watching."

Clay scored his first – of many – tries for the club in a superb match at Whitebank against the high-flying Hawks in July. In a real humdinger, Roughyeds triumphed 24-23, a late try by Crowley, out wide on the left, proving crucial. It wasn't the last time Hunslet would rue the presence of Josh in Oldham colours in 2014. The final four league games saw three more wins, the first being against London Skolars at the Queen Elizabeth II stadium in Enfield. Agoro excelled in this game, scoring a fine hat-trick, the third of which was a 60-metre special which, as Scott Naylor put it, "effectively won us the game." A victory over Hemel – at the third time of asking – a defeat at fourth-placed Gateshead and another comfortable win over the All Golds took the team in to the play-offs in good heart. The slip-up on Tyneside was a disappointing one as it meant Roughyeds would finish third, below York and Hunslet in the final table. It, therefore, appeared as though both these teams would probably have to be beaten away from home if Oldham were to reach another Grand Final.

The play-off campaign began with a Friday evening trip to Hunslet and it resulted in arguably Oldham's most impressive display of the year to date. Playing a tough and physical team on their own ground it promised to be a long night for Roughyeds if they were not at their very best. Supporters need not have worried about that, however. Despite falling behind 12-0 in the early stages of the game, Oldham hit back magnificently, with tries by Ford, Bloomfield, Langtree and Ward, to lead 25-12 midway through the second half. Despite two late converted tries by the Hawks, the visitors hung on to win 25-24. It was a superb victory. The biggest talking point of the game, however, was the one point drop goal, kicked by Josh Crowley, which ended up separating the two teams.

With Oldham attacking in the final third of the field, the half-time hooter sounded with Josh in possession. Crowley told the *Oldham Chronicle:* "The hooter went and I suppose I just acted instinctively. Going for the drop goal seemed to be the right thing to do and seeing as I scored, I suppose it was. It was the first goal I have ever kicked - and there is every chance it will be the last." The Hunslet half-backs were the Coyle brothers, James and Thomas, once of Oldham. As well as they played, and they did their utmost to make the Hawks tick, it was Palfrey and Roper, dictating play superbly, who took the half-back honours on the night.

The victory meant Roughyeds would have just one more away trip to negotiate before reaching the Grand Final – and we already know how playing away from home in sudden-death football has inspired the team to great things over the years. However, it appeared York City Knights away was a genuinely tough task. In 2014, they had finished top of the table with five points to spare, beaten Hunslet three times, hadn't lost at home since April and smashed Roughyeds 54-12 in July.

In a repeat of the magnificent play-off victory at the Huntington Stadium in 2009, Roughyeds ripped into their hosts from the off once again. Sensational tries by Nield, a fully-recovered Thompson, Cookson and Langtree - the latter a long-range special - saw the team lead 24-0 at half-time and there was no way back for York from there. Although they did muster two converted tries, a fifth Roughyeds score from Tyson put the finishing touches to yet another Oldham away-day play-off classic. The final score of 31-12 was as emphatic as it suggests. If the Hunslet victory had been good, this was undoubtedly even better. This was the match in which David Cookson received a badly gashed head injury fifteen minutes into the second half but wore a huge grin, as did the other players, as they celebrated with the travelling fans after the game. Chris Hamilton told the *Oldham Chronicle:* "Nobody knows more than us what it is like to lose in a Grand Final, so there is still a lot of work to be done. It was a fantastic performance at York. The way we have gone about these play-off games has been nothing short of exceptional and full credit must be given to everyone concerned. In two heavy defeats in the league at York and Hunslet we conceded a total of 92 points and scored only 24, so what we have done in the play-offs has been truly amazing. We have earned the right to appear in the Headingley final and I do not think anyone can deny us that."

So Oldham returned to the scene of their 2007 Grand Final defeat to Featherstone Rovers, for the 2014 equivalent against Hunslet Hawks. York had faltered badly in the play-offs, losing at home to Hunslet a week after their defeat by the Roughyeds, so it was another encounter against the men from South Leeds that stood between Scott Naylor and his dream of taking his team in to the Kingstone Press Championship.

The two previous games between the teams had seen Oldham victorious by just one point each time, that is how closely matched the two teams were. It was no surprise to anyone, therefore, that the Grand Final was another close, tense affair and after 80 minutes, the scores were locked at 16-16. Steve Roper, after great work by Jon Ford and Josh Crowley, Dale Bloomfield and Danny Langtree had scored tries for Oldham with Jimmy Watson, James Duckworth and Thomas Coyle replying for the Hawks. The competition rules stipulated that the match would go in to golden point extra-time, with the first team to score being the winner. In other words, there were no second chances, no opportunity to hit back once a try, goal or drop goal had been conceded. It is an agonising way to lose a match of such importance and as the teams took a few minutes break after the final hooter at 80 minutes, you could have cut the tension with a knife. Both sets of players had given their all and were now being asked to continue with absolutely no room for error. Somebody was going to become a hero, all with the Roughyeds at heart prayed it was a man wearing red and white. It so nearly was.

Only a short time into golden point time, Roughyeds got into the Hawks half and looked to set up for the drop-goal we all craved. It appeared that time stood still for an instant as Roper's attempted one-pointer left the half-back's boot and sailed toward the posts. Sitting in the North Stand, I heard some of my fellow Oldham fans, away to my left and directly behind the flight of the ball, yelp in delight as it appeared at first glance as though the kick was going over. Divine intervention was required but when we needed it most, it wasn't forthcoming. The ball drifted wide and, as we feared, the Hawks went back up field and, to the fans consternation, former Roughyed Thomas

145

Coyle, of all people, slotted home the winner. Our hearts were broken once more, it was such a cruel way to lose.

Captain Palfrey said: "Of course, it was gutting to lose, and particularly so after losing the previous year. Looking back though, I would say the 2013 defeat hurt more. Hunslet were a very good side. I would say that we did exceptionally well in 2014 to get as close as we did." Jon Ford said simply: "It was hard to take!" It certainly was.

For prop-forward Jason Boults, a stalwart of the team since 2007, it proved to be the end of his outstanding Oldham career. The Grand Final was his 193rd and final appearance in an Oldham jersey. It is such a shame that he couldn't have gone out on a winning note.

12. Promotion at last

"I was delighted to attend Oldham's big day when they beat Keighley Cougars to guarantee their promotion to the Championship in 2015. It was also a good day for my dry cleaners because in presenting the trophy to the Oldham team, I was soaked by the champagne that accompanied it. I went home wetter but richer for the experience, it was a great day for Oldham."
Brian Barwick, Chairman of the Rugby Football League and Super League Europe (Ltd)

"2015 was the best year of my life!" That was how Lewis Palfrey summed up the year in which Oldham finally achieved their long-time goal of promotion from rugby league's third tier. Not since the relegation season of 2006 had an Oldham team graced the division below Super League but, due to the fantastic achievements of everyone concerned in 2015, that is where the team would be playing a year later.

The agony of losing six Grand Finals in eight years was all forgotten on a balmy September day at Whitebank when a ground record crowd of 1,405 witnessed the Roughyeds finally winning a match that carried with it the reward of promotion. It was not a Grand Final as such, played on a neutral ground as the previous six had been. Classed by the RFL as a Promotion Final and contested by the top two teams in Kingstone Press League One at the end of the regular season, it nevertheless thrust the winners into the promised land of the Kingstone Press Championship. Having completed the league season with a magnificent winning run of 13 straight wins, which ensured the team finished top, the Roughyeds needed to beat second placed Keighley Cougars and stretch the run to 14 and the job would be done. The questions on everyone's lips in the week leading up to the final were, 'Can they do it?' or 'Will the big game curse strike again?'

"We never once contemplated the possibility of not winning the Promotion Final," said Palfrey in 2017. "We not only knew we were capable of beating Keighley that day, we actually knew we would beat them. As a team we felt invincible in League One in 2015."

When looking back on the year in question it is easy to see why the squad were so confident. It was a magnificent year. Only five matches were lost all season, one of them against Championship high-flyers Sheffield Eagles in the Challenge Cup fourth round and one to North Wales Crusaders in the new Ipro Sport League One Cup, both in the first quarter of the season. Only three league games, out of 22 played, were lost. The matches at Barrow, Keighley and at home to Crusaders were the only times the team were beaten in an otherwise golden year of big wins and exciting triumphs. The defeat by the Welsh outfit on 7 June, 2015 was the last time Roughyeds had their colours lowered in the rest of the season, spanning three and a half months and 14 matches.

There was no indication of the great excitement that was to follow later in the year, however, when the season began in February with a testimonial match at Whitebank for Neil Roden, which brought to a close his testimonial year. In bitterly cold sleet and snow a Legends side took on a Select team to say farewell to a man who had given the best part of his career to the club. Neil said: "The game was played on one of the coldest days I have ever played rugby in. It was a good day though despite the weather and I was grateful to everyone involved and to the people who turned up to watch, whose support I really appreciated."

Following their two year partnership with Salford, Oldham changed direction ahead of the 2015 season and joined forces instead with leading Super League club Huddersfield Giants. The *Oldham Chronicle* reported on the new link-up as follows: "Roughyeds seized the chance to work with the Giants, who have been one of the top clubs in the sport's elite division in recent seasons. A chance to work in tandem with the Giants, who topped Super League in 2013 and finished third last season, was considered too good to refuse. Both clubs believe the partnership will be of mutual benefit, especially in terms of dual-registration. A key element of the new link-up is the friendship of Giants head coach Paul Anderson and his Oldham counterpart Scott Naylor, who played for several seasons together in the all-conquering Bradford Bulls side between 1999 and 2003. The Giants boss is also known to Oldham chairman Chris Hamilton, who once managed an England team in which Anderson played.

Chris said: 'Paul and Scott are good friends and another plus for us is that Huddersfield have an excellent record in terms of bringing players through their ranks and into the first team. From the outset, our discussions with Giants have been very positive. They know how close we have been to getting out of Championship One, or League One as it will be known in 2015, and they want to help us to achieve that goal. They are also aware, thanks to the connection of Scott (Naylor) and Paul (Anderson) and also to feedback from Nathan Mason, their young prop who was on loan with us over the last two seasons, that we have a very good set-up at the Oldham club. They have mentioned certain players who will be available to us and that sealed a decision we felt we had to make. We are very much looking forward to working with them.'

148

Giants managing director Richard Thewlis said: 'We are sure this will be a mutually beneficial working relationship. The Oldham club has good coaches and a very professional set-up and that will enable our young players to go there and make progress as they strive to become fully-fledged Super League players. We have a good relationship with Oldham already and we are determined to make this work well for both clubs, happy in the knowledge that our players will be looked after by Oldham in the right environment. We are well aware of the Grand Final disappointments Oldham have suffered in recent seasons and we hope this partnership will help Roughyeds to achieve their aim of returning to the Championship.'"

Coventry Bears RLFC were admitted to the league for their inaugural season in 2015 and as luck would have it, Oldham were drawn to play them in the first round of the League One Cup and in the third round of the Challenge Cup. These two cup ties were played before the League One season had started, so were Coventry's first two games as a member of the RFL. Predictably, following the previous year's Grand Final loss and with inclement weather too, the crowds at Whitebank for the two games against the Bears were 291 and 256 respectively. It was a worrying time for the club.

The squad was strengthened ahead of the season by making George Tyson – impressive whilst on season-long loan in 2014 – a contracted player, by bringing in former Salford front-row forward Adam Neal and by snapping up young outside backs Jack Holmes and Jarrod Ward. Tyson and Neal, in particular, had superb seasons and both played a huge part in the team's eventual success. Speaking in 2017, Neal said: "The promotion year was extra special for me personally because I took a year away from rugby league the year before. Returning to the game in such a successful team enabled me to start enjoying my rugby again. The lads at Oldham are a great group, the fans are special and the staff behind the scenes helped to make it such a good year. The promotion really topped it off nicely."

Oldham-born Ward had spent time in the youth systems at Salford City Reds, Bradford Bulls and Halifax but spent part of the 2014 season playing for Gloucestershire All Golds on loan from the Shay. He started the season with a bang with three tries in the two Coventry games, but his stint as a Roughyed was a short one. In June 2015, after making just 12 appearances, he announced he would be leaving to take up the offer of full-time employment in the South of France.

In the second round of the League One Cup, the new dual-registration agreement with the Giants paid immediate dividends when Jodie Broughton, drafted in on the wing, raced in for two tries as Roughyeds won 32–10 at Barrow, no mean feat. The Sheffield Eagles Challenge Cup defeat, played at Doncaster's Keepmoat Stadium,

Sheffield's home ground for the season, followed and a powerful Eagles side won 44–20, although Oldham fought back well late in the game and never gave up. Adam Clay continued his fine form from late 2014, and scored seven tries in the four cup-ties to confirm what Oldham fans already knew – that he was a winger of real ability at this level.

The Kingstone Press League One season began on Good Friday, 3 April, with the traditional Bank Holiday clash away to Rochdale Hornets. Roughyeds left Spotland triumphant after a fine 23–16 win, with Josh Crowley scoring twice. Following the semi-final loss to Crusaders at Whitebank – played on a Wednesday evening – four wins followed, against Coventry Bears – for the third time in seven weeks – London Skolars and Gloucestershire All Golds, all at Whitebank, and away to South Wales Scorpions. Another new signing, centre Tom Ashton, formerly with Sheffield Eagles, made a try-scoring debut in the Bears game, Jack Holmes scored twice against the Bears and the Scorpions, Jon Ford crossed the line four times against the Skolars and Steven Nield scored a hat-trick against the All Golds.

At this point, the team had its stickiest spell of the year, losing three of its next four matches as already mentioned, the only league losses all year. Despite the indifferent form, Adam Clay continued to run in the tries, two at Barrow, one of his former clubs, and three in a home win over Newcastle Thunder, the successor to Gateshead Thunder. But it was in the next match against Oxford at Whitebank on 14 June that the phenomenal winning run of 14 matches began. Each one is described below:

Game 1: 14 June 2015 Oldham 64 Oxford 0

It was vital the team didn't slip up for a fourth time in five games in this one, as the fans knew only too well. It was never likely to happen. The team were determined to reinforce the fact that the recent losses were just a blip and playing some excellent football, they put a gallant Oxford team to the sword, scoring 12 tries. In fact, the 64 point winning margin was the largest in Scott Naylor's two-and-a-half years at the club. Holmes continued his good recent form with a hat-trick while Clay and George Tyson scored twice and Phil Joy, Adam Files, Gareth Owen, Liam Thompson and Kenny Hughes also crossed the visitors' line. Lewis Palfrey, making his 100th career appearance, kicked eight goals.

Naylor said: "Oxford had won four of their previous six games and had a real dig. They were big, aggressive and quick. We scored some quality tries from good rugby, several out wide. It was important to win and reach a high level of performance. We achieved both."

It was a big day for yours truly also because my first book, *From Watersheddings to Whitebank – An Oldham Rugby League Memoir* had been published by London League Publications Ltd not long before and

I was kindly given permission by Chris Hamilton to sell copies to fans inside the ground that day, and, indeed, at every other home game during 2015. That was a great gesture by the chairman.

Game 2: 21 June 2015 Swinton Lions 26 Oldham 32
Swinton were unbeaten at their Sedgley Park home prior to this visit from the Roughyeds. A brilliant first-half display from the Oldham forwards, with second-row pair Danny Langtree and Josh Crowley particularly impressive, created the platform for the team for a 22–4 lead at the break. Tries from Tyson and Clay plus one each from the second-rowers and three Palfrey goals ensured Swinton would have it all to do in the second half. They came out a different team after half-time, however, and reduced the deficit to 22–20 before a second Tyson try and three more Palfrey goals took Oldham clear again. Sam Gee, deputising at full-back, had a blinder, as did Palfrey and Adam Neal.

Scott Naylor commented: "This was a great result for the club. It was a big challenge against a team unbeaten on home soil this year, but we came through with flying colours. There were times in the first half when we looked like a Championship side. We showed lots of determination and inner strength to pull away again when they got to within two points of us. If we take these qualities through to the end of the season, it will be interesting to see where we finish."

Game 3: 27 June 2015 Gloucestershire All Golds 30 Oldham 42
The club had signed young St Helens half-back David Hewitt in the lead up to this game and he crowned an impressive debut with two tries. It was also his cross-kick to the corner that enabled Clay to score the first of his two tries early in the game. Other Oldham try scorers were Phil Joy, Langtree and Holmes with another seven goals from the skipper Palfrey. Leading 36–12 soon after half-time, Oldham took their foot off the gas and allowed the home side to score three tries, two conversions and a penalty to make the arrears just six points. It was too close for comfort but a late try from Holmes settled nerves to ensure the league points would be heading Oldham's way.

"Another win, another step in the right direction," summed up the coach. "The first half was good, we were patient and we gradually got on top. Our performance seemed to drop a bit after the break and we suddenly found ourselves under pressure. But a lot of credit must go to the All Golds for that, they are a vastly improved outfit. Former Oldham player Lee Greenwood, their coach, is doing a fabulous job."

Game 4: 5 July 2015 Oldham 34 York City Knights 12
This was the archetypal game of two halves. York dominated the first and led 12–6 at the break but, buoyed by Naylor's half-time pep talk,

Roughyeds blasted the City Knights into submission when playing down the Whitebank slope in the second half. Key to the team's resurgence was Oldham's front-row, led by the irrepressible Michael Ward and backed up admirably by Joy and Neal. In a match played in constant summer rain, kicking was a successful option for both teams. But it was the home side's dominance down the middle – Ward and Joy both crashed in for tries from close range – that helped to create the platform for Crowley to score twice out wide with Holmes adding another. Palfrey kicked five goals to pass the 500 point mark for the Roughyeds.

Lewis Palfrey scoring under the posts at Whitebank in 2015.

Adam Neal in action at Whitebank.

(Both photos David Murgatroyd).

Left: Phil Joy takes on Barrow's Craig Briscoe at Craven Park in 2015.

Middle: Liam Thompson congratulated by teammates in a win away to North Wales Crusaders in 2015.

Bottom: Richard Lepori in celebratory mood in the same match.

(All photos David Murgatroyd).

Naylor was in buoyant mood after the game. He said: "York are a very good team. They were very impressive in the first half when I thought they had the edge on us. We had a good chat at half-time about what we needed to do to change things round and it seemed to work well. At the start of the second half, when they led 12–6, it was a case of both teams banging heads and waiting to see who cracked first. We had talked at half-time about the need to work harder, to be more aggressive and to be more direct. Happily York rarely got anywhere near our try line in the second half. I am seeing a different, more mature, Oldham now and we are looking better at controlling and managing certain situations. From the moment we levelled things up at 12–12 I felt we had the ascendancy. We kept it for the rest of the game and that is a good sign of mental maturity. We tend to forget that League One this season is unbelievably tough."

Game 5: 12 July 2015 Oldham 38 Rochdale Hornets 18

This was a typical derby battle, rough and tough, and it was credit to Oldham's exuberance on attack that took the game well beyond the visitors. Hornets started well, as York had a week earlier, and led 8-0 with a try and two goals from Paul Crook. Roughyeds fought back and scored tries before half-time from Clay, dual-registration man Jake Connor, and Palfrey. The first half is best remembered, however, for a brilliant try-saving cover tackle by Holmes on Hornets young half-back Danny Yates as he sprinted clear down the slope. It was a fantastic piece of defending and reading of the play from the Oldham left winger. In the second half Crowley was at his mercurial best, terrorising the Hornets rear guard time and again. Although Rochdale sneaked ahead 18–14, they had no answer to Oldham's sweeping attacks down the slope with another dual-registration man Jacob Fairbank, Gee, Owen and Crowley adding further tries. Owen's try was a gem. From a play-the-ball deep in Rochdale territory, he dummied, shimmied and sneaked through the smallest of gaps to bring the house down.

"Our performance was very similar to that against York and I am really pleased with how we played," said Naylor. "We are finishing games very well indeed. We are dominating in the last 20 minutes and that is a nice thing to have in the locker. The game was neck and neck for long spells. It was a typical derby and excellent viewing for the fans. We are immensely proud of beating Rochdale home and away because it is such a huge thing, and it means such a lot, to our fans, our chairman, sponsors and to everyone associated with the club. We are playing a good brand of rugby, working hard and doing all the right things. The challenge for us now is to keep things going in the right direction, to keep playing well and to be in a position in which we can keep ticking off games one by one and seeing where we finish up at the end of the regular season."

Game 6: 19 July 2015 London Skolars 6 Oldham 32
In a match played on an artificial pitch – a first for Roughyeds – at the New River Stadium, the team never looked in danger of losing against a big and physical Skolars outfit. A touch of class from another dual-registration man, centre Oliver Roberts, in which he slipped a peach of a pass to Holmes on the left wing enabling Jack to send Palfrey behind the posts, was the highlight of a dour first-half in which Roughyeds dominated but failed to turn their superiority into points. A typical barnstorming try from Michael Ward pushed Oldham into a 12–0 lead at half-time before the Roughyeds pulled well clear in the second half with further tries to Palfrey and Ward and two more to Steve Roper and Thompson. Lewis kicked four goals. It was good to see youngsters Tom Dempsey and Richard Joy – younger brother of Phil – given an outing in this one.

The coach's view: "It was an ugly win. To be able to win when nowhere near your best is a nice quality to have. All teams have days when they don't perform as well as they can do, but today was all about getting the job done and ticking off another win box – and for that the boys deserve a lot of credit. London Skolars is one of the toughest places to come to. You've got the early start and the long journey and that's before you even start on the mental side of things. Skolars are probably the biggest side in the division, but we matched their physicality and all their effort."

Game 7: 26 July 2015 North Wales Crusaders 6 Oldham 23
The *Oldham Chronicle's* description of this superb win for Roughyeds best sums up how good a victory this was. "A fistful of 'F' words can best describe a fabulous win in North Wales that put Oldham fans in seventh heaven (seventh consecutive win). Forceful, fantastic, fastidious and fearless are among the words you could use to describe Roughyeds performance in Wrexham. They won 23–6 to inflict Crusaders' biggest league defeat of the season and end their rivals' five-game winning run. It was Oldham's sixth win in eight games away, avenging 18–16 and 38–28 defeats by the Welshmen at Whitebank."

Crusaders were many people's pre-season favourites to gain promotion following their relegation from the Kingstone Press Championship a year earlier. However, Oldham clearly hadn't read the script as they were on fire from the kick-off, going 12–0 up with tries from Neal and Gee before the home side had touched the ball, apart from having to kick off. Neal and Phil Joy were magnificent in the opening half with Ward, Thompson and Gee particularly providing

155

wonderful back-up. A third Oldham try, from Clay, following a Palfrey kick, and a Roper drop-goal put the finishing touches to a win that really made supporters believe anything was possible in 2015.

The *Oldham Chronicle* reported: "Scott Naylor emerged from a victorious Oldham dressing room at Wrexham and said: 'That was good; that is why we do it! This has to be one of the happiest and most fulfilling moments since I've been at the club. When they beat us twice at Whitebank we were lacking a little bit mentally, but we came here this time with absolutely no fear whatsoever. Our aggression was controlled, but right on the limit. Our attitude and effort were stunning. We controlled the game in the second half. We played as we wanted to play and we thoroughly deserved the win. It was a great team performance. The lads have been unbelievably committed to the cause and they deserve all the credit. To do what they did against a quality side on their own pitch was absolutely great. I couldn't possibly be any prouder of them."

Game 8: 2 August 2015 Oldham 38 Keighley Cougars 8
Like North Wales Crusaders, the Cougars had been relegated from the Kingstone Press Championship in 2014 and were fancied to be pushing for promotion. Like Crusaders they had already beaten Oldham in 2015 – 32–24 at home in May – but there was absolutely no chance of an encore for the Yorkshire side here. This Oldham team was now made of sterner stuff than it had been three months earlier and were determined to stretch their winning run to eight games. Admittedly, Keighley were missing two key men in veteran half-back Paul Handforth and player-coach Paul March who was injured in the pre-match warm-up, but they were taken to the cleaners by an Oldham side brimming with style and confidence and looking every inch a team destined to be champions.

Again the pack were immense, Joy, Neal, Ward, Langtree, Crowley, Gee and Thompson were unstoppable. The Roughyeds led 18–4 at half-time, playing up the slope, with tries from Gee, the returned Richard Lepori and Holmes and followed that with another three – by Palfrey, Langtree and Thompson – after the break.

Scott Naylor's verdict: "We have got to keep on winning, but it's in our own hands now. We are training well, playing well and having some luck in keeping players healthy."

Game 9: 9 August 2015 Hemel Stags 6 Oldham 70
Since 2009 the club points in a match record had been shared between Andy Ballard and Chris Baines. On a summer's day in leafy Hertfordshire, however, Lewis Palfrey scored three tries and kicked 11 goals for a grand total of 34 points, to join the two current incumbents

156

at the top of the hit parade. With Oldham in the kind of form they were in, there was little chance of Hemel putting a stop to their relentless march. Lewis was full of praise for his team-mates when I mentioned the record to him. "Of course, it was a proud day for me to become joint record holder but without the quality and quantity of tries the team scored that day I would never have been in a position to match it. I was a bit disappointed in a way though because I missed a really easy kick too, which had it gone over would have meant I overtook the other two lads!"

Langtree and Ward scored two more tries each and Owen, Hewitt, Tyson, Thompson and Gee also crossed the Hemel line as Oldham managed the highest points total since Naylor took over. It was good to see Tom Ashton back after four months out with a major knee injury.

Scott Naylor commented: "After a slow start, we had spells where we were very good. The second half was better than the first, but it's another one ticked off."

Game 10 16 August 2015 Newcastle Thunder 16 Oldham 28

This was undoubtedly one of the toughest assignments in the 14 match run against a Thunder side, under the leadership of Papua New Guinean Stanley Gene, and playing on an artificial pitch at Kingston Park, the home of Newcastle Falcons Rugby Union Club. The result was in the balance until the last few minutes with Oldham tentatively hanging on to a two-point lead. But the winning mentality and mental toughness that a long run like this generates helped Roughyeds cross the line with two late tries by Jon Ford, his second of the match, and Ashton. Earlier Newcastle had led for much of the first hour with centre Macauley Hallett, on loan from Hull Kingston Rovers and later to star for Swinton Lions, Batley Bulldogs and Dewsbury Rams, one of their try scorers. He and Oldham's Sam Gee were dismissed for fighting late on, but the Roughyeds fans were singing once more as the final hooter sounded.

Chris Hamilton praised the team's inspirational commitment and character in what he described as the "toughest game we have had for a long time." He said: "We could easily have lost. Thunder were strong, physical and in our faces and for starters we had to match that. We wore them down and on the back of that we scored some cracking tries, demonstrating that we are much better at game management than in previous seasons."

Game 11 23 August 2015 Oldham 28 Barrow Raiders 12

If the previous match on Tyneside had been tough, then this match was equally so. Barrow came determined to end Oldham's long winning run and deservedly went 12–0 up inside 20 minutes, playing up the slope. It was not the first quarter the fans had expected. At this point, a freak thunderstorm erupted around Whitebank – not for the first time on match day in 2015 – and from then on the classy rugby the Raiders had been playing was deemed impossible by the conditions. Oldham needed to score at least once before half-time and they did so, Ashton scoring out wide on the left, to leave the half-time score 12–4.

What a turn around after the break! With Michael Ward playing like a man possessed, and scoring two powerful tries, the Roughyeds edged their way back into it. They still trailed with just 11 minutes remaining when teenager Hewitt demonstrated his class with a stunning solo try close to the posts when he took the Raiders defence on when they were expecting a short kick near the line. Barrow wilted after that and Ward's second try and another to Liam Thompson saw Oldham home.

Hewitt outlined: "Our pack came out for the second half with all guns blazing and Barrow's forwards started to tire after taking a pounding for 20 minutes. On defence they began to leave a bit of space so when I saw some I went for it."

The squad were given a few days off after this record equalling win – Mike Ford's side in 2001 had also won 11 matches on the bounce – and Scott Naylor said: "Just getting away from me for a week will do them a world of good. We have not had a break since late May and with each successive win the pressure builds on the lads because everybody raises their game to try to knock us off our pedestal. That is a long time between breaks and for a few days at least they need to get right away from rugby and get away from me. I have told them they will not be hearing my voice for a bit because I will make a point of not contacting them. I cannot speak too highly about these guys. They have been absolutely outstanding as a group, every one of them without exception. Their attitudes, work ethics, pride in performances and pride in the badges on their jerseys is reflected in the way they play and how they constantly challenge themselves as individuals and as a team. They deserve the highest praise and credit from everyone associated with the Oldham club."

Game 12: 6 September 2015 Oldham 28 Swinton Lions 16
John Duffy's Swinton team arrived at Whitebank on the back of a fantastic winning run of their own, nine straight games, only two less than Oldham's 11. Duffy, and his Oldham counterpart Naylor, were two excellent coaches adept at squeezing the very best out of their respective teams, qualities that would stand both in good stead in the Kingstone Press Championship a year later. In late 2015, however, they met at a jumping Whitebank – the crowd of 1,004 was the best at the venue for more than two years – in a match in which something had to give. Would the home side's long run end at 11 games or could they stretch it further, thus setting a club record of 12?

It looked good early on because the Roughyeds went 10–0 up but soon after half-time, the Lions, playing down the slope, had moved smoothly into the lead and looked capable of extending it further. But no-one in the ground was betting against Naylor's battlers turning it around. With the forwards, particularly Joy, Owen, Ward, Langtree and Thompson playing out of their skin, the halves Palfrey and Roper were able to shade their battle for midfield dominance with the Swinton pair, Ben White and the talented Chris Atkin. Sure enough, two tries from the mercurial Langtree, an outstanding forward at this level, and another by Clay plus three Palfrey goals wrapped up the match in spectacular fashion in the last quarter. The result meant that barring a mathematical miracle, Oldham would finish top and would meet the team finishing in second place, probably Keighley Cougars, in the Promotion Final.

Scott Naylor said: "Swinton are as good as we are. It would not have taken much for our league positions to be reversed. Today was immense for us as a club and as a team, and to be honest I was worried before the game because I know how good they are. All I can say now is that the 17 who played deserve a giant-sized pat on the back for their incredible effort and the way they went about the job.

The way we fought back and then finished them off ruthlessly was similar to what we have done a few times this season and I cannot speak too highly of them for doing that. To have won 18 games out of 21 and still not be mathematically sure of finishing top shows how tough and competitive this league has been this year."

Game 13: 12 September 2015 Oxford 12 Oldham 76
It was fitting that the league programme should end against the team that faced the Roughyeds in the first game of their special winning run back in mid-June. On a day when the team knew that victory would clinch the League Leaders Shield, it never seemed likely that the home side would be capable of standing in Oldham's way. Despite missing several key players, the Roughyeds cantered to victory, scoring 13 tries and, in the absence of skipper Palfrey, a super 12 goals from 13 shots by Roper.

It was a day of great celebration for the Roughyeds' die-hard fans, many of whom travelled to the 'city of dreaming spires' from Oldham but others, no longer resident in the town, from different parts of the south of England. We all rejoiced together as Palfrey, despite being rested for the game, was presented with the Shield after the match by RFL President Doctor Paul Morgan. "I was given a bit of stick by the rest of the lads for going up to collect the trophy even though I hadn't played in the match," smiled Lewis. "But it was for a season's work, not just one day's. The coach ride home was a beauty. We had pizza and plenty of beer and a good old sing-song. It was a great day."

There was lots of back-slapping and jubilation on the pitch and in front of Iffley Road's Oxford University Rugby Union clubhouse, which looked like an old cricket pavilion, after the game as fans, players and coaching staff all mingled and enjoyed photographs aplenty. Only a short distance from the ground was the track that Roger Bannister ran the first sub-four-minute mile in 1954, but I doubt the celebrations back then were any greater. It was the club's first silverware, apart from the Law Cup, since it was formed and it meant so much to everyone. Nobody was under any illusions, however, that the big one, against Keighley Cougars, was still eight days away.

A triumphant Scott Naylor said: "These lads have put in a phenomenal effort since the second week in November when they started pre-season training. I have not had a moment's stress or trauma with them, either individually or as a group. They are a dream to work with. In all my playing and coaching career I have never known as much harmony as there is here. We are all friends. The lads battle for each other as genuine mates and that team spirit has been a massive factor in our performances and our results. We have won 19 out of 22 and there was only 40 minutes in the whole season when I felt we didn't have a go. We have now won 13 on the run to finish top, so these lads have plenty to celebrate. They should stand proud. To finish top of the league, no matter at what level, is a huge achievement down entirely to their attitude, ability, professionalism and commitment."

Game 14: 20 September 2015 Oldham 31 Keighley Cougars 20
So at last, after all the Grand Final disappointments, the team finally cracked it. On a tense, highly-charged and ultimately fantastic day at Whitebank, promotion was clinched to the sheer joy and relief of everybody connected to the club. Some of the scenes and emotions that day will live me forever:
The sight of hordes of Cougars fans, the most ever brought to the ground by a visiting team, piling in through the turnstiles before kick-off;
The eerie silence among Oldham fans, petrified that the big match curse would strike again, when a mistake by the usually imperious Adam Clay gifted the visitors a soft try from a kick in the first half;
The joy when first Adam Neal and then Danny Langtree scored tries in quick succession before half-time;
The sight of Lizzie Jones, widow of the late Danny Jones, the former Keighley star who died four months earlier playing the game he loved, holding her two babies and cheering the Cougars on, only three weeks

after her brilliant and inspiring rendition of *Abide with Me* at the Challenge Cup Final;

The exhilaration as George Tyson crashed over to score and then Lewis Palfrey dropped a goal to give Oldham a 23–10 lead midway through the second half;

The frustration as future Oldham dual-registration player Tyler Dickinson created a try from nothing for the excellent Paul Handforth to keep Cougars in the game;

The sight of Oldham's fans, all totally immersed yet horribly powerless, willing the team to succeed and urging the players on by shouting and singing in a way they would never contemplate doing anywhere else;

The unbridled joy among those same fans when Clay made up for his earlier error with what proved to be the match-clinching try after a wide pass from Gareth Owen was knocked towards his own line by a desperate defender;

The heap of Oldham bodies diving on top of Clay after the try, sheer jubilation and unbelievable relief that the job was almost done;

The wonderful feeling of ecstasy when the hooter sounded and we knew the job was definitely done;

The pride and happiness as Lewis Palfrey was presented with the Kingstone Press League One Championship trophy by RFL chairman Brian Barwick, and the champagne corks popped as he did so;

and the amazing sight of vice-captain Sammy Gee leading the victory celebrations on the pitch, despite having been overlooked by coach Naylor for the big game.

Scott Naylor was happy to take a back seat after the game and let others do the talking. Chris Hamilton told the *Oldham Chronicle:* "The win at Swinton in June is when we turned the corner. The lads came of age that day and since then they have been absolutely outstanding. This was a typical Oldham performance against a very good Keighley team. We have done that quite a few times this season. We haven't panicked if the opposition had the ball. It has been about game management and being in control. For once, everything has fallen into place. I think Scott and Oldham are a good fit. He is a good coach and he is in a good club. He has not changed the culture of the club because we had a good culture before, but he has done in terms of the quality we have been able to bring in, which includes people who thoroughly respect him. I am so happy we have done it. We are going to enjoy this and nobody can argue that we don't deserve to go up. I was confident before the game, without being over confident. The only time Keighley threatened us was when they got offloads away, but we knew our fitness and everything else would count and it did."

Speaking in 2017, captain Palfrey said: "We were so very confident in 2015 as a team. Although that is exactly what we were – a team – I would like to pick out a few players who were absolutely fantastic for us. Firstly Danny Langtree, what an unbelievable forward he is. He is massively under-rated in my opinion and could have played in Super League if things had gone his way in his younger days at St Helens. I believe he is now one of the best back-row forwards in the Championship. Secondly Richard Lepori, best known for running with the ball from the back and making breaks. But what the fans don't know about 'Lippy' is that he is a wonderful organiser when playing full-back. He reads the game so well and never stops barking out orders to his team-mates, where to stand, what to watch for, to push over to the right or the left etc. He is like a little general. He has a massive impact on the team. And George Tyson, what a competitor this guy is. In 2015, I felt bullet-proof playing stand-off on the right side with George, at centre, and Danny in the second row outside me. It really was a fantastic year. And finally my vice-captain Sammy Gee. I felt so bad for Sammy when he was left out of the team for the Promotion Final. He had been my number two, and been a very good one too, since we came to the club in 2013."

Sammy told me recently about his emotions on Final weekend. "I will never forget the day before the big game when 'Nobby' (Naylor) named his team and I was not in it. I was heartbroken, but our goal was to get promotion and it was undoubtedly a team effort throughout the year." I asked Sammy about the victory celebration on the pitch and how he came to lead it. "Oh, the heartache had gone by then," he smiled. "The lads on the day did it, I was immensely proud of them and of what we had achieved all year. And besides, no-one sings our winning song as well as I do!"

Gee continued: "Being vice-captain of the team since the start in 2013 is a huge honour. I love being at Oldham and have done since I first signed. 'Palf' [Palfrey] was a great captain and is a great guy. Being his, and the team's, vice-captain is something I am absolutely thrilled about, and I have loved every minute."

Gareth Owen had a terrific year, making 25 appearances and became a key man around the rucks. He said: "2015 was the perfect year. After the major disappointment of losing in golden point time in 2014 and the losses in the previous finals, that season was massive for the club. They had been so close to promotion so many times and it was amazing to be a part of the side that finally got over the line. It was also huge for me personally, my first full year at Oldham. We got on a roll in the second half of the season and winning became a habit. I am sure it was great for the fans to see. The final itself was a wonderful day for everyone involved. I would like to applaud the fans because they really helped to push us over the line that day. A fair amount of beer got drank that night."

With the League One League Leaders Trophy at Oxford in 2015.

Sam Gee leading the 2015 Promotion Final victory celebrations,
despite not being selected for the big game.

A lap of honour for the victorious squad.

(All photos by David Murgatroyd).

Prop Adam Neal, in his first year at the club and a try-scorer in the final, commented: "The fact that the game was played at Whitebank was a big help to us. That was our reward for finishing top of the league, of course. It was always a great place to play, very unforgiving to visiting teams. It was my first go at promotion with Oldham but for the group it was a long time coming. This only made the day all the more special for everyone involved."

Full-back Richard Lepori had rejoined the club mid-season, but became crucial to the team in the run-in. "It was third time lucky for the lads and the coaches since Scott and 'Spanner' took over at the beginning of 2013. I am proud of what was achieved, the 14 match winning run to end the year was tremendous. Scott and 'Spanner' were good to work for. In my opinion coaching is getting people to buy into what you are trying to do. I worked with them prior to joining Oldham and they know how to get the best out of me. I have a strong relationship with them both as people as well as coaches. I owe a lot to them for giving me an opportunity in 2013 when I was leaving the Castleford under–20s side."

The final word to 'Spanner' himself: "It was important that we improved as a team year on year so to win promotion in 2015 was crucial for us. Scott is a very knowledgeable person and has a vast experience of not only the game but how things work within the game. He has his ways of delivering his philosophy but always let me put my points across and he always welcomed my side of a discussion whether it was selection or potential signings or moving players to different positions to get more out of them. I have a lot of respect for him."

13. Challenge Cup magic

Saturday 16 April 2016 is a day that will never be forgotten by everybody with the Oldham club at heart. This was the day that the club's introduction to the Kingstone Press Championship was put on hold while the fifth round of the game's most prestigious competition, the Challenge Cup, took place. Having seen off Cumbrian amateurs Kells 40–6 in the fourth round, the Roughyeds had been drawn away to Hull Kingston Rovers in the next round, the fourth time in six years they were facing a Super League club.

As has been covered previously, the first three of these cup ties, against Hull FC in 2011, St Helens in 2012 and Bradford Bulls in 2014 had ended in heavy defeat. The match at Craven Park in 2016, however, had an entirely different outcome. In one of the biggest cup shocks of all time, the part-time Roughyeds entered the passionate and partisan surroundings of the Robins' home in East Hull and blew their full-time opponents away with a fantastic display that had even Rovers fans applauding.

Graham Jowett, the Hull KR representative in the *Songs of Praise* Wembley choir that year, was at the game. He remembers the match: "I went to the game full of confidence that Rovers would win and progress to the sixth round. However, on the day Oldham were stronger and faster in every position. Rovers had no answer at all. The speed and sheer commitment showed by Oldham amazed me. It looked like they were the Super League team, not us. I did not hear one Rovers fan saying that Oldham did not deserve to win, they were undoubtedly the better team and wanted to win more it seemed. Although I am a huge Rovers fan, I came away in total admiration for Oldham."

On a personal level, I was distraught at having to miss this most fantastic of Oldham Rugby occasions due to work commitments and, in fact, I spent the afternoon watching Bangor and Aberystwyth Universities playing our great game on a small rugby union club pitch in Anglesey. Suffice to say, however, my mind was definitely with the boys on Humberside. I mentioned in *From Watersheddings to Whitebank – an Oldham Rugby League Memoir* how I missed the two biggest games in the modern history of the old club, the tour match against Australia in 1986 and the shock Challenge Cup defeat of Wigan in 1987 and here lightning had struck for a third time. You can imagine my utter amazement and joy when I arrived home and saw the result.

Skipper Lewis Palfrey praised Scott Naylor for a tremendous pre-match speech: "Rovers were in a bad run of form in Super League at the time and Scott told us that losing can become a habit, one that is not always easy to break. He said that if we were able to start the game well and put them under a little bit of pressure early on, they would inevitably begin to feel the tension, particularly if their fans started getting on their backs too. I was lucky enough to win the coin toss and chose to play with a strong wind, blowing off the North Sea, behind us in the first half. We got on top almost immediately and eventually scored four cracking tries before half-time. That first half showing increased our confidence and set us up well for the second period."

Irish international Will Hope, with three appearances in the 2015 European Championship behind him, scored the first try. Having played in Naylor's first game in charge, away to North Wales Crusaders in 2013, on dual-registration from Salford and then again in the run-in to the League One title in 2015, the back-row forward was now a contracted Oldham player. Bursting strongly onto a short pass from Gareth Owen close to the line, he crossed without a finger laid on him. The Rovers defence was all at sea and it was a sign of things to come.

Soon after, a precise grubber kick to the line by Steve Roper was pounced on ahead of several defenders by Richard Lepori to extend the Roughyeds' lead. More was to come from the buoyant visitors, however, clearly warming to the task. Roper, enjoying his best 40 minutes in an Oldham jersey, skipped past a posse of would-be tacklers to score by the posts after taking a long Kenny Hughes pass and then, almost on the half-time hooter, great work by Danny Langtree out wide created room on the flank for Adam Clay. The prolific wingman needed no second invitation to dive over in the corner. Roughyeds fans must have been rubbing their eyes in disbelief because rarely had their team taken the game to supposedly superior opposition with such aplomb.

In the second half, the home side rallied briefly but a try from industrious second-row man Gary Middlehurst, a splendid acquisition early in the campaign, and a second to Lepori late on – from an Owen kick – sealed the 36–22 win in style. The celebrations that followed 'Lippy's' clincher became one of the season's iconic rugby league images as players danced in delight behind the try-line and in front of the travelling fans. It was rare for a team from outside the top flight to beat a Super League team at any time, but for an outfit who were in League One only a year earlier and who were still attempting to find their feet in the Championship to do it, in the Challenge Cup, against the previous year's runners-up and in their opponents' back yard was nothing short of remarkable.

Lepori said in 2017: "Nobody gave us a chance before the game so to go there and win was special. That, coupled with my two tries, undoubtedly make it the biggest and best win of my career to date."

Gareth Owen, creator of two tries, recalled: "The feeling of winning that game cannot be described. We were a bunch of lads, part-time professionals, who went there and put in the performance of our lives.

The win against Hull Kingston Rovers

Will Hope scoring Oldham's first try.

Steve Roper celebrating.

(Both photos David Murgatroyd).

We had nothing to lose because we were massive underdogs and that helped us, I believe, to beat a team that realistically we had no chance of beating."

Sam Gee described the win as "amazing, a day I will never forget." He said: "I still look back on it a year later and smile. I have a lot of friends who are not rugby fans but I was bombarded by calls and texts from them. It was one of the best feelings I have ever experienced as a rugby league player." Michael Ward described the win simply as "a great feeling and a great memory."

The following appeared in the *Guardian:* "As the final hooter sounded and the winners celebrated with the small pocket of travelling fans, there was a firm reminder in that moment of why the Challenge Cup still matters. Genuine upsets have been few and far between in recent years, but when Oldham's players return to their day jobs, they will be celebrated as heroes. Last year's beaten finalists Hull Kingston Rovers had crashed out at the first hurdle to part-time opposition, but that should not overshadow a wonderful afternoon for the visitors – a side who have struggled to get to grips with life in the Championship, let alone competing against Super League sides. But here, the Roughyeds, who were 40-point underdogs with some bookmakers, had too much class for a Rovers side who looked worryingly short of ideas and, perhaps even more worryingly, passion. The six tries Oldham scored were of supreme quality as they moved into the last 16 of the competition, where they could meet one of Super League's top sides.

'For me, as a coach, that is as good as it gets,' said Oldham's Scott Naylor, a winner of the Cup as a player with Bradford. 'We are not a wealthy club and days like these and getting into the next round helps the club massively in a financial sense.'"

The cup excitement was far from over following the triumph on Humberside however, as the draw for the sixth round paired Roughyeds with one of the best teams in the land, Warrington Wolves. Following the club's promotion to the Kingstone Press Championship, it was announced before the new season started that 'home' games would have to be staged away from Whitebank, because the tiny ground failed to match minimum ground requirements for the second tier as stipulated by the RFL.

Consequently, all 2016 home games were played at Bower Fold, a smart compact stadium and the home of National League North football club Stalybridge Celtic. It was also the venue that Roughyeds took on St Helens in the Challenge Cup in 2002.

So it was at Bower Fold that the Wolves tie took place on 7 May 2016. Michael Ward and Sam Gee take up the story of another great day in the club's history, although the result was not the reason why. 'Wardy' explains: "Warrington are a fabulous team with international

168

players galore and reached the Challenge Cup Final at Wembley in 2016. So it was a huge thrill to face them. Not only that, but for the first 20 minutes we definitely matched them, there was nothing in it at all after the first quarter of the tie. I was delighted to score a try in that period which put us in front. That was a great feeling too."

Sammy commented: "It was fantastic pitting our wits against one of the best teams in rugby league. We matched them early on but they hit top form in the second half and got away from us. They are a great side. Their coach Tony Smith came into our dressing room after the game and heaped praise on us. He understood how tough it is for part-timers to take on full-time athletes like them. It was a nice gesture and he bought us a few crates of beer too, which we appreciated."

Smith was quoted after the game as follows: "Oldham really challenged us in that first half and it took us a while to click into gear, which was down to them bullying us around. I was pleased that they got another try at the end – a last minute effort by Gareth Owen - as it was a harsh scoreline for the effort they put in during the first half."

Scott Naylor said: "Tony [Smith] came into the dressing room and gave them compliments on some of the structures that they had and a lot of the things that they do. He said he didn't want them to lose confidence in the Championship and to take today's defeat in the right way. Just for him to come into the changing rooms was amazing because when he left and closed the door, you could see from the look on some of my lads' faces that they were in awe."

So Oldham's 2016 cup adventure was over. The team had made the wider rugby league world sit up and take notice with the win away to Hull KR. It was labelled by some sections of the media as one of the biggest cup shocks of all time which is some accolade. Despite everything else that took place in 2016 – and there were many ups and downs in the Championship campaign – it is the Rovers win that the year will best be remembered for. It was a magnificent day in the 20 year history of the club.

Prior to the beginning of the Kingstone Press Championship season against London Broncos at Bower Fold on 7 February 2016, the club had moved to top up its coaching staff with the appointment of another man with strong Salford connections, Peter Carey, to work alongside Scott Naylor and Lee Spencer. 'Spanner' explains the thinking: "As a coaching team we were continually looking to improve. We did so in League One but in moving up to the Championship we had to take things to another level. Coaching is about getting the team to perform, but as part of that process individual player development is crucial. Pete had a wealth of coaching experience that was only going to benefit us. I pushed for his appointment because I have a lot of respect for him, just as I do for Scott."

Pre-season photo-shoot at Spindles Shopping Centre in Oldham in 2016.

Left: Richard Lepori scoring against Batley Bulldogs at Bower Fold in 2016.

Right: Jamel Chisholm showing the Batley Bulldogs defence a clean pair of heels at Bower Fold in 2016.

(All photos David Murgatroyd).

Gary Middlehurst prepares to take on Sheffield Eagles centre
George Tyson at Bower Fold in 2016.

Michael Ward celebrates scoring against Warrington Wolves in the
Challenge Cup. (Both photos David Murgatroyd).

Nobody was under any illusions about how tough the Championship was or how big the gulf is between the third and second tiers of the game. The task was made even harder when two of the stars of 2015, Adam Neal and George Tyson, were enticed away from the club by the lure of full-time professionalism by Championship rivals Sheffield Eagles. Eagles had finished 2015 in third place after the regular 23 match campaign, behind Leigh Centurions and Bradford Bulls. Their coach Mark Aston had earmarked the two Roughyeds as men that could help his side to build further on the great progress they were making as a team and as a club. Oldham wanted Neal and Tyson to stay, but knew they couldn't, or wouldn't, stand in their way when the opportunity to go full-time presented itself to them.

To partly compensate, the club swooped to sign former Salford City Reds, Barrow Raiders and Halifax forward Jack Spencer – son of assistant coach Lee Spencer – and former Leigh Centurions and Barrow Raiders pack man Craig Briscoe, a man who had impressed both Naylor and the Oldham players when he opposed them for Barrow in 2015. Agonisingly, for both club and player, Briscoe badly injured a knee in a pre-season friendly at Barrow and although he returned midway through the season, he suffered a major recurrence against Workington Town late in the year, which sidelined him for the whole of 2017 also.

Craig tells the tale of his wasted two years: "I had only been on the field at Craven Park a few minutes. I was stood up in a tackle and an opponent came in to chop my legs. My foot stayed where it was and my knee went. An MRI scan confirmed I had ruptured an anterior cruciate ligament. A consultant, however, decided I had stretched it, not ruptured it, so after two months of rehabilitation I was back playing and it felt fine. I played six games with no problem and in the next, against Workington, I came on as a substitute after 30 minutes with the instruction to work very hard in the run-up to half-time.

I took the ball in from first man at a play-the-ball and stepped away from an opponent. As I did so someone else hit me and the pressure of the tackle caused it to 'pop' again. The pain was unreal. I would like to say that the club have always been fully supportive of me throughout the two years even though I haven't been able to play. Even after the operation, which I eventually had, they kept me fully involved which I really appreciated. I really hope I will be able to play again soon and repay them the favour."

Only one of the first five league games was won – a cracking 38–16 win over Dewsbury Rams – but defeats to full-time outfits London Broncos and Leigh Centurions plus the part-timers of Featherstone Rovers and Workington Town kept Oldham in the lower reaches of the division. The game at Derwent Park marked the end of Josh Crowley's remarkable run of 81 straight appearances since he made his debut for the club in Scott Naylor's first game in charge in 2013. Sadly, Josh never played for the club again and eventually joined neighbours Rochdale Hornets several weeks later. The blow of losing Crowley, however, was tempered by the signing of Gary Middlehurst from North Wales Crusaders, a man who played well above his weight and who went on to enjoy a superb season.

Following two disappointing Easter defeats – to Halifax at Bower Fold and Swinton Lions at Heywood Road, the home of Sale Rugby Union Club – the team then enjoyed its best spell of the season, winning four of the next five matches, including the Hull KR cup tie. Established Championship outfits Batley Bulldogs, Sheffield Eagles and Featherstone Rovers all had their colours lowered at what was rapidly becoming fortress Bower Fold in 2016. Former Leeds Rhinos speedster Jamel Chisholm, who once won a sprint to determine rugby league's fastest man, and was snapped up by Oldham after impressing against them for London Skolars a year earlier, scored twice against the Bulldogs and finished the season as the club's leading try-scorer with ten in all competitions. A Palfrey drop-goal proved crucial in a heart-stopping 21–20 thriller against the Eagles, a match in which Tyson and Neal opposed the Roughyeds for the first time since their switch to South Yorkshire.

George remembers the match well: "I had been looking forward to this game since signing for Sheffield. I like to think I am competitive on the pitch and was determined that my old mates, wearing Oldham shirts, would not get the better of me. I was keen to prove a point to them," he smiled. "We had celebrated a lot together in 2015, in what was such a good year for the club. When you go through something like that together, you make mates for life. I had a beer with them all after the game, but during the 80 minutes there was no love lost."

Dual-registration youngster Liam Johnson, an England Youth international in 2013, enjoyed a brilliant performance against Featherstone, culminating in a great match-winning try near the end. As the days ticked away towards the Warrington cup-tie, Roughyeds were looking good.

As often happens, however, the massive effort required against a Super League heavyweight – in Oldham's case two of them in this amazing Challenge Cup campaign – took its toll when the bread and butter of the league kicked in again and results took a nosedive following the Wolves game. A long-range special try by Danny Grimshaw – now a Roughyeds star after appearing against them so often in the past – against Leigh Centurions at Bower Fold was a rare highlight in this period as the cup exertions clearly began to have an impact on the team. The Warrington game meant that a scheduled home match against Bradford Bulls had to be rearranged for a midweek evening meaning that Oldham had to face Dewsbury Rams away, Bulls at home and London Broncos away in the space of eight excruciatingly demanding days in mid-June. Something had to give and inevitably it was the performance levels of the team. The Broncos defeat was the seventh straight league reverse since the Wolves game.

Earlier in this run of losses came undoubtedly the lowest point of the club's season. In 2015, Swinton Lions had stolen the second promotion place – behind Oldham – from Keighley Cougars in dramatic fashion. Despite finishing three points behind the Cougars in the final league table, they beat the Yorkshire side 29–28 in the Grand Final after having snatched a golden-point 18–17 victory over York City Knights in the semi-final.

The Roughyeds had, of course, already been promoted after winning the Promotion Final. So the Lions' elevation to the Kingstone Press Championship meant a series of local derbies between them and the Roughyeds in 2016. Swinton had won the first one at home on Easter Monday and the second was earmarked for Bloomfield Road in Blackpool as part of the RFL's Summer Bash extravaganza. The match turned out to be one of the most remarkable and controversial imaginable.

Roughyeds, playing some exciting attacking football, raced into a 20–0 half-time lead with tries from Kenny Hughes, Danny Langtree and Adam Files and four goals from the seemingly imperious boot of Palfrey. At the break, fans were not exactly celebrating victory, but they were certainly in the best of moods and already looking forward to spending the remainder of the Bank Holiday weekend on the Golden Mile, happy in the knowledge that two more crucial league points were in the Roughyeds' locker.

Unfortunately, things turned very sour in the second half. A resurgent Swinton hit back strongly and began to gnaw away at Oldham's lead with converted tries by Macauley Hallett, Chris Atkin and Rob Lever to reduce the arrears to just two points. To the disbelief of Oldham fans, they took the lead 24–20 with a fortuitous try by pint-sized half-back Matty Beharrell when he chased his own kick close to the line. Did Oldham have anything left to come back from here? Not for the first time, and by no means the last, a rampant surge towards the opposition line by Michael Ward led to a try in the corner from Adam Clay to tie the scores at 24–24. Cue the major controversy.

The crucial conversion from Palfrey, which would have pushed the Roughyeds back in front, appeared to go over to the naked eye and Oldham fans in line with the flight of the ball roared their approval in unison as they awaited the touch judges' flags to go up. Lewis began to turn back towards his teammates content that he had landed a difficult and vital kick at such a crucial stage of the game. Then to

Oldham's chagrin, and in what would have made a good 'What happened next' on the BBC Television's *A Question of Sport*, the two touch-judges waved the kick away, suggesting it had drifted wide of the left-hand upright. Nobody could believe it. Fans whistled in outrage, Palfrey looked perplexed and appeared to appeal to the referee that it had, in fact, gone over. But the controversial 'no goal' decision stood. To add insult to injury, Beharrell, who had a fabulous second half for the Lions, then slotted home a winning drop-goal to give Swinton both points in an unbelievable end to the game.

Palfrey outlined: "I am convinced to this day that the kick went over. To be honest, at the time I didn't even think it was close. As an experienced goalkicker, I usually have a very good idea if a kick is good or not as soon as it leaves my boot. I was never in any doubt about this one. I think the issue was that the ball went above the height of the temporary goal posts which may have caused a problem for the touch-judges. But it was such an important kick, so frustrating.

The Summer Bash defeat hit us very hard in 2016. The change in mood in our dressing room from half-time to after the game was unbelievable. We were all cock-a-hoop at half-time but you could have heard a pin drop at full-time. It was a massive high to a massive low and it took us some time afterwards to recover mentally."

Following the losing run, Naylor's boys got their act together again from late June into July with three important victories, against relegation rivals Whitehaven at Bower Fold 26–18, away to Sheffield Eagles 24–16 on a Friday evening and in a thriller against Swinton at home 26–24. Young Castleford Tigers centre Kieran Gill had joined the club on loan and his tries proved to be invaluable in the race to preserve Championship status. Gill scored a try in each of the three victories mentioned while two powerful tries from 'Wardy' were enough to tame the Lions this time, a win that everybody at the club particularly enjoyed after the events in Blackpool six weeks earlier.

With two games left before the Championship Shield began – a series of seven matches against the other teams in the bottom eight after 23 games – Roughyeds were looking good to stay up, with Cumbrian duo Whitehaven and Workington Town occupying the bottom two spots. A defeat at Odsal in the penultimate league match kept the pressure on, but with a home game to come against a Workington side in deep trouble, fans were still confident that the Roughyeds would be fine. Although Town were struggling, they had in their ranks one of the outstanding players in the Championship in former NRL and Super League star Jarrod Sammut. The little Australian could be brilliant on his day, and as we feared, he proved too hot to handle at Bower Fold inspiring his troops to a shock 32–30 victory.

Danny Grimshaw runs clear to score against Leigh Centurions
at Bower Fold in 2016.

Lewis Palfrey kicking for goal watched by referee Chris Campbell,
the former Oldham player, at Bower Fold in 2016.
(Both photos David Murgatroyd).

Left: Adam Clay races away to score against Swinton Lions in 2016 with Roary the Roughyed cheering him on.

(Photo David Murgatroyd)

Right: A strong defensive line! Oldham prepare to defend against Batley Bulldogs at Mount Pleasant in 2016.
(Photo Dave Naylor)

Oldham had started the day five points clear of Town and would have stretched it to an unassailable seven with victory. However, the visitors' win meant the gap was cut to just three ahead of the Shield. It was a huge setback and kept everybody at the club looking over their shoulders.

The complexities of the system for allocating fixtures in the Shield meant that Workington were asked to return to Bower Fold in the first game, just two weeks after their win there. It was clearly a crucial game, could Sammut weave his magic once more, or would Oldham have learnt their lessons? As it was, the Roughyeds never looked like losing second time around and, with new full-back Scott Turner, signed before the deadline from North Wales Crusaders, producing a brilliant two-try debut, they won 30–16. Thus followed a surprisingly comfortable win at a below par Swinton Lions by 30–8, a match in which David Hewitt, back at the club after a brief spell at Sheffield Eagles, scored twice. A long-range interception try from Adam Clay had fans dancing in delight in this one. Things looked good with five games left.

Three heavy defeats followed however – a depressing 82–0 thrashing away to Bradford Bulls, a 54–24 home loss to an on-fire Sheffield Eagles on Wembley weekend and a 32–18 reverse at Halifax – ensuring that nobody at the club could relax just yet. Whitehaven, in particular, were battling hard and produced a stunning, and totally unexpected, 56–12 win at Dewsbury to really throw down the gauntlet to Oldham in the race to stay up. They had sacked their coach, former Oldham star James Coyle, and put four senior players, including another former Roughyed David Allen, in charge. They still had to visit Bower Fold and it appeared that all could well rest on that game on 11 September. So it turned out. Oldham knew that victory would ensure survival with a game to spare. The Cumbrians knew that if they won, everything would go down to the last game of the season when they were at home to Swinton Lions and Oldham had to visit Dewsbury Rams. In that scenario, nobody would have backed against Whitehaven completing a great escape by beating Swinton. So Oldham knew victory was imperative at Bower Fold.

On a tension packed afternoon, tries from Phil Joy, Liam Thompson and Adam Clay along with four Palfrey goals saw Roughyeds sneak home 20–18 despite a valiant Cumbrian fightback, led by the veteran Allen, in the second half. The last 10 minutes were agony for fans with the visitors only one score from snatching it, but showing commendable maturity Oldham kept possession in the Whitehaven quarter to deny them the field position from which they could have been dangerous.

There were wonderful scenes of relief and joy on the final hooter which confirmed Oldham's survival and, sadly for the Cumbrians, consigned them to the drop. The objective from day one had been to stay in this cut-throat competition and it had been achieved with one game left. It was a wonderful afternoon for everybody at the club.

Club chairman Chris Hamilton said it was a "massive achievement" in regard to the future development of the club. He told the *Oldham Chronicle:* "Coaches, players, staff, volunteers and fans have all played their part across a long season to ensure our survival in this division. The hard work has never stopped. Regular fans know what a massive achievement it is. It ranks favourably with winning promotion, perhaps some people will view it as even bigger. For a variety of reasons we have been on a rollercoaster over the last few weeks, but we have achieved what we set out to achieve and we have done it with a game to spare. I want to publicly thank everyone who has joined us on the ride, fans for their loyal support, players, coaches and everyone behind the scenes. This club means a lot to a lot of people and it is great to follow up our 2015 promotion by holding fast in the Championship. It also means we can press on with our squad building programme for 2017 knowing exactly where our immediate future lies."

Gareth Owen described staying up as a "fantastic achievement". He said: "From day one of pre-season training we all agreed that staying in the Championship was our main target in 2016. It would have been awful if we had gone straight back down after all the euphoria at the end of the previous year. In the end we achieved it with a game to spare so it was a job very well done. With having a long cup run, we did not have the luxury of a break on sixth-round weekend when some of our rivals did. It makes a huge difference having the odd Sunday off because it gives everyone a chance to recharge their batteries and get over niggling knocks. It is testament to the coaches, the medical staff and the players for hanging in there and having such a dig because a lot of the lads were running on empty and playing with injuries towards the end of the season."

Back-row forward Liam Thompson, a mainstay of the pack since 2013, had a fabulous season in 2016 and deservedly won the club's player of the year award: "2016 was without doubt my best season as an Oldham player," he said. "I managed to stay injury free throughout the year and felt full of confidence. At the start of the season it took us all some time to get used to the speed of the game in the Championship but once we adapted we were fine. There are, in effect, two mini-leagues within the main league. By that I mean it is exceptionally tough playing against the top teams, several of whom are full-time. It is a big step up from League One, but when we played the teams around us in the table we needed to pick up points, and thankfully we got enough to stay up. The win against Whitehaven which clinched our survival ranks alongside our promotion in 2015 and the win away to Hull KR in the Challenge Cup as the highlights of my career to date. The lads at

Oldham are the best set of lads I have ever been around in a rugby environment. The spirit and togetherness we have makes it so much easier to cope with training for example, especially during pre-season when a blizzard is blowing."

Prop Phil Joy also had a fantastic season: "Playing at a higher level was a great experience for us all, not least me. The players are much bigger, fitter and faster than they are in League One so it represented a real challenge for us to do well. It was a very good effort by all concerned. I would say the toughest aspect for us, and the biggest difference we found, was having to play at such a high intensity every week. The team spirit we enjoyed as a group certainly contributed to us staying up. Oldham is a great club to be at with good coaches, good players and good fans. It is also my home town club and playing for the Roughyeds is something I am very proud of."

Richard Lepori said: "Survival was always our aim. We are not a big club in terms of finances compared to some of our rivals so to stay up was important to us." Vice-captain Sam Gee agreed: "It was a huge achievement. Many people had us as favourites to go back down after our promotion, and you can understand why because it is a huge jump from League One to the Championship. It went down to the wire, but we survived. I would like to take this opportunity to congratulate our fans too. They are part of the reason I have always enjoyed my time at Oldham. They are with us through the good times and they help us through the struggles. I feel I let them down if I play badly. When we are down as a team, they always pick us back up, they are a credit to our club. They never moan or walk off if we are losing, they stay right there with us, encouraging us. They are an amazing group of people. When I finally hang up my boots, I may well join them on the terraces or in the seats and witness watching Oldham from their perspective!"

The final word has to go to skipper Palfrey, who had led the team for four consecutive seasons prior to moving to Rochdale for the 2017 campaign: "It was a massive effort by everyone to hang on to Championship status. It was our biggest achievement in my four years at Oldham by far. Without being disrespectful to League One, there is no comparison between the two divisions. In League One you can often win despite not playing well or being below your best. In the Championship, in these circumstances you are likely to get a cricket score put past you. I am really proud of my time at Oldham. It is a great club and will always be close to my heart. There are so many great memories. From top to bottom, it is full of good people. I got on famously with everyone. And a word for the fans too. They really are a great bunch, so supportive. They celebrated with us when we won and commiserated with us when we lost. It is not like that everywhere."

14. Fighting for Championship survival

The Kingstone Press Championship threw up even more challenges the way of Oldham and their rivals in 2017 following the promotion from League One the previous year of French outfit Toulouse Olympique and a resurgent Rochdale Hornets. With no disrespect to Whitehaven and Workington Town, the two teams who were relegated in 2016, there is no doubt that the competition was even tougher and more demanding in 2017 than it had been a year earlier.

Toulouse spent two years in the English Rugby League in 2009 and 2010, playing in the second tier having had a request to join their compatriots Catalans Dragons in Super League turned down by the RFL. This only proved moderately successful for Toulouse and in 2011 they returned to French domestic rugby league, before re-joining the English game – in League One – in 2016. They proved what a fine team they were by going through the entire league campaign unbeaten before crashing to a surprise home defeat to Rochdale in the Promotion Final.

They recovered from this blip, however, to clinch promotion following victory over Barrow Raiders in the Grand Final and to take their rightful spot in the Championship for 2017. As a full-time outfit, and with several fine, experienced players in their ranks, including some from the southern hemisphere, it was obvious from the outset of the 2017 season that Toulouse would challenge at the top end of the table.

Hornets, too, had a fine year in 2016 under new coach Alan Kilshaw, a man with experience of coaching in the Queensland Cup in Australia as well as with junior and academy teams at Warrington Wolves. Their impressive victory in the South of France was the culmination of a successful season and meant they would join local rivals Oldham and Swinton Lions in the Championship in 2017. Like Toulouse, they had quality players in their team and served notice of their intent by beating Oldham convincingly at Bower Fold in the 2017 season Law Cup curtain-raiser. Several former Roughyeds wore Rochdale colours in 2017 including former captain Lewis Palfrey, Josh Crowley, Miles Greenwood, Jack Holmes and Gary Middlehurst, who left Oldham after one year and followed his former skipper to Spotland.

Scott Naylor and his coaching staff, meanwhile, had to decide who should take over the captaincy. Eventually, they plumped for local boy Gareth Owen. Naylor told the *Oldham Chronicle:* "He is club captain as well as team captain and for a lad who was born and brought up in the town that is something special. Since he came to the club in 2014, 'Gaz' has been nothing but exceptional. He was made up when we offered him the captaincy and he was as proud as punch to accept. He didn't even hesitate for a few seconds. He jumped at it. He is a captain the other lads will look to, listen to and respect and, as an important member of the team, I know he will do a good job."

Owen commented recently: "When Scott asked me to be captain, it was one of the proudest moments of my career. To captain my hometown club is such an honour. I was shocked when I was asked but absolutely delighted. I know my family are proud of me because my mum and dad have both been keen Oldham fans for many years."

Ahead of the season, two prodigal sons made their much anticipated returns. George Tyson and Adam Neal were very much missed in 2016 during their year at Sheffield Eagles and bringing both back when the Eagles hit financial trouble in late 2016 became a priority. Tyson was delighted to renew his acquaintanceship with old pals. "I jumped at the opportunity when I realised there was a chance it might happen," he said. "I loved my first spell at Oldham and got on well with everyone. Having been here before, I knew I would fit straight back in."

George, whose brother Adam Higson played in Super League for Leigh Centurions in 2017, chuckled when asked about his style of play and preferred position on the rugby pitch: "I like to be competitive and I do my utmost to ensure nobody gets the better of me in one-on-one confrontations. That side of my game comes naturally to me I guess. When I was younger I played most of my rugby in the second row, but I have lost some weight since those days and prefer centre now.

I would jump at the chance to play in Super League one day, like Adam does, but my full focus right now is on Oldham and doing my best for them."

Neal was equally positive about his return: "It was great to come back to Oldham. It felt like coming home. I really missed the club while I was away. The Championship is a tough division and probably tougher than ever in 2017. That is good for the game of rugby league in general because it suggests standards are improving across the whole game. Both individually and collectively, we need to be on our game each week – that is the reality of it."

Other signings included stand-off Scott Leatherbarrow, formerly of Keighley Cougars, Batley Bulldogs and London Broncos, former Wigan Warriors, Widnes Vikings, Barrow Raiders, Halifax and Whitehaven prop forward Ben Davies and young Castleford Tigers outside backs Kieran Gill and Tuoyo Egodo, both on season-long loans, and two players whom the Tigers have high hopes for in the future.

As well as doing their best for Oldham, some members of the squad had an extra incentive for pulling out all the stops when wearing the Roughyeds jersey in 2017. Richard Lepori, Joe Burke – who joined the club in 2016 having played for South Wales Scorpions, Barrow Raiders and North Wales Crusaders – Michael Ward and loan signing from St Helens, Ben Morris, all held high hopes of being selected for their respective countries in the World Cup to be held in Australia, New Zealand and Papua New Guinea in October and November.

Lepori, Burke and Morris played lead roles in the qualifying campaign at the end of 2016 which resulted in Lepori's Italy, Burke and Morris's Wales and Ireland all qualifying from the European section.

The Welsh team, led by well-respected Super League coach and BBC Televison pundit John Kear, had a superb two-match campaign. They thrashed a fledgling Serbia 50–0 in Llanelli in a match shown live by Welsh language television channel S4C and then made people sit up and take notice with a thrilling 20–14 win over a strong Italian outfit in Monza. Burke played in both games, turning out in the second-row against Serbia and starting as a substitute in Italy. He probably won't forget the latter match in a hurry as he suffered a nasty facial injury.

Young centre Morris, then a Saints academy and reserve player, scored twice in Italy to underline what Kear already knew – that he was a player full of potential and more than worthy of a starting spot in his team. So the two victories catapulted Wales to automatic qualification and the mouth-watering prospect of a British autumn with the elite of world rugby league Down Under.

Lepori played on the left wing for Italy during the qualifying campaign, scoring four excellent tries, including a hat-trick inside the first 15 minutes, against Serbia in Belgrade. The defeat to Wales meant the Italians had to overcome Russia in a play-off to earn the right to qualify, thus emulating their class of 2013 who had competed in the last World Cup. The match, held at Leigh Sports Village, saw Italy cruise to a 76–0 win with veteran Australian Terry Campese, son of Wallabies legend David Campese, running the show and enjoying a 24 point haul. 'Lippy' scored two more tries to further push his claims for inclusion in the World Cup squad this time round.

Ireland, with former Roughyed Ged Corcoran as team manager, qualified too, with victories over Spain, by 46–6, in Valencia and over Russia, by 70–16, in Bray. Roughyeds' back-row forward Will Hope played in both games, scoring a try against Russia, as did 2015 dual-registration player Oliver Roberts, who scored a try against Spain and two against the Russians. Hope followed in the footsteps of George Tyson, Adam Neal and David Hewitt by leaving Oldham to join Sheffield Eagles while Roberts became a regular member of Huddersfield Giants Super League squad after his stint with the Roughyeds.

Michael Ward, meanwhile, explains how he cherishes the hope that he may represent Ireland in the World Cup: "I qualify for Ireland through my grandparents on my dad's side and I was named in a 40-man squad in 2016. However, the Irish management were keen to include several Ireland-based lads so I missed out on the final 22-man squad. This time, however, I am hopeful I might make it. Playing in a

World Cup would be a massive thrill." 'Wardy' continued: "Scott Naylor converted me into a prop-forward very early in his time at the club. I had played second-row, loose-forward or centre prior to Scott's arrival. He's a good coach who commands respect, when he speaks everyone listens. He uses me as an impact player coming off the substitute's bench which suits me fine because I don't see myself as the type of player who can play the full 80 minutes, like some of the other lads do. I am more explosive whose role is to try to change the dynamics of a game in short bursts. I like to think it works well. I enjoy scoring tries too, and am hoping I might even finish leading try-scorer this year! Of course, it doesn't matter who scores though, as long as Oldham win." 'Wardy' eventually finished joint-top scorer with 10 tries with winger Adam Clay.

The new-look Oldham took to the field for the start of the Kingstone Press Championship season with a Bower Fold game against Sheffield. The Eagles had undergone a turbulent off-season with news of financial difficulties, ground issues and players leaving, but with wily coach Mark Aston still at the helm, they were unlikely to prove easy-beats for anyone. With a team including Papua New Guinean talismen Menzie Yere and Garry Lo, Australian half-back star Dane Chisholm and Roughyeds old boy Will Hope in the pack, it was always going to be a tough start for Oldham. In a frantic game, Tuoyo Egodo, on his competitive debut for the club, had a battle royal with Yere in the centre positions and definitely edged their personal duel. With Scott Leatherbarrow also impressing on debut, Danny Langtree scoring two tries and David Hewitt sniffing out a cheeky interception try from the back of a scrum – just as he had at Barrow Raiders in a pre-season friendly – the Roughyeds won 26–10 to get the league season off to a flyer. It was a very encouraging start.

Following a narrow 8–6 defeat at Featherstone on a heavy pitch and in terrible February conditions, the Roughyeds played host to London Broncos in the third game, and the first in a long line of serious injuries that hit the squad during the course of the year caused prop Phil Joy to quit midway through the second half. Phil described the incident which would ultimately destroy his season: "It was simply a basic tackle. We were defending our own line, I went into the tackle and dislocated my shoulder. At first I thought it was a 'stinger' but then realised I could not move my arm. It was the most painful injury I have ever had.

I returned against Batley Bulldogs in May and it went again. We knew there was a 50 per cent chance of it coming back out, but we had done a lot of rehabilitation and testing and were comfortable I would get through games. It was an 'end of range' tackle – a tackle where the defender has to stretch, as in a diving tackle, meaning the shoulder becomes more vulnerable to impact – which is something I had to avoid

184

if I could. Unfortunately, luck was against me. The recurrence finished me for the season." The loss of Joy was a body blow to the squad as he was a towering presence in the engine room of the front row.

The match against the Broncos ended in an agonising 20–18 defeat after Welsh international winger Rhys Williams scored a late length of the field try to steal the match for London and break Oldham hearts. There was still time for David Hewitt to strike a post with a last-gasp penalty which would have earned the Roughyeds a share of the spoils. Oldham had dominated the game for long periods and were desperately unlucky to lose. The Broncos are a full-time team and finished second behind table-topping Hull Kingston Rovers, relegated from Super League in 2016, after the 23-match league programme. But they will look back on their early season win at Bower Fold as the one they got away with.

Following defeat away to Hull KR and the disappointment of a postponed fixture against Dewsbury Rams at home – at a time when the Rams were struggling badly in the league – Oldham made the short trip along the A627 to Spotland for the first of four derby fixtures in the Championship against Rochdale Hornets. With on-loan prop-forward Jordan Walne – playing for Oldham four years after his last appearance, on dual-registration, in 2013 – and his fellow front-row man Ben Davies having big games, the Roughyeds appeared to have the game wrapped up when they led 26–14 with just a few minutes remaining.

However the home side showed great never-say-die spirit, as they would again at Summer Bash later in the season, to snatch a point with two late converted tries. It was a feeling of not knowing whether to laugh or cry for Oldham fans at the end of the game – was it a point lost after leading by 12 points so late in the game, or a good point well earned on opposition soil. Either way, it was a point which helped to consolidate the team's push for mid-table respectability in the Championship, which at this stage of the season they looked more than capable of achieving.

The Challenge Cup campaign began for Oldham the following week with a fourth round tie against amateur team Haydock, champions of the North West Men's League, and the lowest ranked team left in the competition. The BBC, as they had been for decades, were the main broadcaster of the Challenge Cup and in 2017, extended their coverage by live-streaming coverage of early-round games via the BBC Sport website. Leigh Miners versus Wigan St Patricks in round one, Pilkington Recs versus Siddal in round two and Siddal versus Toronto Wolfpack, the new club based in Canada and who were embarking on their debut season in the English Rugby League, in round three, were chosen to be screened in the first three rounds.

New club captain Gareth Owen with Chris Hamilton in early 2017.

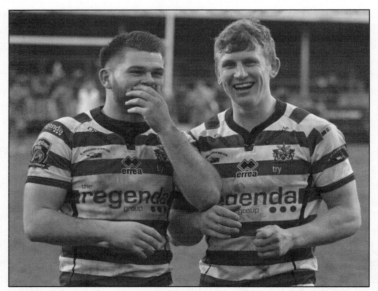

David Hewitt and Gareth Owen share a joke after Oldham's opening day win against Sheffield Eagles in 2017. (Both photos David Murgatroyd).

Left: Welsh international Joe Burke applauds the fans in 2017.

Middle: Sam Gee acknowledges the fans support, ahead of his team-mates, after an Oldham win in 2017.

Bottom: A joyous Kieran Gill scoring his sensational match-winning try against Bradford Bulls at Bower Fold in 2017

(All photos David Murgatroyd).

Oldham were delighted to learn that their tie with Haydock was the game chosen to be screened in the fourth round and so history was made on Saturday 18 March 2017 as a Roughyeds game was screened live on BBC Sport for the first time, with commentary by Dave Woods and Leeds Rhinos star Jamie Jones-Buchanan.

Haydock, coached by former Castleford and St Helens winger Chris Smith and inspired by a guest appearance at training in cup week from former Saints star Sean Long, brought a large travelling support with them and shook Bower Fold to its rafters in the early stages of the game by scoring two excellent tries by Jordan Gibson and Dean Dollin.

Oldham needed to get going or they might have been on the end of a major upset, but that never appeared likely after tries by Lepori, Ward, Tyson and Grimshaw, plus two goals from Leatherbarrow, opened up a 20–8 half-time lead. A second Lepori try, plus others by Burke, Gill and Clay with just a reply by Steven Jones for Haydock saw Roughyeds home comfortably.

Scott Naylor told the *Oldham Chronicle:* "We made the first mistake, gave away the first penalty and let in the first try. Haydock came out with more passion and energy and deserve a lot of credit. The pitch (wet, sloppy and heavy) was a leveller, but you can't take anything away from Haydock, whose pride and passion rubbed off on their fantastic supporters. It took us a while to realise that we were in a game. Once we had done that we never looked likely to have any serious problems."

Chris Hamilton presented Chris Smith with an inscribed glass souvenir of the biggest day in the amateur club's history and said: "Before the game it was a pleasure to work with Haydock officials and especially their club secretary Frank Bradshaw." Of his squad's achievement in becoming the first club from the eighth tier of rugby league to reach the fourth round of the Challenge Cup, Smith said: "It has been a fabulous experience for the boys and it will stand them in good stead as we defend our league title."

After defeat at Batley, the next match saw Bradford Bulls visit Bower Fold in early April. The most exciting climax to a match imaginable saw the Roughyeds pick up another vital two points. The once mighty Bulls – World Club champions in 2002 – had fallen on desperately hard times and had been forced into administration and eventually liquidation in early 2017. A new club was soon born and the RFL invited them to remain a member of the Kingstone Press Championship but with a huge 12-point deduction. Although several players stayed, many others left and the points deduction proved too much for the new-look Bradford side to pull back and they were relegated from the Championship as early as 6 August. Their last-gasp defeat at Bower Fold didn't help their cause one iota, but for Oldham it was a thrilling victory.

With the Bulls leading 22–20 and only seconds left, Oldham's two Castleford Tigers loanees, Tuoyo Egodo and Kieran Gill conjured up a try that had fans in delirium. Egodo, playing on the left wing, retrieved a Bradford kick inside his own half and controlled the ball with his foot. Initially it appeared as though the ball had bounced away from him, but Tuoyo was first to the loose ball, picked it up and set off downfield. Oldham fans in the stand were on the edges of their seats as Egodo broke the first line of defence and approached the full-back. His centre partner Gill had moved outside him at pace and took Tuoyo's pass with the Bulls' defence all at sea. A fast and experienced winger may have gone for the corner flag as the scrambling defence covered across but Kieran was taking no chances on being pushed into touch. Instinctively, he stepped inside the first man, then another, and another. Showing tremendous evasive skills, he swerved past a fourth defender on an arcing inside run and straightened up close to the posts as the last despairing defender made his challenge. There was no stopping Gill now though and his pace and momentum sent him crashing over the line by the side of the posts as the fans went wild on the terrace behind.

Not only was it a match-winning try in the last minute of a crucial encounter, but it was a try right out of the top drawer, a stunning and clinical finish by a young player with a glorious future in the game ahead of him, it seems.

The two youngsters reflected on a magic moment in both of their early careers: "That try defines my time at Oldham," said delighted scorer Gill. "The celebrations in the immediate aftermath were something special, both by the players and the fans. The joy on the faces of my team-mates showed what a great spirit we enjoyed as players and the fans delight was obvious too. It was a special occasion and one that neither I, nor any Oldham fan present, will forget any time soon."

Egodo gave his version of events leading up to THAT try: "It all happened so very quickly. I remember trying to control the ball with my feet and before I knew it I had broken the Bradford line. As I ran in to the Bulls half I heard Kieran screaming at me. I looked up and he was just to the left of me. I knew I had to engage the full-back to give him the best chance of making it to the line. As soon as I offloaded it I knew he would score and win us the game. But it was a great finish by Kieran."

Gill continued: "I enjoyed my time at Oldham very much. Everyone was great from day one and I immediately felt at home. Chemistry is one of the main things I look for within a club. At Oldham it was apparent straight away that there was a bond between everyone."

Londoner Egodo was also very happy at the club: "I began to learn and love playing rugby league at the Broncos and my time there set the foundation for the beginning of my professional full-time career at Castleford Tigers. The opportunity came my way to go on loan to Oldham in order to gain valuable experience and regular game time and I played in some tough and memorable games for them. The win against the Bulls, in particular, was a match I will never forget."

Since the beginning of the year, and even earlier in some cases, Oldham fans had been making arrangements and booking trips for the eagerly awaited springtime visit to the beautiful city of Toulouse in south-west France. The stunning finish to the Bradford game merely whetted everyone's appetites even further for what promised to be a super weekend.

The party I travelled with flew out from Gatwick Airport early on Friday morning, 7 April after we spent the previous evening at my brother Wayne's home in Kent. Other fans flew out on different flights from different airports but all had red and white shirts, banners and flags to the fore. On arriving at the airport in Toulouse, we immediately bumped into keen Oldham fan Dave Naylor, who was already there. We took a bus and then an underground train into the city centre before indulging in a few Friday afternoon beers, chatting to other fans, savouring the beautiful French cuisine and then later finding the two pubs – The Melting Pot and Pub O' Clock – where Oldham fans were gathering. The Melting Pot had rugby league scarves and memorabilia on the walls, not what you expect to see in a pub in France necessarily. It was a great evening mingling with fellow Roughyeds, all excitedly looking forward to the game the following day.

On the Saturday, after a stroll along the banks of the River Garonne, and more chance meetings with people clad in red and white, we made our way to the Stade Ernest Argeles. This was the first time in the 20 year history of the club that the team had played outside of England or Wales and it was very special being there to witness the occasion. Prior to the game, we were delighted to be invited into the Toulouse club boardroom to enjoy French hospitality, wine, bread, ham, cheese and cakes and I was introduced to two people – a couple from the south of England – who were now resident in Toulouse and involved behind the scenes at the club. They were enthusiastic about how well their adopted team were shaping up in the Championship having waltzed through League One the year before. They talked positively about seeing them in Super League in the not-too-distant future – "but not necessarily next year, as when we do go up, we want to be sure we are strong enough to stay up," they acknowledged realistically. I, for one, have no doubt that they will achieve that goal sooner rather than later.

The Oldham team were accompanied onto the pitch by a group of young rugby union players from Tetbury RUFC in Gloucestershire, a club Prince William and Prince Harry turned out for as youngsters. The lads, under–11s, were in Toulouse on a mini-tour of their own and Chris Hamilton invited them to be club mascots for the day after they first contacted him to say they would be there supporting Oldham.

As the match began – with a noisy local band banging drums immediately behind us – it was quickly apparent that Toulouse, brilliantly orchestrated by Australian-born stand-off half Johnathon Ford, a former Cook Islands international team-mate of Tere Glassie and cousin of Byron Ford, and French international scrum-half Stanislas (Stan) Robin, were going to make like extremely difficult for the Roughyeds. In Australian full-back Mark Kheirallah, French centre Gregory White and Australian second-row forward Rhys Curran, they had players of real quality and it was no surprise that they raced into a match-winning 36–0 lead at half-time. Credit Oldham for a much-improved second-half performance which led to tries by Gill, Burke and Lepori to leave the final score 58–18 to the hosts.

Despite the result, fans applauded their troops off the pitch after the players had walked around the inside of the perimeter fence to shake hands with their supporters and thank them for coming. That was a lovely touch and showed that the players appreciated the fans support so far from home.

Another great evening in Pub O' Clock followed when we chatted with leading Super League match official Phil Bentham, who had refereed the game, and RFL representative, George Fairbairn, the former Wigan and Hull Kingston Rovers full-back. Our plane home the following day brought an end to a cracking weekend. Travelling abroad is great fun at any time, but when it is spent supporting your favourite team, with family, friends and fellow supporters, it really is a pleasure, irrespective of the result.

Oldham hit back strongly from their loss in France by beating Swinton Lions 22–18 at Bower Fold on Good Friday. Playing some fine rugby in the first half, they led 12–0 with tries from Gee and Lepori and two goals from Leatherbarrow, before stretching the lead to 18–0 early in the second half with a Ward try and another goal from Scott. The Lions, led superbly by half-back Chris Atkin – later to sign for Hull Kingston Rovers – hit back with tries by former Roughyed Shaun Robinson, Chris Hankinson and Jack Murphy with three goals from Atkin. Two Leatherbarrow penalties kept Oldham ahead, however, and they hung on for two points. It wasn't pretty, rather it was tough and uncompromising, but with Adam Neal – who played the full 80 minutes without a break – outstanding in the forwards, it was a crucial win.

Three days later, a trip to Halifax resulted in another nail-biter, the home side winning 16–14 despite Oldham scoring three tries – by Gill, Burke and Chisholm – to their two. Adam Clay was desperately close to winning the match for Oldham late on, only to be bundled into touch

191

by the corner flag as he went for the corner. So for the third time in 2017, Roughyeds had lost a Championship fixture by two points.

A disappointing Challenge Cup fifth round loss at Featherstone followed before one of the highlights of the year, an amazing comeback win at Dewsbury Rams which had fans wondering how the second half of a match could be so different to the first.

Before half-time, the Rams totally dominated to lead 24–6, despite an early try by Neal for Oldham. After the break, however, the Roughyeds looked a different team, and aided by two remarkable incidents, clawed back Dewsbury's lead and eventually went in front themselves near the end to win 28–24. The try that gave Oldham hope early in the second half, to cut the deficit to 24–12, was a bizarre one. As the visitors attacked strongly, Ward appeared to be held in a gang tackle on, or even over, the try-line. Instead of trying to push him back into the field of play, however, the Rams forwards tried dragging him forward over the dead-ball line. To their consternation, and Oldham supporters delight, 'Wardy' somehow managed to reach out and touch down with defenders all over him.

As Oldham smelled a comeback, a flash of inspiration – or a massive stroke of luck – helped them again. Adam Clay found himself retrieving a stray pass deep inside his own half and on the last tackle and, despite being penned in against the touch-line by a defender, he swung a boot at the ball, hoping to push the Rams back into their own half. Unbelievably, the ball took a wicked bounce, taking it away from the full-back and into touch. It turned out to be a 40–20, and presented Oldham with more attacking possibilities.

Clay told the *Oldham Chronicle:* "Did I mean it? Of course. I opted for the 40–20 instead of a grubber kick up the touchline for me to chase. Seriously, it was a spur of the moment thing. We were under pressure in our own danger zone when I picked up a loose ball near touch. They were on to me immediately so my only option was to put my foot through it and get the ball downfield. Something went our way for a change when it bounced into touch. But I was not going to admit to the rest of the lads that it could have gone anywhere. It has been a big talking point in training this week and it is only outside the dressing room that I admit there was an element of luck about it. Inside, it was intentional — and I won't let the rest of them forget it for a long time!"

As a boy, Adam was a young footballer at Manchester City when Joe Royle was the manager. He added with a smile: "It is a different shaped ball for me these days, but you never lose it. I can still belt it when I have to. When Joe let me go it was the biggest mistake he ever made!" After Clay's wonder kick, tries from Gill, Tyson and Burke – following a defence-splitting break from Leatherbarrow – saw Oldham home.

Left: Roary the Roughyed and his Toulouse counterpart with an injured member of the Tetbury RFC Under-11s.

Below: Fans at Summer Bash in May 2017, holding up pink balloons in memory of those killed in the Manchester Arena bombings a week earlier.

(Both photos David Murgatroyd)

It was a thrilling win and provided a perfect end to April. The Roughyeds were looking good. Unfortunately, May was nowhere near as profitable to the team as April had been. A poor performance in London saw the Broncos hammer them 74–12 with a long-range effort from Tyson the only highlight. Two defeats in the second half of the not-so-merry month of May were even tougher to take for fans. First, a home match against Batley had to be switched from Bower Fold so work could be done on the pitch. It was played at the Manchester Regional Athletics Centre in the Etihad Stadium Campus, the home of Manchester City.

Batley had been struggling, with only one win in their previous six games, and when Oldham went 10–0 up early on and then led 22–10

193

midway through the first-half, it seemed likely the Bulldogs' lean run would continue. A great Clay hat-trick had sparked Roughyeds in that opening half-an-hour, but sloppy defence allowed the visitors back into the game before half-time. After the break, Oldham lost Phil Joy with a recurrence of his shoulder injury and fell apart as Batley pulled away to win 48–28.

The following weekend the horrors of Summer Bash 2016 came back to haunt Oldham once again. In a throwback to the controversial defeat against Swinton Lions a year earlier, opponents Rochdale Hornets overcame a 28–12 deficit soon after half-time when, for the second year running, Oldham appeared to lose belief completely on the big stage after ripping their opponents apart before half-time. Tries from Scott Turner, Tyson and two gems from Lepori, following stunning breaks from Jack Spencer and Danny Langtree, plus six Leatherbarrow goals saw Oldham in control.

It all changed, however, and four Hornets tries saw them home to a stunning 38–28 win. Oldham's cause wasn't helped when the referee, Liam Moore, awarded an eight-point try to Rochdale after Lewis Galbraith was allegedly fouled in the act of scoring. It seemed a harsh call and Oldham heads appeared to visibly go down.

Following the loss at Bloomfield Road, news emerged that Lee Spencer was leaving the club. Chris Hamilton told the *Oldham Chronicle:* "I had a long chat with him, but his mind was made up. He has been fed up for a while. He is also busy at work and has been for some time. He told me he was no longer getting satisfaction and whatever else he wanted out of his job at Oldham. His decision to leave was his alone. It happens. We thank him, wish him all the best and assure him that he will always be welcome at this club."

If May had been disappointing, June was no better sadly, not in terms of results anyway. Away defeats to Swinton Lions at the beginning of the month and to Bradford Bulls at the end of it, were separated by three Bower Fold losses, although in all three home games, Oldham hinted in patches that better days lay ahead. News also came from Castleford that Kieran Gill had been injured on his Super League debut for the Tigers and would miss the rest of the season.

Against champions elect Hull KR, the visitors were stunned early on by a rampant Roughyeds beginning to the game which saw them race into an 18–0 lead after just 10 minutes. Early tries to Burke, Hewitt and dual-registration man, Sam Wood, plus three Leatherbarrow goals gave former Australia coach Tim Sheens plenty to think about. Rovers slowly clawed their way back into it, however, and eventually their class showed, scoring six tries to win 32–24. It had been a rousing display from the home side and fans applauded them off the pitch.

A week later and it was a similar story. This time visitors Halifax led 12–0 but Roughyeds stormed back after half-time to level at 12–12 with tries by Turner and Ward. Leatherbarrow was recalled for a forward pass that would have put Oldham ahead, but the visitors then pulled away to win 30–12, a score that flattered them. Three days later, the rearranged match against Dewsbury Rams was staged when the Rams, having parted company with Australian coach Glenn Morrison and replaced him with veteran Neil Kelly earlier in the season, were enjoying a huge upturn in their fortunes. Despite that, the Roughyeds took the game to them from the off, led 12–6 at half-time and then 16–12 with five minutes left. What followed was heart-breaking for fans, as depleted Oldham, having lost Grimshaw, Turner and Owen to serious injury, were hit with a killer blow when a Leatherbarrow kick was charged down by Rams half-back Gareth Moore who collected the loose ball and scored the decisive try. In what was a vital four-pointer in the lower reaches of the Championship, defeat was a bitter pill to swallow.

Richard Lepori missed the Dewsbury game with an ankle injury which ruled him out until September and the injuries to Turner (concussion for the third time in 2017) and Owen (a foot injury which ultimately required an operation) kept them out for the rest of the year. The injury crisis was certainly beginning to bite.

The beginning of July brought a much-needed win, to end a run of eight straight defeats, and the Roughyeds' first since they won at Dewsbury at the end of April. What a win too. Toulouse Olympique were still very much in the race for top-four qualification and a place in the Middle 8's. They arrived at Bower Fold, however, without star half-backs Ford and Robin and, in truth, looked a shadow of the side that thumped Oldham in France three months earlier. Take nothing away from Oldham though, this was a fantastic morale-boosting triumph. With Lepori and Turner out, Steven Nield played at full-back and did not put a foot wrong in a tip-top display. Nield badly injured a knee at Keighley Cougars in 2015 and, after a long spell on the sidelines, went on loan to Gloucestershire All Golds in early 2017. He was recalled by Oldham to make his long-awaited return to first team action at Bradford Bulls in the previous match and did enough to keep his place against Toulouse. Steven won a clubman-of-the-year award in 2015 for his work behind the scenes while injured and it was great to see him back in an Oldham shirt. He scored the first try and regularly mopped up Toulouse kicks as last line of defence.

It was a rousing show from the team with Liam Thompson playing a full 80 minutes and standing up strong, alongside his colleagues, to anything the visitors threw at them. Tyson and Gee were strong and powerful in the centres, Sam Wood had a fine game at stand-off and Hewitt kicked well under pressure, with Leatherbarrow also absent

195

through injury. The final score of 14–12 was a huge one for the club, because their losing run had dragged them into relegation trouble.

There was more bad news on the injury front, however, with Adam Neal (broken jaw) and Danny Langtree (arm injury) picking up nasty knocks. Neal said: "It is a tough old game. I was very disappointed though because I felt it was a blatant elbow to my jaw and no action was taken. As part-time professionals we have to work as well and being self-employed it has been difficult for me. I guess I have to take it on the chin literally and crack on. As players we choose to play and we know the dangers. I have to focus on coming back and I certainly will be back better and stronger."

Neal was ruled out for several weeks, and although Langtree started the next match against Featherstone Rovers at Bower Fold, he did not look comfortable, picked up another knock and missed the rest of the year. An unprecedented injury crisis now beset the squad. The battered and bruised Roughyeds fought bravely against Rovers, but lost 32–14 to a team described by Scott Naylor as "on the same level as Hull KR and London Broncos, the top two teams in the Championship."

The final two league games before the start of the Championship Shield also ended in defeat against Sheffield Eagles at Wakefield Trinity's Belle Vue stadium and at Bower Fold against Rochdale Hornets. Again Roughyeds fought hard in both games, but in the Sheffield match struggled to contain three-try Garry Lo – a man destined to sign for Super League giants Castleford Tigers – and against Rochdale trailed 18–0 early on before finally succumbing 34–24.

As the 23-match league programme came to an end, Oldham found themselves second from bottom, one point behind Swinton Lions and four behind Rochdale Hornets, with only stricken Bradford Bulls below them. It was going to be a tough seven remaining fixtures in the Shield if Oldham were going to escape the drop, it seemed.

The injury situation was such that several players were brought in on loan prior to the transfer deadline. Wakefield Trinity Wildcats young full-back Luke Hooley, Salford Red Devils teenage winger Connor Williams, St Helens centre Ben Morris and London Broncos pair Kameron Pearce-Paul and Sadiq 'Sid' Adebiyi joined Salford forward Liam Bent on short-term arrangements.

Hooker Matt Wilkinson from Salford and Dewsbury Rams forward Luke Adamson were also snapped up on deals to the end of the season.

The new-look team made its second visit to Belle Vue to face Sheffield Eagles in three weeks in the first Shield encounter. They were well beaten 56–16, but produced a vastly-improved showing in the second match against already-relegated Bradford Bulls at Bower Fold. Although losing 20–16, the Roughyeds recovered from a torrid start when they trailed 20–0 inside the first 30 minutes to reduce the arrears

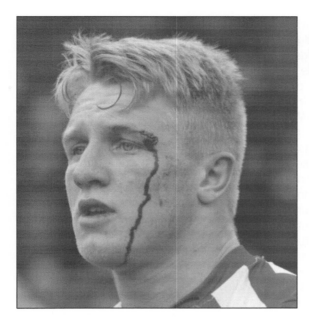

Left: A wounded
George Tyson in 2017.
(Photo Dave Naylor).

Right: Adam Clay scoring a
crucial try against Batley
Bulldogs at Mount Pleasant in
2017.
(Photo David Murgatroyd).

to just four points early in the second half. They were unlucky not to breach the Bulls line again. The defeat kept them in the bottom two but there were signs things were looking up performance-wise.

In the third game at Batley, the renewed spirit evident against Bradford really came to the fore. Trailing 22–0 after Batley had made full early use of their notorious slope, the Roughyeds fought back like tigers and tries from Ward, Gee, Morris – a long-range interception – and Clay, plus three goals from Hooley, drew them level. It was a fantastic point, on a ground where few teams in the Championship win, and when news came that Swinton, Oldham's closest rivals at the bottom, had lost at home to Bradford, there was much optimism among the fans that relegation could yet be avoided. The point drew them level with the Lions although they had a far superior points-difference.

Another trip to Spotland to face Rochdale Hornets was next up, and in a brilliant display, full of guts and pride, the Roughyeds picked up a potentially crucial two points with a much needed 30–24 victory. Joe Burke pushed his claims for Welsh World Cup inclusion with two fine tries and a big game while Hooley showed he is a full-back rich in potential with an assured display, capping a great showing with a match clinching try near the end following a fine Hewitt break. On the same day, Swinton turned the form book upside down with a stunning win at in-form Dewsbury to keep the pot boiling with three games to go.

Oldham then entertained Toulouse Olympique – with Valu Bentley taking on the role of water carrier for the French outfit – and so nearly repeated their victory from early July. The Roughyeds led 12–8 following a Kenny Hughes try and four Hooley goals, but the visitors enjoyed a purple patch midway through the second half when they scored three tries in quick succession. Despite a second try to Hughes and a fifth Hooley goal, Toulouse hung on to win 24–18. It was a battling display from Oldham and on another day, they may have picked up at least a point. But it wasn't to be. Swinton's defeat at Rochdale meant that the clash between the Lions and Roughyeds the following Sunday, 10 September took on titanic proportions. Sadly, that match was lost too, 29–6. Oldham failed to make first-half superiority count and paid the price as Swinton dominated the second half. The loss condemned the Roughyeds – barring a mathematical miracle in the last round of matches – to relegation. It was such a shame after all the promise from 2016. The last match of the year against Dewsbury was largely academic and a 29–22 loss after Oldham had led 22–20 close to the end summed up the season.

Oldham finished two points behind Swinton with a vastly inferior points difference and three points behind Rochdale Hornets. It really was a case of what might have been.

15. Up the Roughyeds!

In this concluding chapter, several people with the club at heart have an opportunity to talk about what Oldham RLFC (1997) Ltd means to them. The club has many good people surrounding it as has been stated by some of the former players interviewed for this book. Staff, volunteers and fans all contribute greatly to the continued existence of the club and long may that continue. A crowd of 3,097 – most of them from Oldham – watched the club's first match, the Law Cup game against our local rivals Rochdale Hornets on New Year's Day, 1998 and 2,943 attended the first competitive game against Heworth in the third round preliminary tie of the Challenge Cup.

Sadly, over the last 20 years, crowds have dwindled to the extent that whenever a four-figure 'gate' is achieved, it is a cause of much rejoicing. However, those fans that do remain in 2017, and attend matches on a regular basis, are dyed-in-the-wool supporters who have Oldham Rugby League Club running through their veins. In some cases, fans have moved to different parts of the United Kingdom, or indeed the world, but have retained their interest in this great club of ours and wish it every success in the future. So here are a few examples of people who will always wish this club well and provide compelling reasons why the club means so much to them. Some provide funny stories and anecdotes of their days following Oldham and I hope they provide an enjoyable conclusion to this book.

Reverend Tony Ford, club Chaplain
I am a lifelong supporter of the club and have missed very few matches over many years. When I did I was always eager to read Roger Halstead's reports in the *Oldham Chronicle*. In 2010, I became, as far as I know, Oldham Rugby's first Chaplain. I came to faith in Christ in the late 1990s and after working for Christ Church, Chadderton as a family worker for a few years I trained for a ministry at Oak Hill College in London. My family and I were delighted to return to Christ Church to serve my three-year curacy and I was ordained into the Church of England in June 2008.

In February 2009, the church was contacted about the funeral of Mick Hough, who had died aged 54. I had known Mick through watching him play for Waterhead ARLFC. He was a tough competitor on the pitch and a great bloke off it. I also knew through rugby of Chris and John Hough, Mick's son and nephew respectively.

My boss and vicar at Christ Church, John Simmons, suggested I do the funeral because of my love for rugby league and for having known Mick. It was a huge privilege to spend time with Sharon, Mick's wife, and the family planning the service and hopefully being of support to them. It became clear that because of Mick's popularity as a person the service was going to have a huge turn-out. It was like a "who's who" of rugby league and Mick had a great send-off.

Just over a year later came the very sad news that Sharon had also passed away, again far too young. This again brought me into contact with the family. John was coach of Oldham's reserve team at the time and he and I discussed the values of having a Chaplain at Oldham Rugby. John spoke to Chris Hamilton and it was agreed we would give it a go.

My first duty was to perform a service of Thanksgiving for our new home Whitebank stadium. After being nomadic for 13 years, we finally had somewhere to call home and it seemed appropriate to give thanks for the provision of the ground and for those who worked to get it ready for the first home match against York City Knights on 9 May 2010.

I love every minute of my role because it is a huge honour to serve the club. We see our players as powerful young athletes who appear unbreakable and yet they suffer pain, heartbreak and anxieties, like we all do. I will not disclose confidential information but some lads have had loved ones die, had marriage break-ups or have had to endure the break-up of their parents' marriage. I have been able to support players' families through some of these challenging times and have also conducted the funerals of some Oldham fans, including that of club stalwart Nigel Marland.

I have been fortunate to be freed up by the Church of England to perform the role which usually involves being at training at least one night a week, being available on match days and at the end of the telephone when needed. When I eventually end my involvement I hope I will be replaced because it is a role that should continue. Most Super League, Championship and League One clubs have a Chaplain now and I hope my presence has been a benefit to the club's staff, players and fans as much as it has been a pleasure for me to be involved with them.

John McAndrew, club employee

I started working for Oldham Rugby League Club as a part-time administrative assistant in 2004. Once I got the job I found out my duties included: running the club lottery; managing the office on match days; managing the car park attendants; managing the stewards; manning the main entrance, selling tickets and assisting sponsors on match days; helping with the attendance turnstile takings and paying wages; and occasionally acting as official timekeeper on match days. I had only wanted a part time job!

However it was not as bad as it sounds and everything seemed to run smoothly. I was based at Boundary Park and I really enjoyed it. In

2006, the team were relegated from National League One without winning a game. I had tipped us to win every game in the club's prediction league, so unsurprisingly, I won the wooden spoon.

Working for Oldham Rugby is never boring, there is always something happening. Having played for the 'old' club in 1959-60 as A N Other in the reserves at Watersheddings, this club is in my blood. I now feel totally at home working here and the present team are a joy to work with. Chris Hamilton never ceases to amaze me how he continues to run the club despite so many hurdles he has to overcome. He never gives up, never stops working and it is a pleasure to work for him.

The Oldham Rugby League Heritage Trust and Hall of Fame

The Trust was formed in 1995 as a result of a group of supporters discussing the formation of an Oldham Rugby League Club Hall of Fame. Initially there were seven inductees, a number which has gradually increased to 19. Consideration was given to all players, past and present, from 1876 when the club was formed, through to the present day. Adjudicators had a tough job. There were some big names, many of the successful candidates coming from periods in the club's history when it enjoyed meteoric success.

The intention now is to add more new members selected from a short list which will be published in early 2018. There is every possibility that it will include players that have served the club well during the period 1997 through to the present day.

The Oldham Rugby League Hall of Fame current membership includes Joe Ferguson; Bernard Ganley; Alan Davies; John Etty; Derek 'Rocky' Turner; Bob Irving; Andy Goodway; Martin Murphy; Herman Hilton; Frank Stirrup; Terry Flanagan MBE; Kevin Taylor; Harry Ogden; Arthur Lees; Jack Read; Fred Ashworth; Mike Elliott; Alex Givvons and Sid Little OBE.

It is perhaps as a direct result of the formation of the Hall of Fame that the Heritage Trust has amassed one of the most important collections of club memorabilia in the world of rugby league both here and overseas.

The Trust has a fine collection of medals, representative caps, jerseys and other articles of memorabilia won by the club and its players in bygone times.

It has commissioned paintings, erected blue commemorative plaques and persuaded the local authority to name streets as a reminder of what has gone before. It has collected and upgraded a library of moving images and held well attended exhibitions at Gallery Oldham which helped to bring the collections to life.

Mike Kivlin on behalf of 'Rugby Oldham'

'Rugby Oldham', or to give its official title 'Oldham Rugby Community and Supporters Trust Limited', was formed in 2005. The club had been forced to play their home games outside of Oldham and the initial aim of the trust was to try to help to facilitate a return to the borough for the team. While the acquisition of the Whitebank Stadium was a major step in the right direction for the club, the refusal of the RFL to allow Kingstone Press Championship fixtures to be played there in 2016 and 2017 highlights the fact that the need for a better facility in the town still exists. We fervently hope the provision of a rugby league dedicated stadium, suitable for the game at all levels, doesn't always remain the pipe-dream that probably it is at present.

In 2008 we were a major sponsor of the club's new reserve team, an arrangement of which we are justifiably proud. We have periodic meetings with Chris Hamilton and always champion the views of the fans. We also try to raise the profile of the rich history of Oldham in rugby league by celebrating notable anniversaries.

We have a membership in excess of 300 people, which is the envy of many other rugby league trusts. We are members of the Supporters Direct organisation and are affiliated to the All Party Parliamentary Rugby League Group.

The trust has always tried to support the game in the town at all levels. In the amateur game we regularly sponsor the man of the match award – the Ben Powell trophy – at the Oldham Standard Cup Final. We have collaborated with originally the Service Area and latterly the Oldham Amateur League to organise the Oldham Junior Finals Day. We also administer the 'Rugby Oldham' Open Age and Junior Challenges which compare our local clubs against each other even though they play in different leagues. The most consistent local player also receives the Man of Steel award, currently worth £500.

David and Nathan Murgatroyd, father and son, club photographer and Roary the Roughyed respectively

David: Partaking in a role you enjoy, for a team you love, is something special. Photography and Oldham RLFC are my utopia. In 2008 the club was looking for someone with an interest in photography who would be willing to help out. Without hesitation I put my hand up and offered my services. Nine years later I am still here and have taken thousands of images. At each match I average more than 600 pictures.

My images have appeared in the *Oldham Chronicle*, the *Daily Star*, the *Daily Mirror*, Craig Halstead's first book *From Watersheddings to Whitebank – An Oldham Rugby League Memoir*, the rugby league media, numerous RFL programmes and my claim to fame, the *Official*

Fans at Bloomfield Road, Blackpool for Summer Bash in May 2017.

The Murgatroyd boys – father and son – David (right) with Nathan (Roary the Roughyed) with the League One League Leaders Trophy in 2015.
(Photo courtesy David Murgatroyd).

guide to the Rugby League World Cup in 2008, thanks to Scottish international Mick Nanyn, an Oldham player at the time.

As well as being club photographer I also double up as match day First Aider and post-match host in the social club, both at Whitebank and, more recently, at Bower Fold. I have been the match PA announcer on occasions. The club could not operate week-to-week without its volunteers and we do our jobs purely for the love of the club.

My parents were both Oldham supporters so this club is in my blood. I love the buzz on match day, the excitement, the singing at home before I set off. At the ground I have to calm down a little and act in a more reserved manner. I cannot join in with the fans singing when I am on the side of the pitch, but I must admit every now and then I cannot help myself. One thing I still do, and always will, is cheer when we score a try. I am a fan and that will never change. But until I go blind or until the club find someone better, I will be there clicking away at matches. After all I have the best seat in the house.

Nathan: Being a Murgatroyd goes hand in hand with being a Roughyed. I grew up supporting the team at Boundary Park and now I am privileged to have the role of Roary the Roughyed. I am a quiet, reserved individual – honest – so when I heard the club were looking for a 'mascot' it never really entered my head to apply. My dad, however, had already made up his mind that he was going to talk me into it.

I made my 'debut' at a Rochdale Hornets versus Oldham game and took the costume home after the match. However, it was the worst 80 minutes of my teenage life. Eventually, as I gained confidence I began to love the role. In 2014 we played Bradford Bulls in a Challenge Cup tie at Odsal and I was so nervous about meeting the renowned Bull Boy Mascots. On the day, Bully didn't turn up so I felt 10 feet tall. Now I am never nervous at away games.

I love my job and look forward to arriving at the ground, meeting fans and watching Oldham play. I have a personalised greeting for some fans, either a secret handshake, a big cuddle or even starting a fight with them. A select few always bring sweets and biscuits and of course Roary has to have some. Younger Oldham fans love talking to Roary and I probably know each and every one of them by name. However, when I am out of my costume and I meet the same people they usually walk past without a second glance.

In 2017, I was invited to be part of the club's promotion at Spindles Shopping Centre and I was also invited by Dr Kershaw's Hospice to compete in "Strictly Kershaws" which was great. I have some plans for Roary in the near future and I am looking forward to growing with the club and becoming bigger and better in the seasons ahead.

Sheila and Grant Somerville, volunteers

Sport has character forming qualities and we believe it has a big part to play in developing a good grounding for life. Commitment and effort is needed to be competitive in any physical sport, so we admire the standards achieved by those involved in rugby league at a semi-professional level, when they are combining training with employment and family life. We enjoy supporting these young men and encouraging them to give their all by cheering them on from the sidelines on match days.

We are both proud Oldhamers and our support of Oldham Rugby League Club is longstanding, having watched the 'old' club for many years and now, of course, the 'new' club. Wherever we have travelled with them, from Cumbria to London, from South Wales to Gateshead and other unlikely destinations of recent times, we always enjoy watching the team play, win, lose or draw. We try to give something back by being season ticket holders and performing voluntary roles such as selling programmes and half-time draw tickets. That is something we both enjoy as it gives us the opportunity to interact with fellow fans on match days.

Our desire to see a sound future for the club has resulted in our involvement with the official, but independently run, supporters group ORSA (Oldham Roughyeds Supporters Association), for which we act as Secretary and Treasurer respectively.

The following is a poem we wrote recently. We hope it rings true with lots of fans feelings.

Real Roughyeds
We never see a glass that's half empty, we know our glass is always half full.
And we always see a lovely day, when the weather is cloudy and dull.
We always see a team of winners, real men giving their all, Do or Die!
So you can choose how you want to be, and we think in the end that you'll see,
It's a real big deal to show how you feel, and to stand with your head held high,
So whatever the score, it's never a bore, IT'S ROUGHYEDS TILL I DIE!!!

Dave Naylor, supporter

As a Watersheddings lad, the rebirth of Oldham RLFC was very important to me. I was present when the 'new' team played Widnes Vikings away on February 1, 1998 in the third round of the Challenge Cup. It was the 'new' club's second competitive game and Oldham were beaten 48–8. However, it didn't seem to matter, our team was out there on the park, giving their all for the badge and being cheered by many Roughyed fans.

Today, I manage the club's website and social media accounts as well as assisting with the match-day programme production. It is a labour of love and I am determined that the club's on-line presence should rival the best that any rugby league club has to offer.

Gareth John Hughes, spokesperson for the 'Loud and Proud' gang who follow the team home and away

The feeling after the demise of the 'old' club was one of despair, no hope, no club. Then the news broke that we would reform and play our first game at our local rivals Rochdale Hornets. Entering Spotland and seeing a sea of red and white, with around 3,000 voices chanting, 'Oldham, Oldham' was amazing. To top it off the new team won against the odds. The NFP Grand Final of 2001 was unforgettable for me as it was the last time three generations of my family watched the Roughyeds together. My gran who was 82, and had not been to a game since the 1960s, wore a Roughyeds scarf and joined in with the chanting. My mum was there too. She always tells me off for getting too excited at matches. On this occasion she was out of her seat yelling support at the top of her voice. I was calming her down.

The next few years were up and down for the Roughyeds, but support from the 'Loud and Proud' gang was undiminished. We were a band of brothers and sisters all united in the cause of giving unwavering support to the team. I lived abroad between 2005 and 2012 and missed some of the Grand Final disappointments. However, my pal, Gerry Jones, telephoned me with a match report every Sunday and provided updates about team selection, injury news and transfer news on a regular basis. On returning home, it was like I had never been away. I was welcomed back by some of the most genuine and passionate fans I am privileged to call my friends. Oldham Rugby League is not just a club or a team to us, it is a massive part of our lives.

We are welcomed at all grounds we visit and have made friends at several clubs around the country. Our club rivalries are put aside as we spend time with opposition fans because we appreciate that they love their clubs like we love ours. We may be small in number but with 'Kev the Cabbie' – Kevin Morrow – leading our singing and chanting, people certainly hear us.

At Hunslet in 2013, Oldham got a penalty and kicked for touch. The ball was heading straight towards me and I thought to myself, 'I am going to catch this.' In my mind I was Billy Slater, the world's best full-back. Unfortunately, I lost my balance, fell over a seat and landed head first. The hilarity has never been forgotten by my mates.

Fans outside The Melting Pot in Toulouse, April 2017.

On a trip to London the same year, several of us wore fancy dress. We had a minibus full including Batman and Robin (Gerry and myself). At a motorway service station the two of us burst into the café and I shouted, 'He isn't here, Batman.' Unbeknown to us, the Oldham team were there, enjoying a coffee, all the players trying to keep a straight face. Scott Naylor told us later that he had to get them out quickly to keep them focused on the match because they were laughing so much.

A game that sums up our devotion was the one at Maesteg against South Wales Scorpions in 2014 which was abandoned due to freakish weather. A group of us stood drenched behind the posts and gave a stirring rendition of *Singing in the Rain*. Sam Gee walked over shaking his head in disbelief. "Thanks so much for coming, you maniacs," or words to that effect, he muttered. That gesture meant the world to us.

Gaining promotion in 2015 was special. The relief and togetherness of fans and players and the scenes of unbridled joy will live with me forever. The following year we knocked Hull Kingston Rovers out of the Challenge Cup. That day was topped off by Rovers fans shaking our hands and allowing us the pleasure of having a celebratory sing-song in their staunch supporters' pub.

The Toulouse trip in 2017 was wonderful. On the Saturday afternoon before the game, 50 to 60 Roughyeds fans were outside a bar singing and dancing, with local people and tourists taking pictures with us. A wedding procession passed with people hanging out of sunroofs and windows applauding the fans, who returned the compliment.

As a group we live and breathe our rugby league club. For as long as there is an ORLFC, and irrespective of what division they play in or what venue they play at, we will be there through hell or high water. Up the Roughyeds!

Tony Peet, supporter
It was Summer Bash Day in 2016 and a large group of Oldham fans, myself included, were in Blackpool ahead of the clash between

Roughyeds and Swinton Lions. On arrival at Bloomfield Road my mate Dave Thomas told me that he had volunteered to take part in the half-time challenge which involved him and a rival Swinton fan dressing up in fancy dress and facing each other in an obstacle race, on the pitch, in front of the fans and quite possibly a nationwide televison audience (the match was televised live by Sky Sports). I thought at the time, 'Rather you than me, mate!'

Anyway, as the first-half wore on – with our beloved Roughyeds racing into a 20-0 lead – Dave must have had second thoughts. "Why, oh why, have I volunteered for this," he must have thought. Unbeknown to me, he was hatching a plan – to get me to do it instead! With a few minutes to go to half-time, he gave me a nudge and whispered: "Tony, my old mate, do you fancy doing the challenge for me?" and he rhymed out a number of reasons why he couldn't do it after all. Being an agreeable sort of bloke, I reluctantly said OK. I made my way down to the tunnel and nervously donned my outfit, thinking I can't let my club down here, I have to win this race.

The idea was that the other lad and I were jockeys riding donkeys, as though we were on Blackpool beach. I set off as fast as I could and, to my surprise, built up a sizeable lead. As all jockeys know, however, fences are there to be hurdled. Unfortunately, as I turned the corner towards one such hurdle, my donkey lost his footing and, instead of jumping over it, I fell head first into it, cutting my face in the process. Roary the Roughyed rushed to my aid and helped me up. To my dismay the Swinton donkey had sauntered past me and won the race. I was distraught, far more upset that I didn't win, than the fact I had 'claret' pouring out of me. I guess I can always say that I gave blood in the cause of Oldham Rugby.

Needless to say, my mates loved every minute of it and have never let me forget it, but it was all in good fun. As if I didn't feel bad enough, Oldham's second-half collapse, and Swinton's eventual one-point win, capped a miserable day. Looking back though, I am glad I took part. I represented Oldham, the club I love. That can't be all bad.

Chris Applegate, supporter
I live in Northampton, but love driving north, with my wife Sue and/or my sons, to watch my team play every Sunday. My mum came from Glodwick and used to go to Watersheddings with her dad. She moved south when she married but would always watch *Grandstand* with Eddie Waring, so despite growing up in the south of England, I was always a rugby league fan. It is a long day, five hours driving for those eighty minutes, so why do we do it? Over the last few years my family and I have been welcomed into the Roughyed family. I could never be happier and more proud on a Sunday, wearing my colours and singing

loudly. To me the Oldham fans are the best in the world. Thank you for letting us be a part of it.

On 7 May 2011, Sue and I were sitting in the West Stand at the Kingston Communications Stadium in Hull for the Challenge Cup fourth round tie against Oldham. Why the West Stand, I hear you ask, where you have to have a note from your mum if you are not wearing black and white? We were with our Hull FC supporting friends so we were a tiny blob of red and white amongst all those opposition shirts. Their club mascot, Airlie Bird, spotted us on his journey around the pitch and came up to shake my hand, and his head. Oldham lost, but the lads gave it their all in spite of the selection being injury ravaged. As we left the stadium several Hull fans patted me on the back and said, "Be proud of your lads because they never let their heads drop and your fans because they never stopped singing. They were more supportive, and made more noise, than a lot of Super League club fans do. Well done!" I was so proud that day.

Wayne Halstead, supporter

Living 285 miles from Oldham, watching the Roughyeds is not easy. I have to pick my matches and plan the weekend well in advance. Over the past 20 years, some of those matches stand out more than most. The Northern Ford Premiership final against Widnes Vikings at Spotland in 2001 and the Grand Final loss to Featherstone Rovers at Headingley in 2007 spring to mind. Due to my location in the south-east, 'home' games for me are when Oldham hit the road – London Broncos, London Skolars, Hemel, Gloucestershire All Golds and Oxford. I was present at the Challenge Cup game in Aldershot against the Army, when flying Fijian Ben Seru was so impressive we signed him after the game – only for him to suffer a career ending injury at Wakefield Trinity Wildcats in the next round. That seems to sum up our luck.

I saw us win at Oxford on a baking hot day, the same afternoon that Andy Murray became Britain's first Wimbledon champion since Fred Perry, and numerous games in London, when the family would stay with me and we would mix watching Roughyeds with the London tourist trail. In 2017, we bumped into, and had photographs with, Mike Stephenson ('Stevo') of Sky Sports fame at the Broncos game in Ealing. And we enjoyed the ultimate southern trip, when we broke new ground and played Toulouse in the south of France, enjoying French hospitality more than the result.

There are times, however, when I have to hit the road, or catch a train, to get to an Oldham home game. Our final game at Bower Fold in 2016, against Whitehaven, was one of those. My train broke down at Retford station in Nottinghamshire and was delayed for three hours. I finally arrived in Stalybridge at 2.50pm and got into the ground at

3.01pm – the only time I have ever missed the kick off. But we won that day and secured our Kingstone Press Championship place for another year, so it was all worth it.

I would love to go to every game like some of our loyal fans do, as I did before moving south, but when I am not there I follow every update on Twitter. I am writing this the day after I drove north and saw us lose at Swinton Lions to condemn us to Kingstone Press League One in 2018. But, of course, we all know we will go again next year. In true Twitter fashion #RoughyedstillIdie.

Robert Nixon, supporter

I have been supporting Oldham for 12 years and was interested to learn, in 2017, that Roughyeds had adopted 'Maggie's' as their shirt sponsors. I was keen to do something to help them. I was running in the Manchester marathon in early April 2017 and decided to donate my sponsorship money to them. I was proud, surprised and delighted when the club invited me on to the pitch at half-time in the Bradford Bulls match at Bower Fold, on the same day as the run, in recognition of my efforts.

I started at Lancashire County Cricket Club at Old Trafford and ran via Altrincham and Timperley to Carrington. I missed the first quarter of the Bulls match, arriving at the ground midway through the first half. After my big moment on the pitch, I watched the whole of the second half and was lucky to witness the brilliant match-winning try by Keiran Gill. What a fantastic end to a great day that was! Winning promotion in 2015 is undoubtedly my favourite Roughyeds memory, but I am sure there will be many more to come in the future.

Peter Hilton, supporter

My family connections with Oldham Rugby go back to the 1920s. The great Herman Hilton, a member of the Heritage Trust Hall of Fame, was my great-uncle. My granddad was on the 'old club' committee in the 1950s.

I watch the team regularly and have witnessed the good, the bad and the ugly watching Oldham. My most vivid 'new' club memory is of watching Adam Hughes play in 2007. He was a terrific centre. Two tries he scored while running up the slope at Featherstone, stand out in my memory. Unfortunately we still lost.

I was among many Oldham fans at Swinton Lions when we lost the 'must-win' match in September 2017 and were relegated from the Kingstone Press Championship. That was a sad day but there have been many happy days too. Being an Oldham fan is not for the faint hearted. It is a deep love that we all share.

Robert Nixon's big moment with Roary at Bower Fold at half-time in the
Bradford Bulls game in April 2017 (Photo David Murgatroyd).

John Flanagan, ex-pat Oldhamer and resident of the Philippines, still very
much a Roughyed (Photo courtesy John Flanagan).

John M. Flanagan, supporter

When I lived in Oldham, and even when I moved further afield, I rarely missed a Roughyeds match. In 2008, however, I moved to Singapore and then in 2010 to the Philippines. I married a Filipino girl and have since been involved in charity work for needy people in the Philippines. As a result of this, in 2011, my wife and I were featured on a live nationwide television programme. It was on the country's most popular variety show and I wore my Roughyeds jersey with pride that night. Not many people in Oldham would have realised that our club colours were being paraded across television screens in a distant land. Our story was also featured in the *Oldham Chronicle* a couple of years ago.

I was born in 1951 and my first game at Watersheddings supporting the 'old' club was in 1954 — not that I recall much about it! Later in life I was the reporter for amateur rugby league in the *Oldham Chronicle* for a short time and did the results and a chat session on BBC Radio Manchester. I maintain a keen interest in the 'new' club to this day, always keen to catch up on their results via social media and discuss rugby with fellow fans. I wish them all the very best in the future.

Des Foy, player at the 'old' club

Des is best known locally for being one of the best centres ever to play for the 'old' club. A Great Britain international, he scored 96 tries in 197 appearances in the red and white. He now lives in Ireland and is a Director of Rugby League Ireland, the organisation responsible for running the game in the Emerald Isle. It was apparent speaking to Des that he feels a lot of empathy for the 'new' Oldham club.

"I am sure life outside Super League is tough for every club but Oldham's lack of a permanent home over the last 20 years must have made it particularly difficult to attract players and keep fans happy. Oldham is a rugby league town and this has been reinforced in recent years when I have enjoyed going back and playing EuroTag — a form of touch rugby league — with lads from St Anne's, Saddleworth and Waterhead amateur rugby league clubs among others, at various venues around the town. I always look out for the Roughyeds results first and stay in touch with their progress as best I can."

On his involvement with Tony Benson and Wayne Kerr in Ireland, Des said: "The development trip to New Zealand that Tony helped organise is still regarded as a high point for Rugby League Ireland a decade later. Wayne is actively involved in the Irish set-up and is able to pass on the experience he gained as a player, not least with Oldham, to the Ireland Under-19s in a coaching role. Trying to keep the rugby league flag flying in Ireland is an uphill battle, so I understand what people at Oldham are going through. I wish them all the very best in the future."

212

Appendix 1: World Cup call-ups 2017

All at Oldham Rugby League Club would like to offer their congratulations to Richard Lepori (Italy) and Joe Burke and Ben Morris (Wales) who were named in early October 2017 in their respective squads for the World Cup in Australia, New Zealand and Papua New Guinea. Also to former Oldham players Will Hope and Oliver Roberts (dual-registration) who have been named in the Ireland squad.

Lepori was delighted to hear he had been named by Italy: "I am really excited to be in the squad to travel to the World Cup. It is a once-in-a-lifetime opportunity. I thoroughly enjoyed playing in the qualifying competition last year so I can't wait for the tournament to start. I will do my utmost to train and prepare as well as I can and if selected to play, ensure I play well. I know we will set ourselves high targets and will be disappointed if we don't make it out of the group.

I owe a lot to Scott Naylor, 'Spanner' (Lee Spencer) and Pete Carey, the coaches at Oldham, for everything I have achieved in the past few years."

Appendix 2: Appearances and scorers

1998	App	T	G	DG	Pts
Craig Barker	13	2			8
Jason Clegg	15				0
Sean Cooper	15	4	1		18
Paul Crook	10	1			4
Richard Darkes	20	5	8		36
Craig Diggle	2	2			8
Chris Eckersley	21	15			60
Michael Edwards	20	6			24
Neil Flanagan	20	3			12
Andrew Fleming	2				0
John Hough	21	7			28
Emerson Jackman	5	2			8
Afi Leuila	20	8			32
Martin Maders	13				0
Mick Martindale	16	5			20
Joe McNicholas	4				0
Adrian Mead	19	5			20
Joe Naidole	15	1			4
Mike Prescott	6	1			4
Andy Proctor	11	1			4
Brian Quinlan	8	1	17		38
Darren Robinson	8	2			8
Paul Round	20	3			12
Graeme Shaw	18	2			8
Ian Sinfield	16	1			4
Nathan Varley	21				0
Steve Wilde	17	6			24
Chris Wilkinson	13		34	3	71

Second Division:
P 20 W 10 D 1 L 9 F 399 A 383 21 pts 5th out of 8

1999	App	T	G	DG	Pts
Craig Barker	8				0
Josh Bostock	7	3			12
Paul Brassington	6	1			4
Keith Brennan	7	3			12
Daniel Brown	31	14	42		140
Leo Casey	28	1			4
Jason Clegg	30	5			20
Michael Coates	6		1		2
Gary Coulter	6				0
Jim Cowan	1				0
Paul Crook	22	3			12
Richard Darkes	11	2			8
Mick Farrell	15	6	1		26
Stuart Fraser	2				0
Danny Guest	5				0
John Hough	30	7			28
Emerson Jackman	29	4			16
Afi Leuila	19	3			12
David Lewis	1				0
Martin Maders	4				0
Mick Martindale	10	2			8
Joe McNicholas	31	8			32
Adrian Mead	31	8			32
Laurent Minut	19	2	10		28
Joe Naidole	10				0
Emmanuel Peralta	26				0
Mark Perrett	15	1			4
Mike Prescott	23	1			4
Brian Quinlan	11	1	4		12
Paul Round	20	4			16
Jim Salisbury	3		7		14
Graeme Shaw	22	3			12
Ian Sinfield	8	1			4
Nathan Varley	11	1			4
Daniel Webster	7				0
Danny Wood	6	1	12	1	29

Northern Ford Premiership:
P 28 W 5 D 2 L21 F 449 A 999 12 pts 17th out of 18

2000	App	T	G	DG	Pts
Warren Barrow	23	12			48
Keith Brennan	5	1		1	5
Mark Campbell	27	5			20
Leo Casey	24	1			4
Jason Clegg	29				0
Dean Cross	4	4			16
Gavin Dodd	1				0
Lee Doran	5				0
Phil Farrell	21	5			20
Peter Ferris	5	1			4
Kevin Fitzpatrick	1				0
Mike Ford	22	6		3	27
Anthony Gibbons	30	16		1	65
David Gibbons	32	10			40
Danny Guest	20	2			8
Joey Hayes	30	17			68
Chris Holland	18				0
John Hough	33	18			72
Kevin Mannion	26	3			12
Shayne McMenemy	22	3	3	1	19
Joe McNicholas	11				0
Steve Molloy	6	1			4
Tate Moseley	3	1			4
Chris Naylor	1				0
Tom O'Reilly	9	1			4
Andy Proctor	26	1			4
Pat Rich	31	10	108		256
Neil Roden	19	6		2	26
Wes Rogers	10	1			4
Graeme Shaw	2				0
Mark Sibson	33	23	13		118
Ian Sinfield	20				0

Northern Ford Premiership:
P 28 W 19 D 1 L 8 F 734 A 513 39pts 6th out of 18

2001	App	T	G	DG	Pts
Danny Arnold	11	4			16
Gareth Barber	7	1			4
Warren Barrow	5	5			20
Keith Brennan	17	12		2	50
Leo Casey	22	2			8
Jason Clegg	33	3			12
Dean Cross	7	3			12
Gavin Dodd	16	7		1	29
Lee Doran	7				0
Chris Farrell	26	2			8
Phil Farrell	34	5			20
Mike Ford	20	1		2	6
Anthony Gibbons	32	13			52
David Gibbons	30	17			68
Danny Guest	26				0
Joey Hayes	10	5			20
Bryan Henare	11	6			24
John Hough	27	5			20
Gavin Johnson	1				0
Daryl Lacey	24	5			20
Kevin Mannion	27	7			28
Shayne McMenemy	1				0
Joe McNicholas	14	8			32
Paul Norton	31	3			12
Andy Proctor	20	2			8
Pat Rich	34	7	146		320
Neil Roden	34	16		6	70
Mark Sibson	23	18			72
Ian Sinfield	25	1			4

Northern Ford Premiership:
P 28 W 21 D 0 L 7 F 780 A 416 Pts 42 4th out of 19

2002	App	T	G	DG	Pts
Gareth Barber	38	17	80	1	229
John Braddish	23	7	63	2	156
Keith Brennan	27	9	9		54
Stephen Brown	1				0
Chris Campbell	12	4			16
Leo Casey	4				0
Jason Clegg	38				0
Will Cowell	25	5			20
Gavin Dodd	30	7			28
Lee Doran	38	13			52
Phil Farrell	20	6			24
David Foster	6	5			20
Anthony Gibbons	26	7			28
David Gibbons	32	10			40
Jon Goddard	37	10			40
Danny Guest	30				0
Joey Hayes	11	6			24
Bryan Henare	33	8			32
Tommy Hodgkinson	2				0
John Hough	37	10			40
Gavin Johnson	9	1			4
Simon Knox	3				0
Daryl Lacey	3	1			4
Joe McNicholas	34	16			64
Steve Molloy	27	2		1	9
Anthony Murray	5				0
David Newton	2				0
Paul Norton	25	5			20
Andy Proctor	8				0
Neil Roden	36	20		7	87
Mark Sibson	35	19			76
Ryan Stazicker	2				0

Northern Ford Premiership:
P 27 W 13 D 3 L 11 F 748 A 553 Pts 29 9th out of 18

2003	App	T	G	DG	Pts
Paul Anderson	22	8			32
Gareth Barber	26	13	32		116
Keith Brennan	21	5		1	21
Chris Campbell	9	5			20
Jason Clegg	3				0
Will Cowell	12	2			8
Gavin Dodd	29	14			56
Lee Doran	31	14			56
Phil Farrell	25	8			32
Jon Goddard	25	5			20
Danny Guest	19				0
John Hough	27	5			20
Chris Irwin	12	4			16
Gavin Johnson	5				0
Nick Johnson	4	4			16
Iain Marsh	25	4			16
Lee Marsh	5				0
Craig McDowell	4				0
Martin McLoughlin	21	1			4
Joe McNicholas	9	2			8
Steve Molloy	29	2			8
Dane Morgan	25	6			24
Chris Morley	27	4			16
Anthony Murray	5	1			4
Paul Norton	10	1			4
Chris Percival	3	1			4
Dan Potter	4	2			8
Neil Roden	27	7		3	31
Adam Sharples	1				0
Darren Shaw	13				0
Ryan Stazicker	18	4			16
Simon Svabic	30	5	81	2	184

National League One:
P 18 W 7 D 2 L 9 F 404 A 500 Pts 16 5th out of 10

2004	App	T	G	DG	Pts
Gareth Barber	28	8	17		66
Keith Brennan	26	5		2	22
Chris Brett	1				0
James Bunyan	14	7			28
Adam Clayton	1				0
Will Cowell	17	7			28
Gavin Dodd	27	15			60
Lee Doran	31	3			12
Martin Elswood	20	2			8
Phil Farrell	19	5			20
Craig Farrimond	6	1			4
David Gibbons	2				0
Jon Goddard	30	13			52
John Hough	12				0
Gavin Johnson	6				0
Nick Johnson	31	25			100
James Lomax	1				0
Iain Marsh	16	12			48
Lee Marsh	26	15	20	1	101
Martin McLoughlin	22	2			8
Steve Molloy	15				0
Dane Morgan	22	10			40
Danny Nanyn	1				0
Pat Rich	10	2	49		106
Mark Roberts	4				0
Neil Roden	22	16			64
Jon Roper	9		20		40
Adam Sharples	7				0
Paul Southern	15	1			4
Simon Svabic	11	2	25		58
Ian Watson	20	6	5	7	41

National League One:
P 18 W 10 D 0 L8 F482 A 503 Pts 20 4th out of 9

2005	App	T	G	DG	Pts
Gareth Barber	22	8	1		34
Ricky Bibey	21				0
Keith Brennan	2				0
Will Cowell	10	4			16
Gavin Dodd	26	17			68
Martin Elswood	13	2			8
Craig Farrimond	4				0
Tere Glassie	23	6			24
Jon Goddard	19	7			28
Andy Gorey	7	3			12
Simon Haughton	14	7			28
Ian Hodson	15	1			4
Chris Hough	13	3	4	1	21
John Hough	20	1			4
Nick Johnson	25	12			48
James Kirkland	14				0
Carlos Mataora	24	3			12
Rob Mills	8	1			4
Damian Munro	17	12			48
Danny Nanyn	10				0
Paul Norman	14	2			8
Mark Roberts	13	2			8
Andy Sands	2				0
Adam Sharples	9				0
Simon Svabic	23	9	10	2	58
David Tootill	2				0
Marty Turner	23	8	84	1	201
Alex Wilkinson	22	5			20
Dana Wilson	22	3			12

National League One:

P 18 W 6 D 1 L 11 F 455 A 545 Pts 13 7th out of 10

2006	App	T	G	DG	Pts
Paul Ashton	11	3	7		26
Andy Bailey	9				0
Chris Baines	17	1			4
Gareth Barber	17	5	24		68
David Best	14				0
Jason Best	1				0
Matthew Bottom	13	2			8
Mike Callan	9				0
Chris Campbell	4	3			12
Ged Corcoran	14	1			4
Wayne Corcoran	16	3	5		22
Craig Dean	6				0
Phil Farrell	6	1			4
Andy Gorey	22	10			40
Dean Gorton	23	6			24
Danny Guest	5				0
Alan Hadcroft	8				0
Gareth Hayes	24	1			4
Ian Hodson	23	2			8
Chris Hough	12		4	1	9
John Hough	19	1			4
Carl Jones	6				0
Ken Kerr	1				0
Tom Kilgannon	9	3			12
James Kirkland	7				0
Danny Ligairi-Badham	1				0
Chris Maye	18	3			12
Danny Nanyn	9				0
Paul O'Connor	3	1			4
Chris Percival	10	8			32
Carl Redford	2				0
Mick Redford	8	1			4
Mark Roberts	14	1			4
Adam Sharples	2				0
Simon Stephens	2				0
Simon Svabic	22	5	1		22
Andy Wallace	2				0
Alex Wilkinson	16	4			16
Desi Williams	11	4			16
Sion Williams	8				0
Lee Wingfield	15	5			20

National League One:
P 18 W 0 D 0 L 18 F 220 A 944 Pts 0 10th out of 10

2007	App	T	G	DG	Pts
Paul Ashton	11	3	27		66
Chris Baines	22	2			8
Jason Boults	25				0
Matty Brooks	17	2			8
Geno Costin	25	8			32
James Coyle	14	6			24
Andy Crabtree	24	1			4
Byron Ford	10	12			48
Ian Gordon	5				0
Andy Gorey	10	2			8
Ian Hodson	23	6			24
John Hough	2				0
Drew Houston	25	6			24
Simeon Hoyle	28	2			8
Adam Hughes	16	22	12		112
Gareth Langley	30	13	35		122
Craig Littler	27	6			24
Richard Mervill	31	3			12
Gareth Morton	7	4	29		74
Paul O'Connor	14	4			16
Mark Ogden	5	1	10		24
Stuart Oldham	1				0
Lucas Onyango	23	18			72
Rob Roberts	12	5		1	21
Adam Robinson	10	3			12
Neil Roden	34	10		2	42
Wes Rogers	10				0
Lee Sanderson	8	1	20		44
Ian Sinfield	24	2			8
Kris Smith	10	5			20
Warren Stevens	5				0
Mike Stout	4	1			4
Said Tamghart	29	4			16
Tony Tonks	20	3			12
Alex Wilkinson	30	12			48
Lee Wingfield	4	1			4

National League Two:
P 22 W 16 D 0 L 6 BP 5 F 661 A 420 Pts 53 4th out of 12

2008	App	T	G	DG	Pts
Chris Baines	26	1			4
Simon Baldwin	8				0
Jason Boults	33	4			16
Matty Brooks	20	1			4
Michael Brown	2	2			8
Daryl Cardiss	14	2			8
James Coyle	37	21	3		90
Tommy Goulden	30	15			60
Tommy Grundy	13	1			4
Danny Halliwell	34	20	15		110
Ian Hodson	14	5			20
Simeon Hoyle	22	5			20
Phil Joseph	33	12			48
Gareth Langley	21	5	8		36
Craig Littler	15	7			28
James Martin	2				0
Luke Menzies	12	1			4
Richard Mervill	35	3			12
Mick Nanyn	32	21	139		362
Paul O'Connor	35	17			68
Lucas Onyango	18	11			44
Rob Roberts	31	7			28
Adam Robinson	25	2			8
Neil Roden	33	12			48
Ben Seru	1				0
Marcus St Hilaire	32	15			60
Warren Stevens	6				0
Luke Sutton	6	1			4
Said Tamghart	34	3			12
Alex Wilkinson	5	3			12

National League Two:
P 22 W 17 D 0 L 5 BP 1 F 716 A 456 Pts 52 3rd out of 12

2009	App	T	G	DG	Pts
Dave Allen	17	6			24
Matt Ashe	7	4	5		26
Chris Baines	29	12	33		114
Andy Ballard	18	17	93		254
Andy Boothroyd	2				0
Jason Boults	20	1			4
James Coyle	20	10	5		50
Thomas Coyle	26	15			60
Stevie Gibbons	7	3			12
Tommy Goulden	23	11			44
Lee Greenwood	21	12			48
Danny Halliwell	17	8	5		42
Ben Heaton	3	1			4
Paul Highton	14	1			4
Jamie I'Anson	27	3			12
Phil Joseph	22	4	1		18
Wayne Kerr	24	4			16
Craig Lawton	5				0
Craig Littler	8	3			12
Luke Menzies	15	2			8
Richard Mervill	12	1			4
Paul O'Connor	28	12	3		54
Lucas Onyango	18	14			56
Paul Reilly	21	6			24
Rob Roberts	12	3			12
Craig Robinson	16	2			8
Martin Roden	10	4			16
Neil Roden	23	7		1	29
Jamie Russo	5	3			12
Marcus St Hilaire	20	11			44
Luke Sutton	1				0
Gary Sykes	19	3			12

Championship One:
P 18 W 10 D 1 L 7 BP 3 F 618 A 449 Pts 35 4th out of 10

2010	App	T	G	DG	Pts
Matt Ashe	22	8	78		188
Valu Bentley	16	3			12
Jason Boults	26	6			24
Mark Brocklehurst	9	6			24
Joe Chandler	28	12			48
Chris Clarke	22	6			24
Dave Ellison	28	7			28
Mick Fogerty	28	19			76
John Gillam	19	16			64
Ben Heaton	27	6			24
Ian Hodson	12				0
Jamie I'Anson	4				0
Wayne Kerr	27	6			24
Craig Littler	3	1			4
Scott Mansfield	4				0
Gregg McNally	12	7	46	1	121
Ben Mellor	3				0
Saqib Murtza	5	2			8
Paul O'Connor	28	19	5		86
Lucas Onyango	28	19			76
Paul Reilly	6	1			4
Craig Robinson	13	1			4
Martin Roden	28	2			8
Neil Roden	21	4		2	18
Marcus St Hilaire	21	3			12
Luke Sutton	9	1			4
John Walker	2				0
Danny Whitmore	25	5			20

Championship One:

P 20 W 17 D 0 L 3 BP 1 F 694 A 438 Pts 52 2nd out of 11

226

2011	App	T	G	DG	Pts
Matt Ashe	1				0
Valu Bentley	25	3			12
Jason Boults	25	4			16
Jack Bradbury	9	3			12
Danny Bravo	9	3			12
Mark Brocklehurst	23	17			68
Callum Casey	9	3			12
Chris Clarke	15	3			12
John Clough	25	8			32
Jamie Dallimore	3	3	2	1	17
Mick Diveney	10	4	33		82
Dave Ellison	17	2			8
Matthew Fogarty	12	8			32
Mick Fogerty	1	1			4
Carl Forber	14	5	63		146
Liam Gilchrist	11				0
John Gillam	9	4			16
Ben Heaton	19	13			52
Andrew Isherwood	17	6			24
Scott Mansfield	1				0
Mark McCully	9	3			12
Steven Nield	1				0
Paul Noone	27	5	2		24
Lucas Onyango	10	7			28
Shaun Robinson	19	8			32
Martin Roden	23	1			4
Neil Roden	23	8			32
Marcus St Hilaire	13	2			8
Luke Stenchion	16	2			8
Luke Sutton	20	3			12
Michael Ward	6				0
Danny Whitmore	15	2			8
Alistair Williams	1				0
Ben Wood	16	6			24
Tom Wood-Hulme	5				0

Championship One:

P 20 W 11 D 0 L 9 BP 3 F 641 A 533 Pts 36 7th out of 10

2012	App	T	G	DG	Pts
Jamie Acton	6				0
Paul Ballard	5	2			8
Valu Bentley	17				0
Jason Boults	26				0
Mark Brocklehurst	13	3			12
Chris Clarke	18	2			8
John Clough	24	8			32
David Cookson	18	5			20
Sam Cunningham	2				0
Jamie Dallimore	23	8	78		188
Dave Ellison	18	3			12
Matthew Fogarty	9	4			16
Rob Foxen	4				0
Liam Gilchrist	16	1			4
John Gillam	9	5			20
Miles Greenwood	25	20			80
Graham Holroyd	5		6		12
Chris Holroyde	2		4		8
Bruce Johnson	8	1			4
Phil Joy	2	1			4
Danny Langtree	2				0
Mark McCully	18	3			12
Chris Murphy	4	2			8
Paul Noone	19	2			8
Lucas Onyango	11	4			16
Lewis Reed	4	1			4
Jack Reid	1				0
Tom Rigby	1				0
Shaun Robinson	8	3			12
Colton Roche	2				0
Martin Roden	16				0
Neil Roden	17	4		2	18
Daniel Smith	4				0
Paul Smith	17	6			24
Luke Stenchion	4				0
Matty Syron	7				0
Alex Thompson	19	12			48
David Tootill	3	1			4
Michael Ward	18	6			24
Danny Whitmore	17	3			12

Championship One:
P 18 W 7 D 1 L 10 BP 5 F 465 A 485 Pts 28 6th out of 10.

2013	App	T	G	DG	Pts
Mo Agoro	22	9			36
Dale Bloomfield	23	11	1		46
Jason Boults	18	2			8
Anthony Bowman	2				0
Niall Bradley	1				0
Dan Brotherton	1				0
Chris Clarke	2	1	1		6
David Cookson	18	5			20
Josh Crowley	24	7			28
Jamie Dallimore	5	4	11		38
Niall Evalds	1	1			4
Adam Files	24	15			60
Jon Ford	15	21			84
Sam Gee	21	4			16
Liam Gilchrist	15	2			8
Matthew Haggarty	9	1			4
Mark Hobson	22	1			4
Will Hope	1				0
Kenny Hughes	19	7			28
Phil Joy	22	2			8
Danny Langtree	23	10			40
Richard Lepori	22	12			48
Callum Marriott	7				0
Nathan Mason	4	2			8
Steven Nield	7	1			4
Lewis Palfrey	22	6	87		198
Neil Roden	6	3			12
Danny Samuel	5				0
Liam Thompson	16	1			4
Chris Tyrer	4				0
Jordan Walne	2				0
Michael Ward	20				0
Tom Whitehead	3	1			4
Danny Whitmore	2		1		2

Championship One:
P 16 W 12 D 1 L 3 BP 3 F 508 A 289 Pts 41 2nd out of 9.

2014	App	T	G	DG	Pts
Mo Agoro	18	18			72
Dale Bloomfield	21	21			84
Jason Boults	20	2			8
Adam Clay	9	4			16
David Cookson	19	7			28
Josh Crowley	25	13		1	53
Alex Davidson	7	1			4
Adam Files	4	2			8
Jon Ford	16	13			52
Sam Gee	17	1	4		12
Mark Hobson	5				0
Kenny Hughes	22	6			24
Phil Joy	23	3			12
Danny Langtree	24	14			56
Nathan Mason	16	2			8
Paddy Mooney	7	1			4
Steven Nield	19	7	2		32
Edwin Okanga-Ajwang	4	1			4
Gareth Owen	8				0
Lewis Palfrey	22	4	59		134
Brett Robinson	15	2		1	9
Steve Roper	16	3	39	1	91
Liam Thompson	12	1			4
George Tyson	16	4			16
Michael Ward	25	7			28
Tom Whitehead	6				0
Danny Whitmore	15	2			8
Ben Wood	14	7			28

Championship One:
P 20 W 15 D 1 L 4 BP 1 F 675 A 457 Pts 48 3rd out of 9.

2015	App	T	G	DG	Pts
Tom Ashton	6	3			12
Jodie Broughton	1	2			8
Adam Clay	23	20			80
Jake Connor	2	1			4
Josh Crowley	28	13			52
Tom Dempsey	8	2	2	1	13
Jacob Fairbank	1	1			4
Adam Files	24	3			12
Jon Ford	16	11			44
Sam Gee	22	7			28
David Hewitt	6	5			20
Jack Holmes	22	15			60
Will Hope	3	2			8
Kenny Hughes	24	2			8
Josh Johnson	5	2			8
Phil Joy	27	5			20
Richard Joy	6	2			8
Danny Langtree	24	13			52
Mick Learmonth	2	2			8
Richard Lepori	7	2			8
Elliot Liku	4	2			8
Nathan Mason	16	2			8
Adam Neal	24	3			12
Steven Nield	8	4			16
Gareth Owen	25	5			20
Lewis Palfrey	26	11	129	2	304
Oliver Roberts	8	2			8
Steve Roper	21	4	18	2	54
Liam Thompson	27	8			32
George Tyson	23	13			52
Jarrod Ward	12	4			16
Michael Ward	25	10			40

League One:

P 22 W 19 D 0 L 3 F 840 A 362 Pts 38 1st out of 14.

2016	App	T	G	DG	Pts
Tom Ashton	4	2			8
Jake Bibby	3				0
Jack Blagbrough	7	2			8
Craig Briscoe	7				0
Joe Burke	22	1			4
Jamel Chisholm	26	10			40
Adam Clay	30	9			36
Josh Crowley	4				0
Tyler Dickinson	18				0
Adam Files	14	3			12
Jon Ford	3	2			8
Lewis Foster	7	1			4
Sam Gee	22	1	1		6
Kieran Gill	12	8			32
Danny Grimshaw	20	3			12
David Hewitt	9	4	5		26
Jack Holmes	14	5			20
Will Hope	23	3			12
Kenny Hughes	27	9			36
Liam Johnson	14	4			16
Phil Joy	28	3			12
Danny Langtree	26	8			32
Kruise Leeming	4				0
Richard Lepori	24	5	1		22
Darnell McIntosh	1				0
Gary Middlehurst	24	4			16
Gareth Owen	31	4			16
Lewis Palfrey	26	1	76	1	157
Steve Roper	12	1	10		24
Jared Simpson	3				0
Jack Spencer	20				0
Tom Spencer	4				0
Liam Thompson	30	2			8
Scott Turner	6	2			8
Michael Ward	31	8			32
Sam Wood	5	2	3		14

Championship Regular season:
P 23 W 7 D 0 L 16 F 401 A 678 Pts 14 10th out of 12
Championship Shield (Includes regular season results):
P 30 W 10 D 0 L 20 F 535 A 918 Pts 20 6th out of 8

2017	App	T	G	DG	Pts
Luke Adamson	16	2			8
Sadiq Adibiyi	11	1			4
Liam Bent	17				0
Joe Burke	25	8			32
Jamel Chisholm	4	1			4
Adam Clay	31	10			40
Ben Davies	20				0
Tyler Dickinson	5				0
Tuoyo Egodo	10	2			8
Sam Gee	25	2			8
Kieran Gill	9	5			20
Danny Grimshaw	19	5			20
David Hewitt	29	5	13		46
Brad Hill	2				0
Luke Hooley	6	1	18		40
Kenny Hughes	31	3			12
Phil Joy	4				0
Danny Langtree	23	4			16
Scott Leatherbarrow	26		65		130
Richard Lepori	15	9			36
Nathan Mason	5				0
Darnell McIntosh	1	1			4
Ben Morris	5	1			4
Adam Neal	24	3			12
Steven Nield	8	1			4
Gene Ormsby	1				0
Gareth Owen	18				0
Kameron Pearce-Paul	7				0
Dan Smith	4	1			4
Jack Spencer	24	1			4
Liam Thompson	20	2			8
Scott Turner	14	4			16
George Tyson	22	9			36
Jordan Walne	1	1			4
Michael Ward	30	10			40
Matt Wilkinson	9	2			8
Connor Williams	5	1			4
Mikey Wood	11				0
Sam Wood	8	3			12

Championship Regular season:
P 23 W 5 D 1 L 17 F 410 A 735 Pts 11 11th out of 12.
Championship Shield (Includes regular season results):
P 30 W 6 D 2 L 22 F 540 A 939 Pts 14 7th out of 8.

Total club appearances

1. Neil Roden   295
2. John Hough   228
3. Jason Boults   193
4. Michael Ward   155
5. Jason Clegg   148
6. Gareth Barber   138
7. Gavin Dodd   129
8. Phil Farrell   125
9. Kenny Hughes   123
10. Danny Langtree   122

Others to top the 100 game mark

11. Lee Doran   112
12. Jon Goddard   111
13. Paul O'Connor   108
13. Lucas Onyango   108
15. Sam Gee   107
16. Phil Joy   106
17. Keith Brennan   105
17. Danny Guest   105
17. Liam Thompson   105
20. Joe McNicholas   103

Total club tries

1. Neil Roden   113
2. Lucas Onyango   73
3. Gavin Dodd   60
3. Mark Sibson   60
5. John Hough   54
6. Paul O'Connor   53
7. Gareth Barber   52
8. Danny Langtree   49
9. Jon Ford   47
10. Adam Clay   43

Total club goals

1. Lewis Palfrey   351
2. Pat Rich   303
3. Gareth Barber   154
4. Mick Nanyn   139
5. Simon Svabic   117
6. Andy Ballard   93
7. Jamie Dallimore   91
8. Marty Turner   84
9. Matt Ashe   83
10. Steve Roper   67

Total club drop-goals

1. Neil Roden   25
2. Ian Watson   7
3. Keith Brennan   6
4. Mike Ford   5
5. Simon Svabic   4

From Watersheddings to Whitebank
An Oldham Rugby League Memoir
by Craig Halstead
Foreword by Chris Hamilton

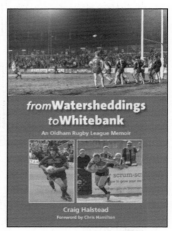

Rugby league has been played professionally in Oldham since 1895 when the great split from rugby union took place. In the ensuing 120 years, teams representing Oldham have graced rugby league grounds in England, Wales, France and Australia. Over that time, there have been many ups-and-downs for Oldham. The highlights include a Championship Final win in 1957, Lancashire Cup Final wins, Second Division Championship and Premiership titles and several promotions. However, there have also been numerous Challenge Cup semi-final defeats, losing finals and relegations.

In 1997, the original club went into liquidation, but in the immediate aftermath of this distressing event, a new club rose like a phoenix from the ashes of the old club. It continues to provide the town of Oldham with a professional rugby league club of which it can be proud.

This book is one supporter's memories, stories, heart-breaking and joyous moments and anecdotes. It provides an insight into how supporting a club – or in this case two clubs – from childhood can provide a lifetime of emotions and experiences, both good and bad.

Craig Halstead first saw an Oldham match, aged 5, in 1971 and has supported Oldham's rugby league team ever since. He attended many matches at Watersheddings, the original club's home, regularly took in away matches and now, despite living in North Wales, watches the new club whenever he can.

Published in October 2011 at £11.95. Special offer: £11.50 post free in the UK available direct from London League Publications Ltd or from Amazon.co.uk .
All our books can be ordered from any bookshop @ full price. To order direct from London League Publications Ltd visit our website: www.llpshop.co.uk or write to LLP, PO Box 65784, London NW2 9NS (cheques payable to London League Publications Ltd).
Most of our books are available as E-Books for Kindle from Amazon.

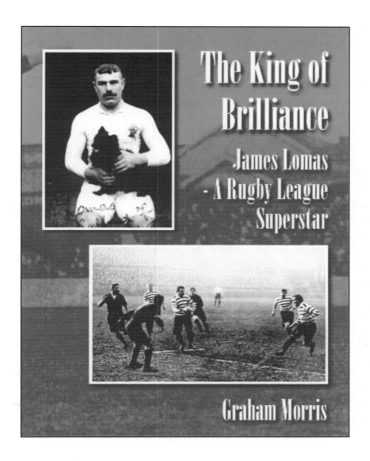

Great book about one of the sport's genuine legends. James Lomas played for Bramley, Salford, Oldham and York, and won representative honours for Lancashire, Cumberland, England and Great Britain. He captained the first Lions team to tour Australia and New Zealand in 1910. This is the first biography of him.

Published in October 2011 at £16.95 (hardback). Special offer: £9.95 post free in the UK available direct from London League Publications Ltd.

All our books can be ordered from any bookshop @ full price. To order direct from London League Publications Ltd visit our website: www.llpshop.co.uk or write to LLP, PO Box 65784, London NW2 9NS (cheques payable to London League Publications Ltd).

Most of our books are available as E-Books for Kindle from Amazon.

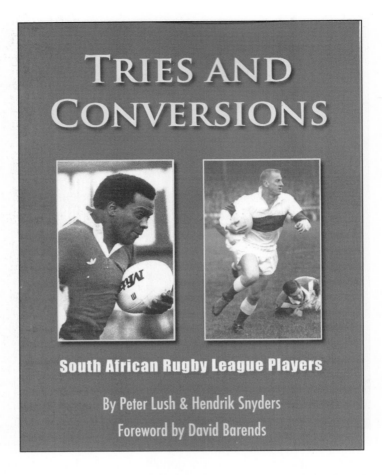

TRIES AND CONVERSIONS

South African Rugby League Players

By Peter Lush & Hendrik Snyders
Foreword by David Barends

In 1910, James Megson and William Mart became the first native-born South Africans to sign for British rugby league clubs. Since then, South African players have made a significant contribution to rugby league. This book is the first comprehensive study of their contribution to rugby league. It covers players who played in Great Britain and Australia. Some were very successful, such as Attie van Heerden and George van Rooyen in the 1920s, Tom van Vollenhoven, Alan Skene, Jan Prinsloo and Len Killeen in the 1950s and 1960s, and Mark Johnson and Jamie Bloem in the Super League era. But there were also players who never made it after switching codes to play rugby league, and their stories are also told here.

Published @ £14.95, available for just £8.95 post free in the UK direct from London League Publications Ltd or from Amazon.co.uk . Credit card orders via www.llpshop.co.uk; payment by cheque to PO Box 65784, London NW2 9NS. Available in bookshops at £14.95.

Also available as an E-Book for Kindle from Amazon.